Changing the Curriculum
A SOCIAL PROCESS

Preface

No one can trace the development of the school curriculum down through the centuries without noting that important changes have occurred. Whether all of those changes have resulted in progress will not be discussed in these pages. The plain facts of the matter are that not enough progress has been made. Changes have not occurred with sufficient rapidity nor in sufficient amount to meet a situation which all students of the culture today recognize: that cultural maladjustments within this industrial civilization are increasing at a frightening rate. Harry Elmer Barnes' declaration that we stand today with our mechanical foot in an airplane and our social foot on an oxcart remains the most graphic description to date of our predicament.

In all thinking about the problem, however, the danger of oversimplification must be avoided. Sociologists for some time have been pointing out that we moderns are not dealing merely with an enormous lag of social arrangements behind technological advances. There are great variations in the rate of change among our social institutions themselves. It is not nearly so difficult, for example, to change an institution like the school as it is to make a change in a social arrangement like marriage. Then, too, science has not made an even advance on all fronts. This is another source of maladjustment within the culture. Nor is scientific advance always ahead of social invention, as some take for granted in the case. Russia is an excellent example of the reverse process.

This newer view of *maladjustments within the culture,* a refinement of the older concept of the "social lag," is accepted for the purposes of this book. Almost all persons see in education our only means of correcting the worst of these maladjust-

v

ments. Organized education through the medium of the school curriculum must be depended upon to do its share of this task, whatever that share may be.

In contrast to the great need is the fact still remaining that changes in the curriculum of American schools have not kept pace with developments in the surrounding society. "Not once in a century and a half of national history," wrote Rugg [1] in 1926, "has the curriculum of the school caught up with the dynamic content of American life."

Since 1926, and especially since the depression of the '30's, increasing numbers of educational leaders have written on this theme. Representative examples from the literature are *The Educational Frontier*, edited by William Heard Kilpatrick [2]; *Democracy and the Curriculum* [3] and other yearbooks of the John Dewey Society; George S. Counts' *Dare the Schools Build a New Social Order?* [4]; Pickens Harris' *The Curriculum and Cultural Change* [5]; and *The Changing Curriculum* edited by Henry Harap, [6] and, most recently, Counts' *Education and the Promise of America*. [7] These books were designed not only to establish the need for drastic changes in the curriculum but also to point out desirable directions of change.

It is not the purpose of this volume to repeat the work of those individuals and groups. It may be assumed that the case for more thorough-going curriculum change has been well made, and the proposed character of that change may be accepted as reasonable. Our concern may then be with the process of bringing about the changes which seem desirable.

The first step in studying the process of curriculum change might well be to examine the process as it now commonly

---

[1] Harold Rugg in *Curriculum-Making: Past and Present*. Part I of the Twenty-Sixth Yearbook of the National Society for the Study of Education (Bloomington, Ill., Public School Publishing Company, 1926), p. 3.

[2] New York, D. Appleton–Century Company, Inc., 1933.

[3] Third Yearbook (New York, D. Appleton–Century Company, Inc., 1939).

[4] New York, John Day Company, 1932.

[5] New York, D. Appleton–Century Company, Inc., 1937.

[6] New York, D. Appleton–Century Company, Inc., 1937.

[7] New York, The Macmillan Company, 1945.

operates in American schools. Once the weaknesses of the present approach are analyzed, it should be useful to turn to the students of social change in the larger culture. Their findings should be helpful in acquiring some understanding of the basic process of influencing social change.

The task then remaining will be to apply the lessons learned from various kinds of experiences with curriculum-making and from the conclusions of social scientists, in order that curriculum change may be understood as a social process over which members of our society can have more intelligent control. The imperatives of the current world situation make it either unintelligent or immoral, as the case may be, to continue to operate in the field of curriculum development in many of the ways commonly employed at present.

This book is addressed, primarily, to members of the administrative and supervisory staffs in schools, although there are many implications for teachers as well as for community adults and learners. It is not that superintendents, principals, supervisors, and curriculum directors are more important than any other group. But their positions as status leaders in terms of the rest of the school system put them in a position to facilitate or to impede wise curriculum development, as the case may be. Sins of omission and sins of commission can both be so great, as far as this group is concerned, that curriculum change may turn out to be no social process at all. On the other hand, the zeal and skill of a superintendent of schools or of other administrative and supervisory agents may offset many other unfavorable factors that promise to operate against change in a particular school system.

The present volume is limited to curriculum change at the local community level. It is recognized that local educational leaders will find it desirable to utilize resources outside their own communities and to help local personnel and constituents to feel themselves a part of a larger enterprise. Such considerations are within the limits of this work. It is not proposed, however, to discuss state programs of curriculum change.

*   *   *

It is always difficult to give proper credit to the many individuals whose ideas and experience become embodied in a book of this type. I am indebted to teachers and other educational leaders throughout the country with whom I have worked and talked, singly and in groups, to professors in whose classes I have received inspiration, and to colleagues at Teachers College from whom I have learned much.

Special credit is due Hollis L. Caswell of Teachers College, Columbia University, whose idea it was that a more fundamental analysis of the process of curriculum change was needed. His advice has been depended upon throughout the writing of this volume.

Florence B. Stratemeyer and George S. Counts, also of Teachers College; William H. Burton of the Graduate School of Education, Harvard University; Charles E. Prall, director of the Commission on Education of the American College of Hospital Administrators and the American Hospital Association; and Dorothy Gray of Queens College, New York City, all read the manuscript critically and gave valuable suggestions.

I appreciate also the courtesy of publishers who granted permission to quote copyrighted materials and of those who contributed the documents that form the Appendix of this book—William H. Burton; C. Leslie Cushman, associate superintendent of the Philadelphia schools; J. Cecil Parker, coördinator of curriculum of the San Francisco schools; Margaret L. Gordon, principal of the J. J. Smallwood School, Norfolk, Virginia; Hazel A. Kier, intermediate supervisor, Kansas City, Kansas schools; and members of my college classes.

Finally, I am indebted to G. Robert Koopman and Paul J. Misner, who collaborated with me on an earlier work, *Democracy in School Administration*. The basic line of thinking developed with those individuals has been extended and applied to the process of curriculum change in the present volume.

A. M.

Contents

PAGE

PREFACE V

FOREWORD by Hollis L. Caswell xi

CHAPTER

I   CRYSTALLIZATION IN EDUCATION I

II   CONTROL OF THE PROCESS OF CHANGE 15

III   HUMAN MOTIVATIONS AS A FACTOR IN CHANGE . . 32

IV   CONDITIONS OF EFFECTIVE GROUP ENDEAVOR . . 61

V   SOCIAL INVENTION 99

VI   LEADERSHIP 149

VII   CONCLUSION 187

APPENDICES

A   Excerpts from Professional Logs 195

B   Basic Assumptions for Curriculum Planning in the Public Schools of Philadelphia 200

C   Curriculum Development in Maine as Based upon the Individual 212

D   Some Suggestions for Participating in Coöperative Thinking Through Group Discussion . . . 219

E   A Supervisor Takes Special Responsibility in the Induction of New Teachers 222

F   A Project in Developing Accumulative Records for Teachers 228

SELECTED BIBLIOGRAPHY 231

INDEX 235

ix

Foreword

The gap between theory and practice in American education is a characteristic frequently remarked and commonly regretted. The difference also between superior and average practice is very great. How to close these gaps is the problem of curriculum improvement. It is this important matter that is the central concern of this book.

During the past twenty-five years organized curriculum programs in cities and states have been one of the principal means relied upon to move educational practice ahead. A large majority of the states and most cities of size provide for curriculum programs. Viewed in the large, organized curriculum work has approached the problem of change as a simple matter. Great reliance has commonly been placed on courses of study. In fact, in many cases the writing and official authorization of courses of study have been considered the principal and adequate means of curriculum change.

However, during recent years it has become increasingly evident that curriculum improvement is by no means as simple a process as implied by the typical curriculum program. This process is, in fact, most complex, partaking of all the intricacies and difficulties of any effort to achieve directed social change. It is evident that a much more fundamental approach is required.

In this book Dr. Miel has made an important contribution to understanding the basic factors involved in modifying the curriculum. Her critical analysis of procedures of curriculum development and appraisal of these procedures in terms of broader conceptions and factors in processes of social change will be found of great value by anyone concerned with improving the curriculum. The work of students of society is utilized most effectively in deriving generalizations which should guide the curriculum worker. Applications are made in clear and illuminating fashion to practical problems of curriculum improvement.

It goes without saying that this book will be of major interest to curriculum directors and directors of instruction, but it should have a much wider appeal. Superintendents, principals, and supervisors will find it a source of first importance in setting their sights for curriculum improvement. Classroom teachers who are involved in organized curriculum work should also find it of value in providing an orientation which will make their work most fruitful.

HOLLIS L. CASWELL

Changing the Curriculum
A SOCIAL PROCESS

CHAPTER I

Crystallization in Education

Somewhere in South America there is a tribe of primitive people who, though living on perfectly dry ground today, nevertheless persist in building pile dwellings for themselves.

It has been the problem always of those who would help to bring about curriculum change to persuade people to give up their pile-dwellings-on-dry-ground. This clinging to what was once a good arrangement long after it has ceased to serve any useful purpose whatsoever is the commonest form of *crystallization*. Crystallization has been described as a good beginning that has turned in upon itself. Or it may be defined as the point reached when an idea or habit is accepted uncritically so that it limits the integrity, autonomy, and opportunities for self-expression of individuals and groups.

Crystallization of curriculum practice is a recurrent phenomenon in American education. It is also a complex one. It is not always easy to determine when a constellation of habits in an educational institution is making for a desirable economy of effort and providing a useful basis of continuity to individual and group living, or when it represents an area concerning which all thinking has stopped and which is serving as a deterrent to constructive action. Therefore, it should be rewarding to students of curriculum change to learn something of the nature of this phenomenon of crystallization in order to gain the ability to deal with it. In this chapter, accordingly, we shall examine some of the manifestations of crystallization in the curriculum of American schools.

THE GRADED SCHOOL AS A CONTRIBUTOR
TO CRYSTALLIZATION

One good example of the way in which crystallization works in education is the development of the graded school. Before the Civil War, education was expanding at a rapid rate. As schools began having to accommodate large numbers of children, various systems of classification were experimented with. Finally the scheme of grading the school was discovered. It spread rapidly, not only among city schools where such a plan was a real boon in the early days of organizing mass education, but also to one-room rural schools where it could never have been appropriate. This method of classification started a whole chain of events, each of which helped to fix the pattern more securely than before. Textbooks began to be graded, and there appeared first readers, fourth-grade arithmetics, eighth-grade spellers, and so on. At first by trial and error, later by "scientific experimentation," "proper" grade placement of subjects and subject-matter was determined. The college relieved its crowded curriculum by forcing some subjects into the high-school curriculum; congestion at that level was reduced by passing on a number of courses to the elementary school. Algebra became fixed in the ninth grade, long division in the fourth grade, beginning reading in the first.

Since the system began with grade one, the kindergarten had a hard time establishing a place for itself in the free public school. As the elementary school terminated traditionally with grade eight, rural schools still find it difficult to make what should be a simple reform, the sending of seventh and eighth graders to a central secondary school. The 8–4 plan was finally broken in many city schools by the junior-high-school movement. But that change had chiefly the disappointing result of moving departmentalization farther down into the grades.

With the grade pattern so firmly established, most attempts at curriculum change have been at the level of juggling within the system. Few persons have had the vision to try to break the pattern itself, much less had success in doing so.

426

TITLE IN BCL 2nd ED.

Changing the Curriculum

A SOCIAL PROCESS

by

ALICE MIEL

Assistant Professor of Education and Research Associate
Horace Mann-Lincoln Institute of School Experimentation
Teachers College, Columbia University

New York and London
D. APPLETON-CENTURY COMPANY, INC.

This one example illustrates the chief characteristics of crystallization: (1) a commendable beginning turned inward; (2) the shutting off of thinking in a certain area; (3) the tendency to spread to all kinds of schools; (4) the tendency to become interlocked with other aspects of the curriculum; (5) the tendency to persist stubbornly (especially if written into state laws); and (6) the tendency, if once broken, to be replaced rapidly by another crystallization (in this case, departmentalization).

CRYSTALLIZATION THROUGH THE TEXTBOOK AND SCHOOL SUBJECTS

Another interesting illustration of the operation of crystallization in curriculum matters is the development of the American textbook and the related development of school subjects during the nineteenth century. New instructional materials were badly needed at that time, for the curriculum was being enriched by the rapid addition of new courses.

Rugg [1] gives some interesting figures in this connection. Between the years 1787 and 1870 no fewer than 149 new titles of subjects or courses found their way into the printed programs of the secondary schools, 75 of them being interposed in the three years between 1825 and 1828. Three hundred and sixty different histories had been published in America before 1860.

From the middle of the century on, textbooks were prepared largely by college professors who were narrowly specialized. Gradually the curriculum became oriented around those subjects of specialization. "Furthermore," says Rugg [2] in commenting on this development, "the professors because of their . . . grounding in cautious research methods . . . tended to concentrate their attention upon the past. . . . Having a fear of unsound generalization, hence a fear of the contemporary in

[1] Harold Rugg, *Curriculum-Making: Past and Present.* Part I of the Twenty-Sixth Yearbook of the National Society for the Study of Education (Public School Publishing Company, Bloomington, Ill., 1926), Chap. II, pp. 20–21. Quoted by permission of the Society.
[2] *Ibid.,* p. 31.

history, the new, the unauthenticated in science, they more and more neglected the vital affairs of current life."

Even though some of those weaknesses of textbook writing have been corrected in more recent years, the subjects which textbooks helped to entrench in the curriculum remain with us. It is only in the past two decades that any considerable number of persons have been able to think outside the subject frame at all. Another result of the "textbook movement" is a group of publishing houses and authors with large financial interests in curriculum.

THE ACTIVITY PROGRAM AS A MANIFESTATION OF CRYSTALLIZATION

A third example from our own day is perhaps the best illustration to be found of the replacement of one crystallization by another. It all came about when educators began to take seriously the principle that children learn by doing. Pioneer individuals and groups started to experiment with ways of utilizing this principle in curriculum-building. Many of the experiments were so successful that numbers of other educators became convinced that here was something they should be trying out in their own schools. Gradually a new pattern crystallized. It went by different names, but in the early 1930's *the activity program* was the current favorite.

A whole dictionary full of new terms and a great body of educational literature grew up around the *unit of work* as the central feature of the activity program. Things reached the point where an elementary teacher viewed the playground as the place where children might learn a colonial dance when they were studying their "Colonial Unit"; a music teacher offered, as her contribution to the children's study of the city water supply, to teach "Row, Row, Row Your Boat" and "Flow Gently, Sweet Afton"; while a third teacher claimed room on the bandwagon because she used the activity, flashcards.[3]

[3] To be fair to a commendable curriculum innovation and to the many educators who made creative use of the newly popular curriculum prin-

Distortions and counterfeits of the original idea behind the activity movement made thoughtful people everywhere begin to question some of the newly crystallized practices. Heads of certain large city school systems, however, saw in the procedures, now routinized and mechanized almost beyond recognition, hope of accomplishing the prodigious task of modernizing their elementary curriculum in a relatively short time. In some cases the activity program was installed at once by administrative *fiat*. In others, it was tried out experimentally in selected schools for a time, then installed in all schools with exact procedures indicated to teachers for beginning specified units of work and carrying them through to a "culminating activity." Of course, the new program met with resistance at first. Innovations are difficult to accept when people have been finding their security by operating in habitual ways. But it is almost certain that, ten and twenty years from now, those who were hardest to convince in the beginning will be the staunchest supporters of the activity program when word comes that it is time to revise the curriculum once more.

To gain some idea of the extent to which schools are encrusted with crystallizations large and small, one has only to start listing the obvious phenomena that the school and only the school exhibits. One might start with the orders given to children—"Stay out until the bell rings," "Don't come in after the bell rings," "No talking," "Don't leave your seat without permission," "Don't help anyone else," "Sit still," "Wait until recess." Then one might list school marks, grade norms, the eight-, nine-, or ten-month term, schooling from ages five to seventeen, school open from eight to four, boys' lines and girls' lines, readers, "schoolhouse" brown, and so on with a long list.

---

ciple, it should be stated that thereby a number of promising changes have been effected in the program of many schools. In fact, the activity concept as analyzed by Lois Coffey Mossman in *The Activity Concept* (The Macmillan Company, 1939) and others continues to provoke thoughtful reëxamination of practice and to contribute to desirable changes in the school curriculum. It is against mechanization and distortion of a valid curriculum principle that this discussion is directed. It is a wasteful procedure to replace an older crystallization merely with a newer, fresher one.

CRYSTALLIZED PROCEDURES FOR CURRICULUM-MAKING

Perhaps the most important form of crystallization in curriculum development has been the standardization of procedure for making changes in the curriculum which began to take shape in the 1920's. That was the period when local school systems such as those of Los Angeles, Winnetka, Denver, Detroit, St. Louis, and Baltimore were commencing to give serious attention to problems of curriculum change.

Toward the end of that decade books and studies dealing with principles and techniques for curriculum-making commenced to appear. A glance at the table of contents of a representative work published in 1929 reveals the nature of the pattern that was emerging. The author promises to consider such questions as:

How should the curriculum organization be set up?
How should the duties of the aims committee be performed?
What procedure should production committees follow?
How should a new course of study be installed?

Following the publication of such books came almost a frenzy of curriculum activity in the '30's. A study made by the United States Office of Education in 1936 revealed organized curriculum-development programs under way in more than seven-tenths of the cities over 25,000 in population.[4] A great many such enterprises were being carried on in smaller centers also. Most of those programs had been initiated since 1932.

By 1934 the pattern for curriculum-making that is most familiar today had become fixed and widespread. Evidence of the fact that curriculum development had been reduced to a formula calculated to work in any school system of size is a study by Trillingham, who set about to learn how curriculum programs were organized and administered at that time in a number of large cities throughout the country.[5] This, in brief,

[4] Reported by Henry Harap, Ed., in *The Changing Curriculum* (New York, D. Appleton–Century Company, Inc., 1937).
[5] C. C. Trillingham, *Organization and Administration of Curriculum Programs* (Los Angeles, University of Southern California, 1934).

is the pattern he discovered and which he then recommended for general use in sizable school systems:

1. The superintendent of schools initiates the curriculum program and is ultimately responsible for the curriculum.
2. In direct charge is a curriculum director, assisted by a curriculum specialist or consultant who is "to aid and stimulate teacher groups" and "critically evaluate the progress of the curriculum program."
3. A curriculum council or cabinet is chosen by the superintendent to determine the philosophy of the school and general guiding principles, "to set up general objectives of the program," to serve as a clearing house, and, finally, to approve work submitted by various committees.
4. An aims committee has the job of formulating the aims of education and determining the program of studies to be offered.
5. A production committee for each subject and each division becoming active determines subject aims, subject content, pupil activities, materials, and so on.
6. A course-appraisal committee for each new course of study oversees the try-outs of new materials.
7. A course-installation committee sees to it that the course is properly installed after study by the principals and teachers who are to use it.
8. A continuous course-improvement committee keeps bringing the course up to date.

Weaknesses in Procedures as Crystallized

This plan for organizing and administering curriculum programs deserves careful study, for it represents perhaps the most dangerous type of crystallization in the whole curriculum picture today. The most obvious weakness of the procedure recommended by Trillingham is its underlying assumption that the curriculum is a series of documents periodically to be added to, revised, brought up to date. In other words, at the time of Trillingham's study, *curriculum* was still synonymous with *course of study*, in the realm of operation if not in the realm of theory.[6]

[6] That some shift in thinking has occurred in the decade since Trillingham's work is attested by the following report in the *Curriculum Journal*, Feb., 1942, p. 53: "Some of the most important curriculum developments in the Bakersfield (California) city schools are those that do

In the second place it is taken for granted that superintendents of schools, curriculum directors, and curriculum specialists shall launch all curriculum programs, selecting the personnel of working committees, evaluating the progress of those committees, and taking full responsibility for the results. This method of work violates the fundamental principles of democratic participation. It looks, indeed, as if here were the type of curriculum program which Saylor [7] characterizes thus: a program "planned in terms of course of study preparation, but organized so as to promote acceptance of the completed course by teachers through participation of representative teachers in its preparation."

A third observation regarding Trillingham's proposals is that there is an unquestioned assumption that curriculum revision in the sense here employed must be a system-wide activity. The possibility of autonomy for individual schools within the system is given no consideration.

A fourth observation has to do with the recommended first steps in curriculum revision. First a philosophy must be written down by one small group; next it must be broken down into principles or objectives; at this point new groups take over to break objectives into smaller bits called "aims." These are worked out for different subjects and grade levels of the school system. The whole procedure is based on connectionism in psychology—reduce the desired response of the pupil to a convenient unit of behavior, then set a stimulus situation to produce and fix that response—an additive rather than a developmental approach.

---

not ordinarily receive attention. For instance, workshop facilities have been developed where supervisors have adequate room to hold meetings within their offices and space where projects may be assembled and work in various types of art, poetry, and so forth may be carried on right in the workshop by teachers. . . . The supervisors of music and art, the material for the testing program, the circulating library, the central library for circulating books for children, as well as the Audio-Visual Aids Department are all housed in one place where the teachers may come and go into either of the laboratories for assistance."

[7] J. Galen Saylor, *Factors Associated with Participation in Coöperative Programs of Curriculum Development* (New York, Bureau of Publications, Teachers College, Columbia University, 1941), p. 2.

A final observation is that two groups of persons seem to have been entirely ignored in this master plan of participation in curriculum development. Those groups are the learners themselves and their parents and other adults in the community who have a stake in educational undertakings.

FAULTY CONCEPTION OF CURRICULUM UNDERLIES CRYSTALLIZED PROCEDURES

This whole formula for organizing and administering curriculum programs, which is still in common use today,[8] is based on a faulty definition of the curriculum. A year after Trillingham's report came the publication of Caswell and Campbell's influential work, *Curriculum Development*.[9] This book set forth a broad conception of the curriculum which cleared the air with regard to conflicting definitions of that term and should have freed curriculum workers from the limitations of mere course-of-study preparation. As refined in a later book by Caswell,[10] this now generally accepted definition of the curriculum reads: "The curriculum is . . . composed of the actual experiences which children undergo under the guidance of the school." [11]

[8] For evidence of the truth of this statement one has only to consult the department "News from the Field" in the *Curriculum Journal* during its last year of publication (1942–1943).

[9] Hollis L. Caswell and Doak S. Campbell, *Curriculum Development* (New York, American Book Company, 1935).

[10] Hollis L. Caswell, *Education in the Elementary School* (New York, American Book Company, 1943), p. 188.

[11] This definition is essentially the one accepted for the purposes of this discussion. The writer is aware that some educators have begun in recent years to regard the curriculum as all of the experiences children have under any circumstances. The latter definition is the result of a belief that curriculum workers, in selecting and organizing learning experiences for and with children, have tended to ignore the influences of the child's out-of-school living. Those advancing the idea hope that a definition of the curriculum so broad as to erase the lines between the child's school experiences and those outside the tutelage of the school will guarantee wiser planning of those experiences.

The writer is in entire sympathy with the point of view that all of each child's experiences must be taken into account in curriculum-planning. But it should be quite possible to do so without blurring the word *curriculum* until it loses its root character. As a word that meant in the

The fact that course-of-study preparation is still the most common activity in the field of curriculum development shows that the full implications of the newer definition of the curriculum are not as yet grasped by any great number of people. If it is true that the curriculum is composed of the experiences children undergo, it follows as a corollary that *the curriculum is the result of interaction of a complex of factors, including the physical environment and the desires, beliefs, knowledge, attitudes, and skills of the persons served by and serving the school;* namely, the learners, community adults, and educators (not forgetting the custodians, clerks, secretaries, and other "nonteaching" employees of the school).

If this corollary is studied carefully it will be seen that curriculum change is something much more subtle than revising statements written down on paper. To change the curriculum of the school is to change the factors interacting to shape that curriculum. In each instance this means bringing about changes in people—in their desires, beliefs, and attitudes, in their knowledge and skill. Even changes in the physical environment, to the extent that they can be made at all, are dependent upon changes in the persons who have some control over that environment. In short, the nature of curriculum change should be seen for what it really is—a type of social change, change in people, not mere change on paper.

INSIGNIFICANT RESULTS FROM CRYSTALLIZED PROCEDURES

The faulty conception of the curriculum that underlies most of the curriculum programs to date is one reason for reëxamin-

---

original Latin "a racetrack" and as a word that has for centuries been associated with schooling, it must, to be true to itself, it seems, connote something planned and planned for, a somewhat limited segment of life, not all of it.

The definition here accepted does not limit the curriculum to experiences which children have within the four walls of the school or within school hours. It does mean, however, that a quarrel between a mother and a father on Saturday night will not be considered as part of their child's curriculum, important as that quarrel is in its *implications for that curriculum.* The curriculum is here limited to those experiences for which the school has some responsibility and which it has some opportunity of affecting.

ing current procedures in curriculum-making at this time. A further reason for reëxamination of the pattern of curriculum development as it has crystallized in our day is that this pattern has produced such insignificant results. In spite of all the attention and energy that has been directed toward solution of curriculum problems during the last two decades, it is rather generally agreed that there has been relatively little fundamental change in the curriculum of American schools in the years when rapid advances in technology have been making drastic changes in the whole culture surrounding the schools. When careful study was made of 1,175 selected courses of study produced by representative school systems during the years 1930 to 1940, one of the major findings was that "there is a great dearth of the kind of new content which is needed for our times." [12] Although certain favorable trends were discovered, the following facts were considered significant: [13]

1. There is a persistent attempt in the majority of courses to utilize traditional subject matter to satisfy new needs.
2. Part of the new content that has been introduced is in many instances not significant. It is as academic as is the remainder of the course. . . .
3. Some of the new material does not provide for a sufficiently thorough analysis of the problem involved. Like many other innovations, some of the material seems to have been introduced merely because it was novel.
4. There are glaring shortages in content in certain fields. For example . . . in social studies there is little or no mention of advertising and its widespread influence, art, child labor, housing, insurance, installment buying and consumer education, social security, dictatorships and many other vital problems today. . . .
5. The underlying philosophy of many of the courses prevents the content from assuming full significance. For example, the idea that science should remain "pure" stultifies the social emphasis that might otherwise be present. . . .

In short, existing courses have been overhauled slightly and a few new courses have been added to the curriculum as a result

[12] Herbert Bruner and Others, *What Our Schools Are Teaching* (New York, Bureau of Publications, Teachers College, Columbia University, 1941), p. 207.
[13] *Ibid.*, p. 209.

of all the curriculum activity that has been in vogue. In view of the need, however, changes have been superficial indeed.

A still more recent study by Hopkins, Stratemeyer, and Woodring shows that not even did a second world war succeed in bringing great reality into the school curriculum, if one may judge by representative curriculum materials produced during that period. In the introduction to a *List of Outstanding Teaching and Learning Materials 1942–1945* these observations, among others, are made: [14]

> Two major concerns of school people seemed to stand out. They were minimum essentials and character education. Frequently they were referred to under different names but the intent was the same. There was more discussion than agreement. There were vague feelings that the subject essentials were not adequate and that character was more than the overtones of a traditional program. Yet there was little attempt to clarify and implement these feelings. The old essentials still prevail.
>
> Experiences and needs of children were generously suggested as a means to orient them to the subject matter of the courses of study. Such experiences and needs were rarely used as a basis around which to build a curriculum.
>
> The use of community resources was suggested in many instances as desirable in teaching and learning. The emphasis in general, however, was upon books as the normal and desirable resource and upon book learning as the basic essential for educational achievement.
>
> The effects of the war period appeared in two ways: first, in the new areas of study such as aviation and meteorology, and second, in the new emphasis given to old subjects, especially health and physical education, mathematics, and science.

Again there is evidence that changes in the curriculum are too few and too insignificant.

Read in the light of the foregoing comments on courses of study prepared in the decade of the '30's and since, Rugg's summary of methods of curriculum-making current in 1926 has a familiar ring: [15]

---

[14] Prepared by L. Thomas Hopkins, Florence Stratemeyer, and Maxie N. Woodring for the Department of Supervision and Curriculum Development, National Education Association (Washington, D.C., 1945).

[15] Rugg, *op. cit.*, p. 427.

Partial, superficial, and timorous "revision" rather than general, fundamental, and courageous reconstruction characterizes curriculum-making in the public schools . . . the existing program is always taken as the point of departure. . . . Thus curriculum-making becomes a process of accretion and elimination. There is little, indeed almost no movement under way in public schools to initiate curriculum-making from the starting point either of child learning or of the institutions and problems of American life. For over fifty years, tinkering has characterized the attack on the curriculum. In most centers the situation remains essentially unchanged.

If such are the results of mechanical curriculum procedures, efficient as they may appear to be on paper, it is evident that the process of curriculum change needs study.

FAILURE TO BENEFIT WIDELY FROM INNOVATING PRACTICE

Parallel with the development of the standardized curriculum program as just described has been experimentation on the part of pioneering individuals and groups in an effort to improve the experiences which children have under the guidance of the school. There is a growing number of schools employing a more functional approach to curriculum change. Not a few of them have arrived at some rather creative solutions to persistent educational problems. Their experience is valuable to others, and there are available many accounts of the changes such schools have made. Elsie Ripley Clapp's *Community Schools in Action* is a good example.[16] There are also *The Community School*, edited by Samuel Everett,[17] and *Youth Serves the Community*, edited by Paul Hanna,[18] as well as recent yearbooks of the Department of Supervision and Curriculum Development of the National Education Association and issues of *Progressive Education*, particularly those for the years 1939–41.

Such accounts of promising practices are stimulating and worth while. But, in most cases, the innovators have failed to record for the benefit of others the detailed steps they took in making basic curriculum change possible in their schools. Since

[16] (The Viking Press, New York, 1939).
[17] (D. Appleton–Century Company, Inc., 1938).
[18] (D. Appleton–Century Company, Inc., 1936).

there has been a dearth of careful analyses of how fundamental changes have been brought about in people and in their ways of working, schools have borrowed from those who have blazed the trail whatever they could most easily lay hands on—often the outer shell only. Thus another impulse toward crystallization of curriculum practice has resulted.

It is recognized that out of experimentation by pioneers in education and dissemination of their findings through imitation considerable progress has been made. Indeed, it would be quite wasteful for each individual or group to pioneer for itself in all aspects of living. The question is whether or not crystallization is an inevitable result of trying to profit from the experience of others. Is there not some way in which the value of human experience may be transferred to others without the stultifying effect of borrowing ready-made solutions?

The writer is convinced that there are better ways of bringing about curriculum change than have yet been widely employed in American education. There has long been a need to discover those better ways and to bring them together into a form that would be useful to curriculum workers. There is need to learn both how to break down undesirable crystallization in education and how to prevent new crystallizations from setting in.

It is the purpose of this volume to present an analysis of a process of curriculum change based on the assumption that such change is a type of social change. As was pointed out earlier in this chapter, the changes involved when the school curriculum is really modified are actually changes in the attitude and behavior of persons. The changes in those persons must be in the direction of greater flexibility and greater awareness of fundamental issues.

In the next chapter the larger process of social change is discussed. This discussion provides a background for more detailed analysis in succeeding chapters of various aspects of the process of social change, together with implications for the process of curriculum change itself.

CHAPTER II

Control of the Process of Change

In the foregoing pages there has been outlined the nature of the large problem facing all who have responsibility for the school curriculum. The problem, stated in its simplest terms, is the increasing number of cultural maladjustments within this society. Laissez-faire Americans must decide whether there shall be large-scale social planning or millions of persons going jobless; individualistic small farmers must cope with the movement toward large corporate farms; minds conditioned to national sovereignty must plan for a world that knows atomic energy. Because of its unreal character, the school curriculum is not making sufficient contribution to the solution of these and other problems of cultural maladjustment, large and small.

The inadequacy of methods commonly employed in attempts to improve the curriculum was dealt with at some length in the preceding chapter. In the present chapter consideration is given first to the possibility of achieving some measure of control over social change. Next the general nature of an adequate process for directing social change is described. Finally there is presented a brief analysis of factors in the process of change that promise to lend themselves to social control. This analysis should be helpful in determining the factors in the process of curriculum change that should in all probability receive early attention and special emphasis on the part of curriculum-makers.

NEED FOR MORE SOCIAL CHANGE

If there is anything that characterizes the present period in the history of social thought, it is the recognition that change should no longer be allowed to take its haphazard course. Charles A. Beard is one who has long advocated that "endless, unplanned change" be replaced by control of change. And Robert Lynd says, "Casual change is forever missing the boat." He pictures the results of this casual, unplanned change as follows: [1]

... our culture pattern ... is a pattern of *markedly uneven change of unprecedented rapidity in some traits and of marshalled resistance to change in others, and tolerating at many points extreme disjunctions and contradictions.*

Ralph Linton, with his knowledge of cultural anthropology, also testifies that most of culture growth has been unplanned and on the basis of expediency. "The very concept that it can be controlled and directed," he writes, "is so new in human history that we do not know whether it is valid or not." [2]

It is the task of the present generation to test the validity of this concept—to find out to what extent it is possible deliberately to control and direct change. Naturally the task will be difficult. The process of social change as it has operated in history is vastly complicated. It would be unrealistic to expect that a process involving so many unpredictable and interrelated factors could ever be brought completely under control. It will be long before man will be willing to plan continuously in many areas of group living and will acquire the ability to foresee the full consequences of all his acts even in their short-range perspective.

Defeatist Attitude a Hindrance

Yet, it serves no constructive purpose to take a defeatist attitude. Myrdal believes that social scientists have too long been under the spell of Sumner's *Folkways*. He points out [3] that Sumner's theory of the binding effect of the folkways and mores was based largely on studies of primitive people and that it must

[1] Robert Lynd, *Knowledge for What?* (Princeton, N.J., Princeton University Press, 1939).

[2] Ralph Linton, "Potential Contributions of Cultural Anthropology to Teacher Education," *Culture and Personality* (Washington, D.C., American Council on Education, 1941), p. 15.

[3] Gunnar Myrdal, *An American Dilemma* (New York, Harper & Brothers, 1944), p. 1032.

be applied with caution to a "modern western society . . . characterized by . . . a virtually universal expectation of change and a firm belief in progress. . . . Sumner's construction," he continues, "conceals what is most important in our society: the changes, the conflicts, the absence of static equilibria, the lability in all relations. . . . The valuation spheres, in such a society as the American, more nearly resemble powder magazines than they do Sumner's concept of mores."

Sumner, himself, saw opportunity and challenge in the crises he found occurring whenever mores became so fixed they failed to meet new interests and needs of men. On this subject he wrote: [4]

It is in such crises that great men find their opportunity . . . it behooves us by education and will, with intelligent purpose, to criticize and judge even the most established ways of our time, and to put courage and labor into resistance to the current mores where we judge them wrong. It would be a mighty achievement of the science of society if it could lead up to an art of societal administration which should be intelligent, effective, and scientific.

Since Sumner's day, the world has seen many an experiment designed to improve the "art of societal administration." Some experiments have been on a small scale as, for example, attempts at coördination of various agencies in a community. There have been a few of vast proportions such as the T.V.A. in this country. From these, man has learned much and will learn more. Each social discovery that is made, tested, and extended paves the way for further discovery. Conscious attention to this process could yield a rate of increase for social invention similar to the one which the field of technology has experienced with respect to scientific invention. There is need to "invent" conditions that foster much social invention.

There is every reason to have confidence that desirable social changes can and will increase in number and importance as more persons in more communities deliberately pool their wisdom and their efforts to secure such changes. If this confidence has no basis, there is no justification for organized education. The

[4] W. G. Sumner, *Folkways* (Boston, Ginn and Company, 1906), p. 118.

school is one of man's attempts at deliberate social change. Unless some control of the process of social change is possible, the school curriculum has no function to serve.

It is not meant to imply that the school curriculum can, of itself, effect basic social change in the near future. Linton has expressed rather well the limitations within which the educator must expect to achieve: [5]

Under existing circumstances it seems highly improbable that the educator can bring about great or revolutionary changes in our culture, at least as it concerns the generation with which he has to deal. His hope of changing and directing future development must rest upon two things, a series of minor but intelligently directed changes in the existing culture pattern and the inculcation of values whose general acceptance would make for a better society.

Yet, even in the case of factors apparently out of the hands of the professional educator, it is entirely conceivable that ways can be found of achieving more control than now appears likely or possible. For example, we have only begun to explore the potentialities of school-community coöperation. Within the area where curriculum workers ordinarily operate, it is probable that deliberate curriculum change can largely replace unplanned change as more persons make serious attempts to foresee consequences. Factors now operating more or less by chance on schools at the local community level—improved textbooks, professional publications, state institutes, requests from the public, suggestions from teachers—these and other influences can be studied and utilized more effectively.

Deliberate Social Change Must Take on Value

Whether or not our society can achieve some control over social change will depend upon how many persons come to *place value upon deliberate social change*. At present there are wide differences among people in their attitude toward change. We have the George Apleys who complain: [6]

[5] Linton, *op. cit.*, p. 15.
[6] J. P. Marquand, *The Late George Apley* (Boston, Little, Brown & Company, 1937), p. 294.

I wish there weren't quite so many new ideas. Where do they come from? . . . Why is everyone trying to break away from what we all know is sane and good?

George Apley's counterparts are to be found in practically every school, church, club, and legislature in the land.

There are others who may be less satisfied with present conditions than the George Apleys appear to be but who resist change nonetheless. This is the group that can be counted upon to admit the need for change but then to doubt the wisdom of each and every modification suggested. They insist upon having proof in advance of the adequacy of any proposal before they are willing to lend their support to it. They do not seem to realize that man as an individual and men in association must ever act before all the proof is in, that life is therefore propositional, a series of experiments.

But change is occurring constantly whether people like it or not. It is occurring with increasing rapidity, yet with little social control. Things people say they want left unchanged do not remain so. The family is an example of an institution that is changing in response to other modifications in our culture, changing in ways that are causing distress to some of our social scientists.

Instead of resisting change, it seems that people must go out to meet change. They must deliberately plan for and guide social change instead of accepting submissively the stream of "endless, unplanned change" which Beard laments. People must be helped to see that new ways and ideas can usually be made to work if they are thoughtfully selected as the basis of group action and if enough attention is given to making them work.

NEED FOR AN ADEQUATE PROCESS FOR DIRECTING SOCIAL CHANGE

If deliberate social change is to replace haphazard change, human beings in this modern world must learn to give more attention to *process* than they have been willing to do in the past. There exists a variety of attitudes toward process. To some persons the term is merely a source of irritation or bewilderment. These individuals are so impatient for results or have so little knowledge of the relation of means to ends that they will not or cannot give proper attention to process. They believe that, if they have a well-defined goal, there is no reason why they should not aim directly at it—or, as often happens, order some other persons to proceed at once to the goal—without thought of the appropriateness of the means employed. The weakness of this approach is twofold: (1) there is no guarantee that the goal as envisioned will be the one reached if attention to means is lacking, and (2) there is no guarantee that the goal is worth working for if attention to the selection of that goal is not made an integral part of social process.

Another group is so convinced of the futility of trying to direct social change that a laissez-faire attitude is adopted. Their lack of faith in deliberate social change makes them unwilling to devote effort to discovering a process of effecting such change.

A third group of people conceive of process as a number of clever techniques permitting the initiated to gain their own ends no matter what the effect on others. They have up-to-date knowledge of principles of social psychology and of human development, but they exploit this knowledge. Their concern with process turns out to be an active force for antisocial ends.

It is such an abuse, perhaps, that fosters a fourth attitude toward process, one of distrust. For example, Max Lerner sees process as lacking in directional value: [7]

Apart from the negative value of furnishing an antidote against an undue structural emphasis in social thought there is little in process theory itself that makes a valuable instrument of analysis. The mere flux, continuity, becoming finally emerge as ends in themselves, and they tend to inhibit questions of the purpose or direction of the process or of differences of value in it.

When persons are heard to remark that they are not interested in the product but only in the process, they make themselves liable to the criticism Lerner advances. What these persons really mean, in most cases, is that they are interested in a given

[7] Max Lerner, *Ideas Are Weapons* (New York, The Viking Press, 1939), p. 495.

process because it results in a product or products which they value above the products that would result from a different process.[8] Values conceived and achieved from contrasting methods of developing a dramatic production with learners is a case in point. To some teachers certain intangible results in terms of personality development have a higher value than a finished performance, if a choice must be made between the two products.

Many persons are contemptuous of process, yet we cannot hope to achieve deliberate social change without attention to it. Instead of regarding process as unimportant or ineffectual or evil or lacking in directional value, it should be recognized for what it actually is—a means-end continuum with infinite possibilities for effecting constructive social change if the group employing it so desires. No matter what conception of process is held, means and ends go on interacting at all times; means become ends and ends become means toward other ends as the process continues. If desirable results are to be assured from this process of interacting means and ends, equal attention must be given to both. Furthermore, the process itself must contain its own guarantees if it is to be judged sound and adequate. Guarantees that appear to be essential are: (1) the guarantee of security; (2) the guarantee of individual and group growth; (3) the guarantee of accomplishment. In other words, a process shall be judged by its products. Some of these products may be observed in terms of effects on human beings, and that effect may be only a facial expression. Others will be reflected in their deeds. Since these guarantees afford a means of evaluating the soundness of a social process, let us consider briefly the import of each one of them.

The Guarantee of Security

It will not be easy to increase the numbers of persons who value and promote deliberate social change. To do so will mean

[8] Stephen Corey (in conversation) has advanced the interesting idea that a process is actually made up of a number of products exhibiting various interrelationships and configurations. Process, the movement from product to product, is like an electric current in that it cannot be observed but can be tested and studied only through the quality of its products.

that many individuals will have to find security in ways other than those they try to employ at present. In other words, they will have to cease their efforts to find security in withdrawal and retreat to former social conditions; that alternative just does not exist. Instead they will have to find their security in the *process* used to bring social change under control.

Beard gives this description of the situation facing humanity: [9]

Deprived of the certainty which it was once believed science would ultimately deliver, and of the very hope that it can in the nature of things disclose certainty, human beings must now concede their own fallibility and accept the world as a place of trial and error where only those who dare to assume ethical and esthetic responsibility, and to exercise intuitive judgment, while seeking the widest possible command of realistic knowledge, can hope to divine the future and mould in some measure the shape of things to come.

Childs [10] put the same idea in slightly different terms when he said that we need a "society composed of people who can creatively find their controlling ideas and ideals in the ongoing process of experience itself."

Dewey defines this new security in these words: [11]

. . . there are a steadily increasing number of persons who find security in *methods* of inquiry, of observation, experiment, of forming and following working hypotheses. Such persons are not unsettled by the upsetting of any special belief, because they retain security of procedure.

People need the security of group process for another reason also. Living, as has been pointed out by numerous social philosophers, is a lonely business, and man is constantly seeking to establish working relationships with others. Loneliness is, perhaps, on the increase in our culture, especially in urban centers where problems are unusually complex and where impersonality is common. Dewey and Childs are convinced that when "the indi-

[9] Charles A. Beard, *The Open Door at Home* (New York, The Macmillan Company, 1934), p. 20. By permission of the publishers.

[10] John L. Childs, *Education and the Philosophy of Experimentalism* (New York, The Century Company, 1931), p. 133.

[11] John Dewey, *The New Republic*, Feb. 6, 1924. Quoted in Childs, *op. cit.*, p. 44.

vidual does not participate in collective projects of social planning and control, he feels himself submerged and paralyzed by forces too large and blind, apparently, for any control." [12] Participation in joint enterprises that challenge the efforts of each individual is an excellent means of reducing the feeling that one is working alone against overwhelming odds in a confused world.

Since the process to be employed by human beings as they work out solutions to pressing problems is to carry responsibility for the security of individuals, it is essential that that process be selected most carefully. This will entail not only the use of the best techniques now at people's disposal but the invention of new ones also. For example, much more should be known about ways of encouraging and utilizing the different contributions of various individuals in a group. In the words of Howard Lane,[13] we must learn how to operate in such a fashion that "individual talents and tools are . . . prized as assets of the group, and are not claims to the individual's distinction from the group."

The Guarantee of Individual and Group Growth

To be judged successful, the process employed for bringing about planned social change must result in the growth of the persons engaging in it. As H. S. Elliott [14] has said, the "growth of those participating is in proportion to the amount of thought and effort put into what is undertaken." Further, he believes it to be true that "persons in the long run do successfully only what they figure out for themselves." If progress is to be paced more nearly to need, human power to solve problems intelligently must be stepped up enormously.

One way of describing the desired growth is to say that it will

[12] John Dewey and John L. Childs in William H. Kilpatrick and Others, *Educational Frontier* (New York, D. Appleton–Century Company, Inc., 1933), pp. 57–58.

[13] Howard Lane, *Group Planning in Education,* 1945 Yearbook of the Department of Supervision and Curriculum Development (Washington, D.C., National Education Association, 1945), p. 6.

[14] H. S. Elliott, *The Why and How of Group Discussion* (New York, Association Press, 1923), pp. 7–8.

consist of increasing identification of self-interest with the interests of an ever-enlarging group. This is by no means the same as identifying public interests with private ones. If self-interest is increasingly to be identified with the interests of a larger group, certain tendencies in individuals will have to be turned in other directions. Tendencies to seek power and to exploit others will have to be turned into the tendency to be of service to others. The tendency to value achievement as a means of personal aggrandizement will have to be converted into a tendency to value achievement for its contribution to the common welfare. The tendency to be competitive will have to give way to the tendency to be coöperative on more and more occasions. The tendency to be social will have to overcome the tendency to be individualistic.

Democratic Socialization as the Desirable Direction of Growth. There lie in all individuals the potentialities for developing behavior patterns that fall toward one or the other end of the scale of social values just described in differing terms. The direction in which it is desirable that growth occur may be indicated by the term *democratic socialization.* The greatest need of the world today is for more democratically socialized individuals. This combination of words has peculiar significance. It replaces the individual-society dualism of the nineteenth century with a unity that is coming to be understood by more and more twentieth-century minds. Modern thought can advocate the overcoming of *individualistic* tendencies while yet conceiving of *individuation* as a necessary and inseparable part of the process of *democratic* socialization. Attention to the process of individuation, the "Siamese twin" of socialization, is essential if our society is to produce an increasing number of contributive types of people. This point is elaborated in the following passage: [15]

Democratic socialization is not to be confused with national socialization characteristic of totalitarian forms. It is not to be thought of

[15] G. Robert Koopman, Alice Miel, and Paul J. Misner, *Democracy in School Administration* (New York, D. Appleton–Century Company, 1943), pp. 29–30.

as standardizing in nature, and every effort must be made to permit the individual to express himself in a creative fashion. . . . Individuals vary in the way they meet situations both old and new. Individuation as a part of the total process of socialization denotes the way in which the personality establishes a personally satisfying working relationship with society. In other words, individuation represents the growth toward a definite, consistent, and individual way of meeting situations. It recognizes that there are many kinds of social behavior and also that there is a sort of internal consistency to the behavior of a socialized individual. The principle of individuation recognizes individual differences of a biological nature and encourages variety of behavior.

Interpreted in this light, democratic socialization is a meaningful expression of a desirable direction of growth. It suggests an over-all criterion for judging the human products of a process of social change. It helps one to understand the problem of growing up which Snyder poses in these terms: [16]

Man derives his humanity through association with other men. . . . There are, in particular, two characteristic and universal aspects in this process of development, which give us our cue for the guidance of children into social understanding and behavior. These are: (1) growth from dependence on others to self-dependence, and (2) growth from absorption in self to concern for others.

The two growth trends proceed, however, in anything but an even, progressive course. From the cradle to the grave there is, in both, a pull in contrary directions. We want to be free and on our own; but we also want to lean on those who will let us. We want to do for others; but we want to follow our own interests, too. This ambivalence, felt in all of us, makes the human drama, the drama built around values and our choices among these values.

Accordingly such a concept as democratic socialization should be of value in helping individuals to resolve conflicts resulting from this two-way pull.

The Guarantee of Accomplishment

It almost goes without saying that a group will experience little security and will achieve little growth if, as the result of employing a process of change, there are no appreciable results

[16] Agnes Snyder, *Social Studies for Children*, Bulletin of the Association for Childhood Education (Washington, D.C., 1944), p. 9.

to show for efforts expended. Nor can success be postponed until some grand but distant day. The group must have evidence as it proceeds that progress is being made. In other words, a process cannot be judged adequate unless it demonstrates by its works that it is efficient in accomplishing group purposes. The efficiency here referred to is the "stepped-up" variety which results from best use of the strengths of many persons. Koopman, Miel, and Misner describe this type of efficiency in the following terms: [17]

Many persons are skeptical about the efficiency of democratic organization and control. Democracy is accepted as an ideal but is considered to be an impractical theory. The difficulty undoubtedly arises in connection with the restricted meaning which many individuals attach to the term efficiency. To many other persons it is becoming increasingly apparent that democratic control can result in a higher level of efficiency than has ever been achieved. This kind of efficiency is dependent upon the channels for administrative control that may be established. These channels are: (1) purposeful activity; (2) planning; (3) flexibility; and (4) discipline. These channels, then, become the several basic factors of the democratic process.

All this has important implications both for the aspiration levels of individuals and groups and for choice of techniques of co-operative action, matters which will be discussed in some detail in succeeding chapters.

Other Features of an Adequate Process

As persons set out deliberately to bring the process of change under some kind of control, it would seem advisable to study the matter from the three angles just discussed—the promise that the process offers of guaranteeing some amount and kind of security, growth, and accomplishment. A process that contains such guarantees can never be an automatic one, never a formula that is sure to work under any conditions whatsoever. The process employed by any group of persons to achieve given ends must be developed out of the situation in which the group is working. The nature of the group must be taken into account.

[17] Koopman, Miel, and Misner, *op. cit.*, p. 63.

The purposes which the group wishes to achieve must be considered. The means at the disposal of the group and the obstacles faced must figure in the selection of process at every step. In short, there is no standard process in which one can put trust. Creativity is called for at all points. An adequate process is built to suit the situation and the purposes of the group.

Need for Balance Between Gradualism and Rapidity. Furthermore, the most delicate task of timing and strategy is involved, for the process chosen for use in any given situation must achieve a nice balance between *gradualism* and *rapidity*. Gradualism is a commonly accepted principle in directed social change as is evidenced by two interesting catch phrases now abroad. One scholar sees the process of controlled social change as "directed gradualism." Another uses the expression "assisted evolution." Both express a valid principle; namely, that change in social arrangements, which means making changes in persons who control the arrangements, cannot be hurried faster than those persons are prepared to go. Any adequate process will take account of this fact. Otherwise the security of people is threatened.

On the other hand social scientists everywhere are gravely concerned over the *growing* maladjustment in our culture. Lynd gives the following as his two appraisals of the situation: [18]

1. The knowledge which the sophisticated experts possess in our culture is growing at a rate far more rapid than the rate at which it is being institutionalized in the habits of thought and action of the mass of our population.
2. As a culture we are accumulating our disabilities and the resulting strains incident to daily living at a rate faster than social legislation, education, and all the agencies for "reform" are managing to harness our new knowledge in the reduction of these disabilities. We are becoming culturally illiterate faster than all these agencies are managing to make us literate in the use of the potentialities of the culture.

From these two conclusions the validity of a second principle can be established. That principle is that we should attempt to

[18] Robert Lynd, *Knowledge for What?* (Princeton, N.J., Princeton University Press, 1939), pp. 108-109.

progress *as rapidly as necessary*. Otherwise accomplishment lags. Dewey has made a penetrating observation on this point: [19]

There are vices of reflection as well as of impulse. We may not look far enough ahead because we are hurried into action by stress of impulse; but we may also become over-interested in the delights of reflection; we become afraid of assuming the responsibilities of decisive choice and action.

Li Yu Ying had the same thing in mind, no doubt, when he took part in one of the monthly round-table discussions sponsored by the Free World Association. He said on that occasion: [20]

If a state of evolution is judged premature—or if it is premature —every endeavor should be made to make it "ready." It is a matter of education. It is one of the "used and unused" applications in the process of evolution. Therefore, one should not wait for that which is "ready" but see to it that it is made "ready."

The necessary balance to be achieved between the two principles just stated is well summed up by Koopman, Miel, and Misner. What they say regarding the development of a democratically administered school is pertinent here: [21]

The development of a democratically administered school should be as gradual as possible and as rapid as necessary. This principle is apparently paradoxical. Gradualness, however, means that development should be as slow as necessary to allow time to make for finer adjustments that individuals must make. The appropriate rate of growth of each individual must always be respected. Rapidity is suggested in order that progress may not be blocked or ground lost by allowing an organization to remain too long on any one plateau of development. It is from this state of affairs that most human institutions are suffering at present. The most important consideration is that the school (and other institutions) progress rapidly enough to meet social needs.

This advice leaves to those concerned with process in a local community a problem calling for rare good judgment, as do all

[19] John Dewey, *Human Nature and Conduct* (New York, Henry Holt and Company, Inc., 1922, p. 197.
[20] *Free World*, Vol. III, Sept., 1942, pp. 342–343.
[21] Koopman, Miel, and Misner, *op. cit.*, p. 318.

the specifications detailed in the foregoing paragraphs. It is in discovering what all this means in terms of action that art and science must both be employed.

FACTORS THAT MAY BE BROUGHT UNDER CONTROL

In order to ensure that a process of deliberate social change does indeed include the guarantees of security, growth, and accomplishment, it will be necessary to give attention to details of the process. Out of all the complex and interrelated factors involved in the process of social change as it has operated, certain ones appear to lend themselves to manipulation at the local community level more readily than do others. A realistic approach to deliberate social change will make full use of these more manageable factors.

Four such factors, or groups of factors, have been isolated for treatment in the remainder of this volume. They are: (1) the nature of the *motivations* of the persons on whom change depends; (2) *conditions* of effective group endeavor; (3) the extent of *social invention*, and (4) the amount and quality of *leadership* present. These aspects of the process of deliberate social change will be dealt with in turn in the four succeeding chapters. There is no particular virtue or significance to this ordering. It does appear, however, that the chapter on leadership, when read in the light of the treatment in the three preceding chapters, not only takes on more meaning but also serves to unify the separate discussions of motivation, conditions, and invention by placing special responsibility for attention to these factors in the hands of those taking leadership in any social enterprise.

In each chapter there will be both an analysis of the operation of the factor under discussion in directing and controlling change in society in general and implications of this analysis for curriculum change. In all the discussions, human beings will be made the focus of attention, for control of change will come only as more and more persons deliberate on the consequences of individual and group action.

Process as a Configuration

As a chapter is devoted to each of these aspects of process in turn, it must be remembered that the factors in a social situation never operate in isolation but always in a configuration. No part of the process can be improved without affecting the process as a whole; similarly, no part of the process can be neglected; least of all can the problem of directing social change be solved by tackling only one aspect of the process, such as leadership or organization or any one condition of effective group endeavor.

Participants in the process may be encouraged by realization of the fact that, while the area within which people can operate when they deliberately intend to direct and control change is somewhat limited, there is nevertheless a great deal of room for experimentation. Because of the interrelatedness of factors, it may be that this experimentation will have wider effect than is anticipated. It is not impossible that control over the manageable elements in our culture may yet prove to be the tail that wags the dog of "uncontrollable" factors.

Myrdal is optimistic with regard to the results that may be secured if human beings will substitute for a fatalistic and static premise a dynamic one. His sketch of the process that would result from such a substitution makes an excellent conclusion to the present chapter and a challenging introduction to the chapters that follow, where the process of deliberate social change is discussed in detail: [22]

. . . we may consider the same facts that have been observed by Sumner, Park, and Ogburn and add to them an explicit and dynamic value premise (instead of the implicit, fatalistic and static one) and from these deduce a quite different practical conclusion. Recognizing the folkways and mores, for example, and having a desire to *change some of them* in one direction or another, we should be interested in studying the range and degree of inertia; all the exceptions to the folkways; the changes, the flexibilities, and the manageability of some factors in the social system; instead of, as Sumner usually does, stressing and exemplifying the great over-all inertia. On the practical plane we should make not only the negative

[22] Myrdal, *op. cit.*, pp. 1052–1053.

inference that a plan for social change should expect to be time-consuming and to meet strong resistance, but also the positive inference that it has to direct its attack on certain points where the mores are weakest and where people are already beginning to question them (or have a divided conscience with respect to them). We should also infer that it should not attack them directly but should create situations where the people themselves will strain the mores. Similarly, if we recognize the tremendous force of certain processes and sequences we might, with a dynamic value premise, deduce that strategy demands a redirection or stoppage of processes which contain within themselves a motive power in a certain direction, and an effort *against* individuals coming to "adjust" themselves to the processes. Finally, a recognition of the sweep of social trends and of the basic role of invention and economic organization in social causation, coupled with a dynamic instead of a static valuation, would lead one to facilitate the perfection and adoption of those inventions which have the greatest promise of moving society in a desired direction and to seek *social* inventions that would modify economic organization and the effects of mechanical inventions.

Myrdal has made an excellent case for a "dynamic value premise" and gives many practical hints for the student of deliberate social change, among them directing one's attack at points where the mores are weak, redirecting or stopping processes that give negative direction, and giving attention to social invention. Let us now turn to the factor of human motivations and attempt to apply a dynamic value premise to the problem of utilizing and strengthening or redirecting the motivations found in participants in the process of change.

CHAPTER III

Human Motivations as a Factor in Change

One hot summer day, back during the "depression," a W.P.A. worker leaned on his shovel for an instant, wiped his sweating brow, and inquired of the foreman, "Say, how deep are we going to make this ditch?"

"I'll take care of that," snapped the boss. "You go ahead and dig."

This episode reveals the lack of simple courtesy and regard for personal feelings that is all too common in human relationships in a highly competitive society like ours. It also shows abysmal ignorance of the true source of human energy. For too long employees in business and industry, government and schools have been told just to "go ahead and dig." Their managers or bosses or leaders frequently have failed to capitalize on the energy that is generated by even the sketchiest acquaintance with the size and nature of the enterprise in which workers are engaged.

It is certain that great stores of human energy are now being dissipated or are immobilized because of the character of the motivations upon which people operate. In this connection, Arnold[1] makes the interesting proposition that "tiredness is as often the result of doubting the worth-whileness of what we are doing as it is of too much work."

If it is true that strong motivations are a fundamental source of energy, they should be studied as a crucial factor in the process of directed social change, for effective participation in such a process requires the expenditure of a good deal of energy. As someone once said, "What we need to know about human beings

[1] Dwight L. Arnold, "Social Studies Evaluation in the Intermediate Grades," *Social Education*, Vol. VII, Mar., 1943, pp. 117–120.

is what makes them *burn*." What is the nature of the motivations that drive people on to the stage of accomplishment?

The motivations of people are complex and both affect and result from group processes. Gardner Murphy sees two psychological obstacles to a "determined morale" (such as would be a necessary condition of strong, well-directed motivations). The first obstacle is apathy, the second a "hardy skepticism, a disillusioned defeatism which, though very different from apathy, works much to the same end." Murphy [2] declares that we know little about methods of dealing with these two very different sources of difficulty, although he adds that "we can probably cope with apathy with relatively little trouble." A morale program aimed against intelligent, honest, and profound skepticism is another matter, Murphy believes. The skeptic has much ground for doubting that man can affect the course of social change to a significant degree.

The following analysis of the problem of strengthening or redirecting human motivations is designed to suggest possible ways of dealing both with the apathetic and with the skeptical. The analysis puts emphasis on three phases of the problem: (1) the rôle of values; (2) utilization of the factor of dissatisfaction; and (3) the rôle of goals.

THE RÔLE OF VALUES

In Chapter II mention was made of the concern of some persons lest a process that gives no thought to values be employed in effecting social change. At that point the position was taken that any adequate conception of process must provide for consideration of both means and ends. Not only must means and ends be mutually compatible, but the differences of value in various means-ends continuums must be recognized. The desirable situation, from the standpoint of deliberate social change, is that of groups and individuals operating upon the highest possible value level.

[2] Gardner Murphy in Goodwin Watson, Ed., *Civilian Morale* (New York, Reynal & Hitchcock, 1942), pp. 410–411.

Before discussing what are appropriate values for the citizens of a democratic society, it may be well to clarify the way in which values operate in human affairs. Dewey has painted an illuminating word picture to make distinctions among commonly used terms. He refers to the *ideal* as a "comment by the emotions." He looks upon this ideal as a "sense of an indefinite context of consequences." It is from this context that the aim is selected; but the sense of a wider context "enters into the *present* meaning of activity." Continuing, Dewey makes this distinction between the *aim* or *end* and the *value-base* or *ideal:* [3]

The "end" is the figured pattern at the center of the field through which runs the axis of conduct. About this central figuration extends infinitely a supporting background in a vague whole, undefined and undiscriminated. At most, intelligence but throws a spotlight on that little part of the whole which marks out the axis of movement. Even if the light is flickering and the illuminated portion stands forth only dimly from the shadowy background, it suffices if we are shown the way to move. To the rest of the consequences, collateral and remote, corresponds a background of feeling, of diffused emotion. This forms the stuff of the "ideal."

Much as people may delude themselves into thinking that all choice is a matter of sharp, clean-cut decisions taking place in a floodlighted arena, values and aims or goals probably operate in much the way Dewey describes. Values, we may conclude, show us the general "way to move."

Gaps Between Professed Values and Operational Values

Everyone operates at all times upon a set of values, some more clearly defined than others. In fact Americans are conditioned by their culture not only to accept but frequently to act upon certain common values, such as justice, brotherhood, love, generosity, public-mindedness, the worth of human personality, and the method of intelligence. We call all these things good, and we admire people who behave in accordance with them. The difficulty comes in applying these and similar values under novel circumstances or in complex situations where consequences are

[3] John Dewey, *Human Nature and Conduct* (New York, Henry Holt and Company, Inc., 1922), p. 262.

remote. Thus, most Americans were too ill informed of developments in other parts of the world to be aware of the consequences of a blown-up bridge in Manchuria. Rationing was a brand-new experience. Once tried, it appealed to people as a scheme that was basically fair, but a little individual chiseling appeared to each individual chiseler to be harmless and justified for one reason or another. Americans will donate money to starving Chinese and they will contribute old clothing for the destitute people of Europe, but they object when meat disappears from the butcher shops. Perhaps it is that they are unwilling to sacrifice in order that Russians and Frenchmen may have meat; perhaps, on the other hand, they are merely revealing suspicion that a situation has been badly handled, that the missing meat is going not to Europe but to the black market.

The purpose of this analysis is to show that the point at which attention is needed is in the matter of applying high-sounding words and phrases to innumerable practical situations. This will mean finding concrete answers in concete instances covered by such general questions as the following:

Where does justice lie when property values conflict with human values?

Does brotherhood extend to persons of another ethnic group or creed?

Does love extend to the enemy who tortures?

Shall generosity be carried to the point of lowering one's own standard of living if that is the only means of raising the living standards of others?

Will public-mindedness go so far as to make men serve the government that is paying a dollar a year for their services rather than preferring the interests of the company which is keeping them on its payroll?

Is there worth in the personality even of those in the "lower-lower" class?

It will do no particular good to educate people to give respectable answers to those questions as stated. The test comes when Individual A or Group B is called upon to make a judgment and act in a specific instance. Is that judgment and is that action consistent with the democratic ideology to which most people in this country subscribe?

Helping Persons to Improve Their Values

The question remaining is, "How can persons be helped to improve their values?" A clue to the answer to this question may be found in a consideration of how values originate.

Dewey [4] says that value arose as a separate problem "when teleological considerations were eliminated from one natural science after another and finally from the sciences of physiology and biology." This led the way to the experimentalist position that values come out of experience and are tested and revised in experience. The contrast with the older view is well drawn by Childs: [5]

It [experimentalism] contends that it is not tradition and precedent, but the movement of experience responding to changing conditions and expanding bodies of knowledge which should contribute the ultimate criteria of both truth and value.

Individuals can agree on such an origin for the values of the human race and still be of different opinions regarding the way in which the values of given individuals and groups are improved. Some advocate that the first step in a coöperative enterprise should be agreement upon common values.

The desirability of common values is apparent. They tend to unify a group and facilitate adoption of common goals and agreement upon methods of achieving them. In a democracy any group beginning to work together can and should agree fairly readily on such general values as those named earlier in this discussion. But, as can be readily understood from the foregoing paragraphs, it has proved rather wasteful to spend much time verbalizing about such values in advance of experience with them as they operate in actual situations.

The suggestion that it is fruitless to verbalize with regard to values at any length in early stages of group process is not meant

[4] John Dewey, "Theory of Valuation," *International Encyclopedia of Unified Science* (Chicago, University of Chicago Press, 1939), Vol. II, No. 4, p. 3.

[5] John L. Childs, "Experimentalism and Education," *Teachers College Record*, Vol. XLIV, May, 1943, p. 540.

as a denial of the fact that it is better for a group to value justice rather than injustice, love rather than hate, brotherhood rather than intolerance, generosity rather than greed. It is rather to say that only as such values are put to work can their full meanings be seen.

From the standpoint of process it would seem desirable that groups attempt to arrive at common values less by intellectual discussion before launching an enterprise and more by undergoing together many experiences involving valuation throughout the process. Only as values are lived will they come to have real and deep meaning to those who hold them. Only as they come to be deeply held can values exert a strong motivating force and genuinely influence the direction of efforts. If values are deemed important enough, they will prompt the holders to search for ways of realizing them. In fact, Dewey makes this the measure of values: [6]

In empirical fact, the measure of the value a person attaches to a given end is not what he *says* about its preciousness but the care he devotes to obtaining and using the *means* without which it cannot be obtained.

From what has been said regarding the rôle of value in directing social change, it would appear that the problem is rather more than one of agreement upon values, important as it is that coöperating groups have many things in common. The difficult task comes as the group tries to articulate its values in operational terms. This is an indispensable part of any process of change that would guarantee results compatible with democracy. There must be provision, *within the process itself*, for continuous clarification, appraisal, and revision of values. Because of the fact that means and ends are inextricably interwoven, the very choice of process depends upon values held.

Values—Their Implications for Curriculum Change

It has been observed that values are relatively useless as long as they remain verbal abstractions and that, therefore, time spent in early stages of group process on improving verbalization of

[6] Dewey, "Theory of Valuation," p. 27.

values is largely time wasted. Yet, the prevailing pattern of curriculum change as described in Chapter I is based upon exactly the opposite assumption. Many school administrators believe it necessary that each group begin its work on the curriculum by formulating a philosophy of education, a process which they look upon as requiring anywhere from one to two years. Witness the following excerpts from administrators' accounts of their curriculum programs as they appeared in an educational periodical recently.

The report from School A says in part:

The superintendent, declaring —— schools needed a fundamental educational philosophy, appointed a committee of fourteen in the fall of 194–, who spent the school year preparing the twenty "Purposes of Education in the —— Public Schools."

In School B a general representative committee was appointed to

reduce to writing statements of educational philosophy. The statements as set down by this committee were referred to all teachers in the system for criticism and suggestions for revision. After many revisions the statements were approved and adopted as a basis for directing their curriculum efforts.

School C, just beginning a long-time program announces:

Two years will be devoted to the study of basic philosophy at elementary, junior high school, senior high school, and junior college levels.

The approach that is common to these three illustrations violates the principle that excessive verbalization of values should be avoided. It disregards the fact that mere adoption of a philosophy or set of values by a group does not necessarily change the individual's operating values even if each individual has a more direct and active part in the process than is indicated for the teachers mentioned above. It ignores the fact that again and again agreements as to philosophy, made in advance at great cost of time and patience, have broken under the impact of practical considerations in an actual situation. If a process is to contribute to security, growth, and accomplishment, it will not force individuals to squander precious time for results of low endurance value.

Function of General Agreements. As indicated earlier it may be desirable to spend a brief period reaching some general agreements on values as a basis for continuing acts of valuation as group work proceeds. If a group of teachers (not just their principal) so desire, each one might write out a statement of his own philosophy, from which a composite one could be worded. One such composite philosophy, developed in Ovid, Michigan, contained six beliefs expressed in less than one hundred and fifty words. The beliefs covered such things as coöperation between pupils and teachers and between home, school, and community, the purpose of education, the need for centering the program around the child, the need for teaching respect for democracy. The final belief was that "education should never be considered as finished either for the teacher or the pupil." [7]

Even with this commendable start, the Ovid teachers will have to make numerous value judgments with respect to the working of each one of their beliefs. Further elaboration at the time when they were writing down their philosophy would not have saved them from watching their belief about a child-centered program, for example, undergo frequent challenge and illumination as institutional habits and traditions come into conflict with the interests and needs of numbers of children.

The strategy called for has already been implied. Begin with a tentative statement of values held, if so desired, or omit such a step entirely. But, by all means, seek *constantly* to make values explicit. As conflict situations arise, learn the reasons for disagreement and seek for group agreement on some phase of the matter at least. Avoid making decisions of the either-or variety. Learn the technique of finding where on a scale between A and B the group is willing to place itself at a given time on a given issue. Then point up any agreements reached. Make the group feel that unity is *growing*. This advice is equally applicable to

[7] Carl L. Strong and Staff, "A School System Goes Democratic," *The Clearing House,* Vol. XVIII, Sept., 1943, p. 14.

groups of professional educators and to community adults and learners.

UTILIZATION OF DISSATISFACTION

Much more promising in most cases than philosophizing as a way of securing initial interest in deliberate social change is capitalizing upon dissatisfaction. Men do not change their social arrangements so long as they are perfectly satisfied with them. Dissatisfaction with existing conditions seems to be a prerequisite for intentional change. Now it is easy to see that the present period is one in which the *sources* of dissatisfaction are not lacking. Maladjustments in our culture are numerous, varied, and on the increase. Yet, it is not a simple matter to make dissatisfaction function actively as a motivating force in our complex modern society. Dissatisfaction may be present in greater or lesser amounts in different social groups or in different individuals within the same group. The quality of the dissatisfaction, that is the degree of urgency associated with a possible change, will also vary greatly from person to person and group to group. At various times and in relation to various problems different individuals and groups may be arranged on a scale stretching all the way *from* a tendency to be controlled by tradition, habit, inertia, social pressure, fear of and hostility to innovation *to* a tendency to become bored and discontented with the old and curious about innovation.

Even this picture represents an oversimplification, for the motives of those who cling to the old are decidedly mixed. Sumner has made a useful distinction between the conservatism of the aristocracies and that of the "masses": [8]

We must not be misled by the conservatism of castes and aristocracies, who resist change of customs and institutions by virtue of which they hold social power. The conservatism of the masses is of a different kind. It is due to inertia. Change would make new effort necessary to win routine and habit. It is therefore irksome.

[8] W. G. Sumner, *Folkways* (Boston, Ginn and Company, 1906), p. 45.

In utilizing dissatisfaction as a factor in producing change the student of society must learn to deal with these two types of conservatism, the conservatism of those with a stake in present arrangements and the conservatism of those who do not wish to be bothered with change. Then, too, the scale seems not to provide a place for our honest skeptic, who realizes full well the undesirability of present arrangements but who has no confidence that change for the better is likely to come about.

Nevertheless, what Lynd calls a "general emotional receptivity to change" is closely related to the extent and intensity of dissatisfaction present in the population. The problem is partly one of helping people to arrive at a "common definition of the situation" through analysis of conditions and making explicit the maladjustments involved. In the case of the more apathetic persons, much new information and many new experiences will be necessary if they are to become actively dissatisfied. It will be a matter largely of converting a vague sense of discomfort and unrest into strong convictions that certain specific ills should be attacked.

Mary P. Follett believed there was really no such thing as the apathy of the average citizen of which people talk. "Every man has *his* interests," she wrote; "at those points his attention can be enlisted." [9]

In the case of those who cling to established ways because they are the only security they have for maintaining the social power they have acquired there is involved the delicate task of helping them to become dissatisfied with their present definition of self-interest. As for the skeptical, dissatisfaction is already present but will not operate as a positive force unless there is some assurance of success in reducing cultural maladjustment.

Fortunately for human progress, there is a fourth group of persons in whom already exist dissatisfactions of such nature that they are ready to be utilized at once as motivations toward action, other conditions being favorable. This group can be counted on as a nucleus for hastening the process of change.

[9] Mary P. Follett, *Creative Experience* (New York, Longmans, Green & Co., 1924), p. 230.

Dissatisfaction—Implications for Curriculum Change

As with attitudes toward social change in general, emotions with regard to curriculum change are mixed. The wise administrator will study the teachers, learners, and community adults with whom he is in direct contact and will attempt to determine in what stage of readiness for change they are. He will likely find two rough groupings at first—those who are rather dissatisfied with the present school curriculum and those who are apparently rather complacent about it. It will soon be apparent that both of these groups may be subdivided.

Persons Dissatisfied and Willing to Work for Change. Among the dissatisfied are those who are so convinced of the imperative need for curriculum revision that they are willing to make rather drastic changes over a short period of time. Toward this group the administrator has two responsibilities. First, he should determine who are the members of this group and should learn as much as possible concerning their reasons for desiring change and the nature of the changes they would like to see brought about. These persons can furnish valuable support in the initial stages of a program of curriculum development. Second, he must help such individuals to recognize differences in toleration of change and thus secure understanding and patience with a process that may be somewhat slower than they would like. He should be extremely careful, however, not to use these human differences as an excuse for a do-nothing policy. He has a responsibility for hastening the process all he can.

Persons Dissatisfied but Skeptical. The second subdivision of dissatisfied persons contains those who show no great interest in participating in curriculum improvement because previous experience has rendered them skeptical of the productiveness of energy expended in that direction. Perhaps, if they are teachers, they have taken part in earlier curriculum programs that failed to produce satisfying results. Perhaps, if they are learners or community adults, they have received only rebuffs on any occasion when they offered a suggestion with regard to the school program.

It is not surprising that parent and teacher and student groups should contain a goodly number of skeptics. A great many administrators have become able to use the "brush-off" technique with remarkable finesse whenever proposals for change have come from any of the groups mentioned. But even in the cases where administrators have shown an interest in change by inaugurating curriculum programs, the process employed has often been so inept and so contrary to principles of social psychology that the program has defeated its own purpose in the long run.

Toward the skeptical, one responsibility of administrators is, again, to learn who the skeptics are, for they represent a potentially powerful force for change if once they can be convinced that the curriculum can actually be improved through coöperative effort. The administrator should also study their experiences with curriculum development in order to avoid repeating mistakes made in the past. Finally, the administrator should demonstrate that he welcomes their suggestions for change and their help in bringing it about.

Persons Satisfied with Things as They Are. As we turn to the complacent group who exhibit no major dissatisfaction with things as they are in schools, our subdivisions prove to contain, first, those with a vested interest in maintaining the status quo as far as curriculum goes. For example, department heads, special supervisors, and teachers who have specialized in some school subject see that if changes are made in the organization of the curriculum, they may have to make a difficult vocational readjustment. Parents whose children seem destined for college usually desire a high school with a good academic standing and view many changes proposed for the modern high school as a threat to their own children's best interests as they see them.

A second subdivision of the satisfied group contains the persons who are naïve with regard to social realities and uninformed about principles of human development. These individuals live in a sheltered world and are functionally ignorant both of the extent to which maladjustment in our culture is mounting and of the increasing ineffectiveness of the traditional curriculum.

Like all others, persons in the satisfied group should be studied to determine their present motivations. Then, somehow, they must be helped to acquire ever stronger convictions as to the need for changes in the schools. When they have arrived at that state of dissatisfaction, fear of personal inconvenience will already have been greatly reduced. Growth in socialization will have occurred as self-interest has become more identified with group interest.

Various means may be employed to carry on the study here advocated as a basis for planning experiences that will awaken and mobilize individuals. Questionnaires, interviews, and observations of behavior in different situations all are valuable techniques if correctly used. If teachers are invited to show in some way the changes they would like to see made in the school, a rough indication of the amount and nature and location of dissatisfaction may be secured. This may or may not be a wise step to take with community adults and learners at a given stage in their experience with directing change. But certain it is that these persons will not have come into full partnership in the process of curriculum change until they have regularized opportunities to register dissatisfaction.[10]

Methods of Arousing Dissatisfaction. There seem to be three worth-while methods for helping people to begin to see need for curriculum change. One promising approach is through a study of the social scene. There is much evidence that both teachers and administrators are in need of such study on a continuing basis. If the study also engages the attention of community adults and learners, it will be that much more effective in stimulating interest in curriculum change on the part of all who must be sympathetic with change in order for that change to be its most effective.

Now study of the nature of society may be as remote and

[10] While waiting for teachers, students, and community adults to come to the point where they feel free to raise questions and make suggestions without fear of reprisal, the suggestion box as used in industry might be tried. Ultimately participation on a higher level is, of course, greatly to be preferred.

abstract as the formulation of philosophy to which objection was raised earlier. In that case, it will be more academic than motivating. Rather, people should approach community study as amateurs, not sociologists. The study should be begun on a familiar and meaningful level. In other words, social phenomena should be observed and data gathered in the local community. In that event curriculum implications of the findings should be so obvious that they will furnish strong drives for curriculum change.

A good example of approaching curriculum change through attack on problems capable of local study and improvement is the Citizens' Fact-Finding Movement of Georgia, started in 1937.[11] In this study many citizens worked together to discover facts about conditions of life in the various localities in their state. Some of the results had a higher yield than others in implications for the school curriculum. For example, nutrition needs led to activities to improve eating habits; the menace of hookworm led to the growing of vegetables and eventually to home and school beautification. On the other hand, need for dental corrections, though great, provided only a small rôle for teachers.

This project, which has had a real effect on the curriculum of the Georgia schools, illustrates the value of studying the needs of our society through studying local manifestations of those needs. It is desirable for all concerned to achieve an increasingly broad social point of view, but, in the beginning, groups should be encouraged to find an easy place to take hold of the problem of improving our vastly complicated social order. In other words, the uncovering of a social problem based in the local community is more likely to create dissatisfaction and desire for change than consideration of some remote problem.

A second promising approach to curriculum change is to en-

[11] See Charles E. Prall and C. Leslie Cushman, *Teacher Education in Service* (Washington, D.C., American Council on Education, 1944), p. 389. See also Tarleton Collier, "Citizens' Fact-Finding Movement of Georgia," *The Educational Record*, Vol. XXI, Apr., 1940, pp. 131-139.

courage study of human development. A better understanding
of the learning process, of principles of mental hygiene, and
of the nature of growth should in itself motivate much curriculum change. In the case of teachers it probably is better
for study to begin at the local level with children whom they
know. Generalizations and principles can emerge from such a
study and carry fuller meaning as a result.

In the case of the lay person, it may be desirable to depend
more largely upon generalizations and principles in any group
study of human development. Individual adults should then be
helped to make application to the young people they know best.

A third approach is to utilize some dissatisfaction felt by the
persons associated with the school to motivate interest in group
problem-solving. Some persons object to this approach on the
ground that it results in the expenditure of energy on insignificant enterprises. Yet experience has shown that this is not an
inevitable result. Many groups, who have had the benefit of
skillful, evocative leadership have moved rapidly from their
early "low" level of concern to consideration of more basic
sources of difficulty. Since some things are easier to change than
others and since early success is important to high morale, it
seems wise to tackle the simpler problems first.

Choice among the three methods of approach in utilizing
dissatisfaction as a motivating factor in curriculum improvement will depend upon a number of circumstances. In some
instances people need the satisfaction of moving on problems
of real concern to them, minor as they may be. In other situations, where there has been a tendency to amplify petty criticisms into major issues, dissident factions may be united in working toward some goal that is beyond and larger than the trifling
irritations of the moment. This matter is more fully developed
in the paragraphs that follow, where we turn to the problem
of helping groups to set adequate goals.

Cautions to Consider. Two cautions are in order before we
leave the matter of dissatisfaction. It is one thing to help groups
of coöperating individuals to identify problem areas and it is
another to make a teacher or group of teachers feel inadequate

if a problem cannot be produced immediately upon someone's request. Much time has been wastefully expended on problems "manufactured" to save the face of individuals put in the embarrassing position of having to have a "problem."

A second caution is that dissatisfaction should not be regarded merely as a factor operating to furnish initial motivation. It should be utilized at all stages of the process to keep crystallization from setting in. Groups should be encouraged to make use of valuable solutions to problems only so long as they serve a useful purpose. The process of curriculum change should provide for periodic review and evaluation of such solutions as well as regularized opportunities for expression of dissatisfaction at any time by any participant in the process.

THE RÔLE OF GOALS IN HUMAN MOTIVATIONS

We have so far in this chapter discussed the fact that if values have real and deep meaning, they are significant motivating factors. Dissatisfaction was seen as a motivating force of a slightly different type. When made explicit, a dissatisfaction may be the spark that sets off the charge of stored energy. But it is not enough merely to be dissatisfied with what is. Unrest is not likely to eventuate in action so long as men know no alternative to what they have. Therefore, closely related to dissatisfaction as a factor causing men to desire change is some goal or series of goals that promises if achieved to lead to a better state of affairs. The term *goal* is used here in a broad sense. It includes the compelling idea of whose power Urwick writes: [12]

. . . change would be a far slower process than it is, were it not for the fact that many new ideas exercise a kind of hypnotic influence upon their originators and upon many of their followers. The originators not only fall in love with the idea, but often become possessed by it.

It includes also vision of a better world, the prospect of which leads men to plan and work unceasingly. Some of the possibili-

[12] E. J. Urwick, *A Philosophy of Social Progress* (London, Methuen and Company, Ltd., 1920), pp. 113-114.

ties that men see in the years that lie ahead are that increasingly human rights may take precedence over corporate property rights; that we may some day plan production in terms of consumption instead of trying to consume in terms of what people want to produce; that international good-will may become dominant; that social security may become a reality. The word *goal* is also considered in this discussion to be synonymous with purpose, aim, objective, or end. It can be applied equally to the vague and general or to the specific.

The very fact that goals can be of so many sorts shows that goal-setting is a complex activity. In order to play their proper rôle in motivating for social change, the goals toward which any given group of persons is working should possess certain characteristics:

1. The goals should be set by the group for itself.
2. Goals should liberate, not limit, the efforts of individuals and groups.
3. There is need for both specific and general goals, immediate and remote goals.
4. Goals should be flexibly held.

Goals Should Be Set by the Group for Itself

The position that goals should be set by the group for itself has so much support from psychology, both educational and social, that it seems unnecessary to elaborate it here to any great extent.[13]

Mannheim links the idea of self-set goals to freedom in an interesting fashion: [14]

[13] See the following references for reports of experiments revealing that production is increased when groups in industry set their own goals: Kurt Lewin, *Civilian Morale*, p. 61. A report of an experiment by Morrow carried on with two groups of sewing machine workers in a rural area in the South. Goodwin Watson, "The Surprising Discovery of Morale," *Progressive Education*, Vol. XIX, Jan., 1942, pp. 33–41. An interpretation of implications for education of the results of an experiment conducted by the Western Electric Company, Hawthorne Works, Chicago.

[14] Karl Mannheim, *Man and Society in an Age of Reconstruction* (New York, Harcourt, Brace and Company, 1940), p. 373.

Apart from freedom to decide one's own destiny and dispose of one's own property, freedom will depend on the influence one is able to exert in determining the aims which are to be realized by collective action.

It is well established, then, that the motivational value of self-set goals is infinitely greater than that of externally imposed goals. Groups do have the obligation, however, to learn to place their aspiration level at the highest possible point considering their own powers, for the need for rapid social progress is great indeed.

Self-Set Goals—Implications for Curriculum Change

Many administrators reveal lack of faith in the effectiveness of group process for setting adequate goals. As we have already observed, they fear that groups will be everlastingly concerned with insignificant problems and their short-range implications if they are encouraged to set their own goals, especially if they are allowed to do so before going through a long process of arriving at common values. It is this reasoning that lies behind the aims-and-objectives approach to curriculum development that has been so prevalent in this country. The standard mode is for the long process of formulating a philosophy of education to be followed by the outlining of a large number of general and specific objectives that seem to be in keeping with the philosophy agreed upon.

This approach violates the principle that a group should set its own goals. It might appear that, under the procedure in question, selected teachers at least were helping to set the goals toward which they would strive. As a matter of fact, those persons have no part in making the preliminary and basic decision as to whether or not it is profitable for a group to employ the standardized curriculum procedures, which frequently involve spending one or two years struggling with abstractions, arguing over the right word for the right place, and coming out ultimately with a product that is usually used primarily to rationalize existing elements of the curriculum. Is it any wonder that teachers, thinking that this and only this procedure represents coöperative curriculum-making, prefer to be allowed to stay in their classrooms to teach or to plan for the next day?

We pass over the fact that the usual procedure is to give only representative teachers the opportunity to participate in the formulation of aims and objectives that are to form the basis of a course of study for all to follow, and that learners and community adults seldom have a part in the process. If assisting with the formulation of philosophy, aims, and objectives in the standard manner is the highest type of participation in curriculum development that can be conceived, perhaps it is just as well that more persons have not been subjected to it.

Those who have tried to follow the principle that the group should set its own goals report success with the procedure. Hollingshead relates the way in which he learned his lesson.[15] He tried first to interest a group of teachers in developing a common philosophy of education. After a couple of years of rather futile effort, this school principal stumbled onto the fact that teacher interest was readily engaged when the teachers began to attack the comparatively simple problem of how elementary-school children should be dismissed. This problem soon proved to be more complicated than it appeared on the surface, and before long teachers were engaged in discussion of the differing philosophies of education lying back of various dismissal procedures. As this study led on to other matters, the group was finally well launched on a constructive, continuous program of curriculum improvement.[16]

How Growth Occurs. This illustrates the fact that growth comes not as persons work on problems that seem significant only to the status leader, but as they, while taking care of the problems that appear significant to them, learn increasingly to

[15] Arthur D. Hollingshead, *Guidance in Democratic Living* (New York, D. Appleton–Century Company, Inc., 1941), pp. 6–9.

[16] For a delightful account of the adventures of a mythical school administrator as he fumbled for ways of interesting his teachers in the problem of curriculum change, read the story of Joe Brown in the introduction to *Leadership at Work*, Fifteenth Yearbook of the Department of Supervisors and Directors of Instruction (Washington, D.C., National Education Association, 1943).

push their study back to more fundamental sources of difficulty.

Not all groups will need or want to begin with small, specific problems. Their choice of problem upon which to work will depend upon their experience with group goal-setting. If the principle that goals should be self-set is followed, the school administrator can be relatively certain that the group is being allowed to start where its members are and not where he, or someone else, might think they should be.

This does not mean that the status leader does not have large responsibility. His function is to help the group to take up explicit problems which he can see are of such immediate concern and potential import that to attack them will increase the security and sense of satisfaction of the group. Frequently it is out of the behavior of the individuals whom he is responsible for knowing well that the school administrator will get his clues as to appropriate problems for attack. But the formulation and acceptance of the problem must be the product of group thought; otherwise there will be no check on faulty judgments which, considering the unpredictable nature of the data in matters of human relationships, any status leader can easily make.

The chief values of providing for group goal-setting seem to be that (1) the problems chosen for attack will be paced to the readiness of the group and thus will have greater motivating value and (2) the problems will be less likely to be limited to abstract and stereotyped classifications. This latter statement is particularly true if the choice lies between goals set by the faculty of one school and goals set by the central staff of a city system.

Goals Should Liberate, Not Limit, Groups

The position that goals should not place needless limitations upon people is of extreme importance. Taba pleads for predictions (goals) that liberate and do not limit: [17]

The essence of good life includes its unpredictability and its forwardness, the newness of its patterns and the individuality or

[17] Hilda Taba, *Dynamics of Education* (New York, Harcourt, Brace and Company, 1932), p. 107.

uniqueness of its relations . . . this does not mean that one should not foresee human conduct at all. It only means that predictions should be made in terms of liberation and of progress and not in terms of limitations. It means that both the prediction and the control should be alert to the appearance of new possibilities. It also means that the attempt to control should cover general directions, not fine exact outcomes. The absence of exact prediction and strict control does not abandon human affairs to blind chance, or imply lack of all management and conscious direction. The very integration which produces change also produces the patterns of that change. . . .

Margaret Mead recommends goals that do not place ceilings on human endeavors: [18]

We can have no clear vision of a final form which we want society to take; for the minute that we have such a vision we begin to educate, cajole, force people, identified living human beings, to fit into the pattern which we have conceived as good for them . . . If we turn our attention towards processes, towards directions, and away from fixed plans into which we attempt to fit living human beings, we deal immediately with an open-ended system, a system in which we cannot know what the outcome will be. . . .

This "open-ended system," this "lack of a clear vision of a final form which we want society to take" is a source of anxiety to persons who have always found their security in the precise, the definite, the well-outlined. It is difficult for them to accept the idea of working toward an end which no one can clearly describe, even though the steps toward that end are being progressively defined. Yet, according to Urwick, the latter process is the way in which growth actually occurs: [19]

It is one of the conditions of humanity's growth to be always defining and re-defining the good at which it aims, always giving new content to its vague conception of a better social state.

One of the best ways of demonstrating the superiority of open-ended goals is to examine what has happened to a few

[18] Margaret Mead, *And Keep Your Powder Dry* (New York, William Morrow and Company, Inc., copyright 1942 by Margaret Mead), pp. 187–190. By permission of the Company.

[19] Urwick, *op. cit.*, p. 16.

of the fixed limits set by people in the past. Consider, for example, how ridiculous appears to us now Webster's objection to incorporating the Oregon region under the Constitution. "Why," said he, "a Congressman's term would expire before he could reach the Capital!"

In 1934 the Brookings Institute issued a statement to the effect that a 19 per cent increase in production was all that resources in this country would allow. Ten years later production had tripled.

No one knows the ultimate lengths to which the human race can go. Deliberate social change will be hampered as long as people attempt to freeze arrangements at the point where they believe perfection has been or can be attained. Human beings should be given the artist's freedom to "design in materials," to discover through experimentation what may be achieved rather than to be limited by someone's notions.

Liberating Goals—Implications for Curriculum Change

Perhaps the most limiting of all goals in a school system is the end so frequently desired by the central staff, namely that curriculum change shall proceed at the same rate in all the schools in the system. The aims-and-objectives approach to curriculum-building, the issuance of detailed courses of study, the use of administrative *fiat* to effect a change in the curriculum, the adoption of textbooks and selection of other instructional materials in a central office—all these practices are common in city school systems. They come out of lack of faith in the ability of teachers and principals to plan appropriate experiences for learners in their own schools with the help of the adults most closely concerned and with the help of the learners themselves. As a result, many creative individuals are kept from realizing their visions, while persons less ready for change are unduly hurried into new ways for which they are inadequately prepared. Both groups are thus prevented from doing their best work.

The fact that the "aims-and-objectives" curriculum is posited upon a mechanistic theory of learning imposes a further limitation.[20] The curriculum resolves itself into an attempt to realize a multitude of specific aims in an additive fashion in the vain belief that broad general aims are thereby realized.

Defects in Educational Objections. Thompson lists four defects which he finds in current lists of objectives in education: [21]

1. They lack comprehensiveness; they are too narrow in scope to include all the manifold aspects which properly belong to the field of education.
2. They are often listed as abstractions which cannot be made the goal of any desirable activity.
3. They lack dynamics; that is, their pursuit does not move men to action. No one desires them sufficiently to make any effort or sacrifice to attain them.
4. They lack a clearcut organization so that one can distinguish among such levels as broad social objectives, concrete or specific social objectives, teachers' objectives, and pupils' objectives.

Other examples of goals that limit are artificial grade standards, reverence for the intelligence quotient as derived from tests in current use, the subjects considered standard in the curriculum, schedules based on ringing bells, sixteen units for graduation, emphasis on the measurables in teaching, long division in the fourth or fifth grade, fractions in grades five or six— hundreds of items could be listed out of brief study of our institutional habits.

Operating upon a Broad Principle. A contrary approach is meeting with growing favor. Here the concern is not with standardization and with even progress toward numberless fixed objectives. The system as a whole operates on some broad principle that is readily agreed to, such as democratic socialization or helping the young to learn to live the good life. The acceptance of such a broad purpose does not close the matter of

[20] For a detailed analysis of the relation between the "aims-and-objectives" approach and the mechanistic theory of learning see Hollis L. Caswell, "Practical Application of Mechanistic and Organismic Psychologies to Curriculum Making," *Journal of Educational Research*, Vol. XXVIII, Sept., 1934, pp. 16–24.
[21] Merritt M. Thompson, "Levels of Objectives in Education," *Harvard Educational Review*, Vol. XII, May, 1943, pp. 196–211.

values and goals in education; it opens the way for learning what they really may be. A broad end-goal helps to unify all the persons concerned with curriculum improvement and guides them in making the many decisions that are necessary in the process of their coöperative activity. Yet a goal of this nature is open-ended. It does not impose unnecessary limitations but rather requires constant redefinition of the end-in-view and continuous evaluation of steps taken toward the goal.

This newer approach makes no assumption that it is unimportant that teachers and others concerned with the curriculum arrive at common values, that a common philosophy of education is of small moment in group effectiveness in promoting curriculum change. Unless proposed changes can be checked against long-time values, they may be piecemeal and unconstructive. There is a growing belief, however, that common values, a common philosophy, emerge out of experiences with coöperative curriculum development and that all that can be expected at the start is agreement on the general direction in which growth lies.

In line with this tendency to set up a unitary, controlling objective or goal for the curriculum, are the newer practices with regard to development of curriculum materials. Prescriptive courses of study are increasingly being supplanted by teaching aids of various kinds which are developed coöperatively to fill needs teachers themselves see. Other materials that guide but do not limit teachers are curriculum records which make available to others the results of experiences various teachers have had with learners; bulletins giving help with various processes; brief conclusions reached to date by groups of teachers with regard to different areas of the curriculum such as social studies or language arts. Such materials are suggestive; they broaden teachers' horizons by opening up many new possibilities. In short, they liberate by widening the area of choice.

Specific and General, Immediate and Remote Goals

We have been discussing so far the more remote type of goal that serves well to give the general sense of direction which people need. It is valuable to aspire toward such an end as full employment or an enduring peace or the multiplication of democratically socialized individuals. However, goals can be so remote that they fail to give proper guidance as people work along together. Preoccupation with such goals, can, as Lewin observes,[22] make it difficult to "give sufficient consideration to the actual structure of the present situation or to conceive realistically what step in the present world can be taken to achieve this end."

Therefore, people need also concrete plans of action that suggest definite steps that may be taken in moving toward the distant goal. They need a series of specific, short-time goals so that accomplishment can be experienced frequently. But these goals must be viewed in relation to long-time values and goals. Otherwise they can limit vision and preclude intelligent action. That is why it is desirable to have a combination of specific and general goals, long-time and readily attainable short-range goals. In the case of a complex organization, the larger group may hold in common certain broad directional goals in the form of policies upon which the group plans to operate, leaving it to smaller action groups to determine the specific goals likely to contribute to the achievement of the larger ends desired. All organization should provide for this division of labor in order to save the time of the larger group.

Immediate and Remote Goals—Implications for Curriculum Change

The way in which a combination of immediate and remote goals may work has been implied in the earlier discussion in this chapter. A group of persons concerned with the curriculum of a school agree on the broad objective toward which they will work. But this vaguely defined goal is not enough. More specific projects will have to be discovered if groups and individuals are to find rallying points for effort. With all of its ramifications the problem of conservation alone offers countless challenges. Housing needs of a community, need for economic

[22] Kurt Lewin, *Civilian Morale*, p. 67.

coöperation, need for recreational facilities for youth—all these suggest that it is not difficult to discover really dramatic goals within any community.

After these more specific but still large projects have been undertaken, even more specific decisions are called for. A multitude of judgments must be made from day to day, week to week, month to month, and year to year to determine what particular experiences have most promise of helping a particular learner or group of learners to become more socialized or to come nearer to leading the good life. The characteristics of a democratically socialized person, the components of a good life must be defined in terms of operation in a given community if curriculum plans are to provide appropriate experiences for learners.

Examples of decisions which may have to be made in a school are:

1. Is learning to read the most important thing for Robert Brown to do in this year of his life?
2. Is experience in various arts essential for the good life?
3. Will operating the school store be a more worth-while experience for the seven-eight-nines or for the nine-ten-elevens in this school?
4. Should only the best of the children's thank-you letters be sent to the parent who showed slides to Miss White's group this morning?
5. Should every child be required to write a thank-you letter on this particular occasion?
6. Shall music be credited for graduation on the same basis that academic subjects are?
7. In this particular classroom should a student or the teacher serve as a discussion leader today?
8. How can the children in this school be helped to become more responsible?
9. Does academic freedom entitle the teacher to promote racial intolerance or religious bigotry?
10. Shall school time be released for religious education by various religious groups?
11. What is this community's most pressing problem?
12. Shall lunch be served daily to the children? How shall costs be met?

As such questions are met and as answers are obtained that satisfy the group at the time, a growing number of working agreements is reached, agreements which give direction to individuals until new evidence leads to revision of decisions. The making of each decision has entailed weighing and harmonizing of values and thus represents advance toward values held in common. This is a strategy of progressive definition of steps toward an open-ended goal.

Goals Should Be Flexibly Held

Those who find most security in definite, short-run goals are the ones most likely to suffer another type of limitation which goals sometimes impose. That limitation is inability to give up or to change a goal that proves not to be worth the effort of achieving. Many persons, once they have set their goals, are able to revise them only at the cost of great strain. These persons will need help as individuals if they are to learn to consider all goals as tentative and the attainment of them as contingent upon a great many factors. Such persons are often aided by participating on a number of occasions when a group is engaged in the process of reconsideration of goals.

There is a real source of difficulty if goals once adopted are difficult to revise or abandon. No matter how adequate such goals were when adopted, they can effectively forestall experimentation and creativity if they cannot be reëxamined with ease.

Flexible Goals—Implications for Curriculm Change

It is in respect to the difficulty of effecting changes in goals that the standard approach to curriculum-building is particularly faulty, for once general and specific objectives have been outlined at the expense of much time and labor and once they have been made the foundation stones of a detailed course of study for an entire school system, ready modification is out of the question.

Procedures for curriculum development must, to be effective, provide for continuous review of goals set and continuous evaluation of results being secured in pursuit of them, in order that sights may be raised or lowered as the situation demands or that a goal that no longer appears desirable may be abandoned without a major upheaval.

Changes of goal occur in all school systems, but the attendant shock is often great since, as a usual thing, neither teachers, patrons, nor learners have been led to expect and desire change. Much less have they been encouraged to take any initiative in the matter. The nature of the usual curriculum program is such that activity comes in great spurts which necessitate relatively long periods of lull to reëstablish equilibrium. During the intervals of quiescence, individuals tend to grow attached to their present goals and to find security in adhering to them. The greater the length of time between spurts of curriculum activity, the greater the attachment to present goals. The strain involved in revising them is correspondingly great. This is the explanation for the phenomenon of crystallization in education described in Chapter I. A continuous and less spectacular process of change should provide the necessary flexibility in the situation.

Points at which individual teachers may need help are in learning to use a textbook flexibly—to start in the middle or near the end or to use only parts of it as the situation dictates; learning to use all kinds of curriculum materials flexibly instead of adhering to them literally; learning to put the capacities and needs of individual children ahead of the logic of a subject—and many more. Parents will need assistance in understanding such flexibility in school schedules, use of materials, "standards," and the like and in developing necessary flexibility in their dealings with their own children.

SUMMARY

The discussion in this chapter has been concerned with various aspects of the problem of strengthening and directing the motivations of people. It was shown that possibilities of affecting motivations lie in the direction of helping groups to have much experience with valuation, of pointing up vaguely felt dis-satisfactions, and of galvanizing groups to action through the appeal of a vision or idea or goal that provides a focus for ex-penditure of energy.

In the next chapter we turn to conditions that promise to make group endeavor relatively effective. The presence of these conditions have their motivational effects also. In fact, it is diffi-cult to mark as distinctly motivational any parts of the process of deliberate social change. This fact illustrates again the in-terrelatedness of the whole we are now engaged in analyzing.

CHAPTER IV

Conditions of Effective Group Endeavor

In the preceding chapter the rôle of human motivations in group process was discussed at some length. But of what use to help people "get religion" if there is to be no effective outlet for mobilized energy? What is to be the answer to the honest skeptic who does not see how the efforts of a single individual can count for much and who does not have evidence that groups of persons will be able to affect the course of events to a significant degree?

People who are public-minded and eager to serve others are not lacking. Carr declares: [1]

There has probably never been a time when so many people in so many parts of the world were not only looking for guidance, but were themselves so eager to make their own contribution to the building of a new order.

It appears that much motivation for social change is already present. An element that frequently is lacking is favorable conditions for utilizing that motivation. Three conditions favoring group endeavor are discussed in this chapter: (1) organization, (2) group solidarity, and (3) heterogeneity.

ORGANIZATION AS AN ESSENTIAL CONDITION OF GROUP ENDEAVOR

The selection of organization as the first condition for effective group endeavor has been a deliberate one. It has been observed that new arrangements breed new minds. The very act of *participating* with others in organized activity is educative.

[1] Edward H. Carr, *Conditions of Peace* (New York, The Macmillan Company, 1942), pp. 115-116. By permission of the publishers.

Organization provides training in responsibility, giving rise, in turn, to initiative. Moreover, people learn to know the feeling of security and satisfaction that comes from coöperative activity by experiencing that feeling. Dewey has noted that thought is ordered through the ordering of action, while Linton says that "behavior patterns are actually the easiest of all culture elements to modify" and that "most cultural change begins with them." [2] An organization that provides channels for participation of large numbers of persons should be an effective means of changing behavior patterns and therefore should be arranged in the earliest stages of the process.[3]

It is not at all difficult to get support for the claim that organization is of crucial importance in group process. Both Lynd and Dewey have shown its relationship to individual freedom. Lynd writes: [4]

. . . just because of the need of human beings for certain vital freedoms to grow and change, their dependence upon reliable, coördinated, institutional structuring in the culture is correspondingly great. . . .

[2] Ralph Linton, *Study of Man* (New York, D. Appleton–Century Company, Inc., 1936, p. 361). The fact is not overlooked that it is frequently easier for people to change the verbal statements of their values than to operate on the basis of those changed statements. The point here made is that actual cultural change does not take place until people do modify their behavior. It is now being established through new techniques of "action research" that putting people into situations where they cannot help trying out new forms of behavior is a better way to hasten social change than merely to use an intellectual approach. Thus, legislation in recent years has forced industrial management and labor to find new ways of coöperating where exhortation had failed. Legislation has also made it possible for white workers in many instances to have their first experience working with colored people, just as World War II brought colored and white members of the armed forces into close relationship. It is highly probable that to yield maximum value these experiences must be reinforced by intellectual analysis and interpretation, but that does not lessen the worth of actually behaving in new ways. How best to arrange in democratic fashion for people to have opportunities for new forms of behavior and how best to make such experiences fruitful for desirable social change is a comparatively new challenge to our social psychologists.

[3] For a descripiton of teacher growth through such participation, see Appendix A, "Excerpts from Professional Logs," pp. 195 ff.

[4] Robert Lynd, *Knowledge for What?* (Princeton, N.J., Princeton University Press, 1939).

Dewey makes the point in these words: [5]

Individuals can find security and protection that are prerequisites for freedom only in association with others. . . . The predicament is that individuality demands association to develop and sustain it and association requires arrangement and coordination of its elements, or organization—since otherwise it is formless and void of power.

From another source we get challenging evidence of the power and importance of organization for its effect on individual behavior: [6]

Interviewers (factory) had noticed that an individual who is not very capable, or not very well adjusted socially, may behave capably and normally when he works in a human surrounding that suits and sustains him. And, on the contrary, an exceedingly capable and normal human being will behave as if he were neither when he works in inappropriate surroundings.

If organization makes as much difference in individual performance as Mayo indicates, it seems that it deserves serious attention.

At this point cognizance should be taken of the argument always advanced whenever someone urges the value of organization; namely, that a particular *form* of organization cannot guarantee democratic results. It is insisted that it is the spirit in which people enter into association with one another that really matters. Now the importance of a democratic spirit, of real allegiance to humane values is readily granted. One of the sorriest spectacles is autocratic, domineering leadership masquerading under democratic forms of group control. But an equally sorry sight is that of the well-intentioned leader wanting to encourage coöperative endeavor but providing no channels for bringing persons together to plan and carry out ideas and evaluate results of group effort. Without proper organization and means of group attack on problems, the special abili-

[5] John Dewey, *Freedom and Culture* (New York, G. P. Putnam's Sons, 1938).
[6] Quoted from Elton Mayo by W. Lloyd Warner and Paul S. Lunt, *The Social Life of a Modern Community* (New Haven, Conn., Yale University Press, 1941), p. 2.

ties that reside in all members of the group are likely to go untapped.

Although it must be admitted that organization cannot of itself guarantee security, growth, and accomplishment, the desirable type of organization can make a significant contribution to deliberate social change. The following appear to be the characteristics of a desirable organization:

1. It is functional.
2. It facilitates widespread participation and a free-flowing type of interpersonal relationships.
3. It fulfills a constructive social purpose that is the group's own purpose.
4. It provides for continuity of problem-solving.
5. It provides for necessary coördination among groups.

Functional Organization

Ideas about organization are very stereotyped in our country. We have too many notions as to what groups should try to work together, what organizations every up-and-coming community should boast of, what groups we should accept as incapable of undergoing organization, and so on. The weakness of our present forms was revealed over and over again when they were strained by the influx of war workers in community after community. Not only did it prove difficult to blend the old and new members of the community, but organization of the new families within a housing project proceeded slowly and painfully, according to all reports. Out of the experimentation that has gone on in those centers, we may learn some valuable lessons for organizing that great group that usually remains inarticulate in any community.

In no field, perhaps, is social invention more needed than in the field of community organization. There is need to discover types of organization suitable for different purposes. Each community should discover organizational forms adapted to peculiar local conditions.

If De Huszar [7] is right, and there is every reason to believe

[7] George B. de Huszar, *Practical Applications of Democracy* (New York, Harper & Brothers, 1945).

that he is, such organizational forms should be based upon small, problem-centered groups. For example, in Michigan, community organizations have found need for groups to deal with each of the following areas: health, housing, recreation, education, bill of rights, know your neighbor, aid to youth, town beautification, improvements to community services, and studying community needs and resources.[8]

There is need to discover, also, some simple forms of organization suitable for situations where people are unaccustomed to working together on coöperative enterprises. This probably means giving persons opportunity to learn at first in the group that has the greatest sense of common membership, encouraging a branching out when the earlier group seems assured of success. In cases where there is great need for coöperation among groups, the branching out process may have to be hurried more than would otherwise seem best. All such decisions can be made only in light of local conditions and needs.

Functional Organization—Implications for Curriculum Change

Organization for curriculum development in American schools is stereotyped just as is community organization. When Trillingham recommended for all large cities the organization for curriculum-making which he found common to a number of school systems he studied, he was violating the principle that organization must be adapted to the situation for which it is designed. It has not been accident but deliberate appropriation of someone else's pattern that has caused the formation in school system after school system of identical organizations for curriculum development: a central committee on philosophy, aims, and objectives, grade-level and subject committees on specific aims and course-of-study writing, try-out committees, installation committees, reviewing committees, and the like.

[8] "The Community Council in Defense," *Bulletin* No. 3036, Instruction Service Series (Lansing, Mich., State Department of Public Instruction, 1942), pp. 11–12.

Instead of searching for a blueprint of organization for curriculum development, educational leaders will do well to develop an organization suited to peculiar local conditions. If the staff is small, it may be best that it operate largely as a committee of the whole. If the teaching group is sizable, division of labor may be effected through creation of committees. Some prefer a comparatively large number of short-term committees with specific assignments. Others prefer the continuity of planning and the self-propulsion that comes from a very few standing committees with well-defined functions and areas of operation. Some school systems have had success with an organization based upon the three functional groups to be found in any school—professional personnel, learners, and community adults.[9] No matter what plan of organization is selected, there is special value in letting it develop with new needs rather than beginning with an elaborate structure for which there is little use at the time.

In one Negro school in the South, the teachers learned early that a good way to get things done was to enlist the coöperation of the parents by giving them an opportunity to share the community burdens. When trucks parked on the sidewalk before a white business concern near the school and made it necessary for the children to walk out into a dangerous street, the school staff invited the parents to help them get the condition remedied. Success in this venture led the parent group to take action readily a second time when it was pointed out that trucks headed for the city water plant were speeding down the street past the school and constituting a hazard for the children. On a third occasion the parents lent their aid in getting a light for the back yard of the school. The school principal had tried in vain to secure this simple remedy for vandalism on the school grounds.

The teaching group concluded that they were wise in first

[9] For detailed descriptions of this and other types of organization, see G. Robert Koopman, Alice Miel, and Paul J. Misner, *Democracy in School Administration* (New York, D. Appleton-Century Company, Inc., 1943), Chs. 4, 6, 7, 8.

showing the benefits of group action, then gradually perfecting an organization to accomplish more.

As the implication of the four remaining characteristics of desirable organization are examined, other recommendations of general nature will be made. Also it is shown in a later section how the principle of beginning with a group that has the greatest sense of common membership may be applied to curriculum development.

Widespread Participation and Free-Flowing Interpersonal Relationships

Reference has already been made to the fact that a large section of the population in each community remains unorganized. Carr finds that World War II revealed much social power in people in a similar situation in England and pleads for utilization of this material in time of peace: [10]

. . . the civil defence and other services organised during the war have revealed in the British people an immense reserve not merely of devoted service, but of initiative and capacity for leadership, which had never been tapped by our peace-time organs of local government. The problem is to utilise this material and evoke this local patriotism in time of peace by giving to such voluntary services and organisations a real function to perform in our local administrative system. Such cooperation of citizens in the business of administration is a truer form of self-government, and may represent more of the essence of democracy, than voting in a multiplicity of local elections. . . . The determining factor in making democracy real and effective is not to multiply the number of direct channels through which popular authority flows, but to create among the maximum number of people a lively sense that they, and people like them, are administrators as well as administered, and that the conduct of government is part of their business and their responsibility.

The apathy of a large section of the community and their lack of organization for expression may well be a more serious limitation on community coöperation than the differences between organized groups in the community. Moreover, some in this great unorganized section of the population are in more

[10] Carr, *op. cit.*, p. 164.

serious state than apathy and helplessness. Rather, they qualify for inclusion in what Agar calls "masses" and which he says [11] "consist of all those who no longer participate in the creative life and thought of the community: all the cynical, all the hopeless, all the angry, all the frightened. These are the frustrated men and women who no longer can, or no longer will, take part in the work of carrying forward a civilization."

If we wish to stop this social waste and enlist the support of large numbers of people in the task of "carrying forward a civilization," we must find ways of helping those people to feel that a share in social control is possible for them. The innovations in community organization that are lauded at present represent attempts to bring already organized groups into harmonious relationship, usually through the agency of a community coördinating council. This is an important step and much good can come of it. However, changes in social arrangements can be more profound and can come with greater rapidity if ways are found for securing appropriate participation of all the community in attacking common problems. Furthermore this result must be accomplished without developing additional divisions within the community. Thus there is need of organization for enlisting and directing the good intentions and energies of people into channels which seem most likely to guarantee results.[12] Such organization must be based on democratic principles and techniques in order that unhampered communication among people may go forward.

Facilitation of Participation—Implications for Curriculum Change

On no count can the common desire for uniformity in school systems be condemned more readily than for its effect on the amount and quality of participation that results. As long as curriculum development proceeds primarily on a city-wide

[11] Herbert Agar, *A Time for Greatness* (Boston, Little, Brown & Company, 1942), p. 47.

[12] Apropos here is Robert Lynd's terse reminder that "denial of right to prevent free assembly does not mean there will be assembly." *Op. cit.*, p. 217.

front, participation of teachers must necessarily be limited to representatives of individual building faculties, or worse still, to representatives of a district composed of several schools.[13] Participation of learners and community adults in a city-wide program is rarely practiced. Again the experience could be afforded to only a handful of persons on a representative basis and hardly seems worth recommending if wider and better opportunities for participation can be found.

If really widespread participation is desirable, there appears to be no better way than to make the individual school the unit of participation, the primary action agency in curriculum change. This plan has a number of advantages, as will appear in the discussion that follows. But from the standpoint of participation alone it is worth consideration. If an individual school faculty is made responsible for developing, with the aid of all available resources, the best possible curriculum for the learners to be served, the principal and every individual teacher can have an important part in the process. Every learner can have an important part also, although appropriate participation for him will be of a somewhat different character from that of the professional personnel. If the individual school is made the basic unit for curriculum development, we can also go a long way toward solving the problem of how to help give form to that large, unorganized group present in every community.

Advantages of the Autonomous Individual School. Let us examine briefly how an individual school organization may provide, for the three groups concerned, participation that represents an improvement in quality and amount over the typical school situation.

The first suggestion is that the individual school be a relatively small unit in order that face-to-face contacts may be facilitated. It should be remembered that if a school faculty

[13] The need for coördination of the parts of a school system is not overlooked. This matter is discussed on pp. 79–82. For a thoughtful statement of the relationship between the individual school as an organic unit in curriculum development and citywide plans set up on this foundation see Appendix B, "Basic Assumptions for Curriculum Planning in the Public Schools of Philadelphia," pp. 200 ff., prepared by C. Leslie Cushman.

consists of thirty persons, a good working group, there may be anywhere from 500 to 750 learners and from 1,000 to 1,500 parents or guardians to be organized, to say nothing of the adults with no children in school, yet who have an important stake in the program of the school. If it is impossible under existing conditions to plan school units of this size or smaller, it is possible to organize "schools within a school" to get somewhat the same effect.

The second suggestion is that, within the school unit, organization should provide for as wide participation as possible. For the faculty this means regular meetings of the group as a whole for determining lines of direction of effort and general policies upon which the faculty will operate, for group study and for other purposes. It also means the appointment of committees to carry special responsibilities assigned by the faculty.[14] Typical committees deal with teacher affairs, community relations, and curriculum. Every teacher should have an opportunity to participate in carrying out various of these assignments.

For the student body this means some all-school assemblies for the purpose of building group solidarity, a representative council to serve much the same purpose as the faculty meeting, and, in addition, a number of subcouncils or committees to extend opportunities for student participation. While these committees may deal with problems ranging from articles lost and found to running the school newspaper, such experiences are a legitimate part of the curriculum and have their effect on other parts of it.

Coördination of Community Participation. The same general scheme may be utilized for community adults. The general parent-teacher meeting may be used as is the school assembly for the purpose of building group solidarity. It is rather difficult to secure the attendance of non-parents at such meetings, but continuous effort should be expended to that end. It may be of some help if a more inclusive name can be chosen for the organization.

[14] The matter of division of labor is further discussed in a later chapter. See pp. 140–141.

The executive committee of the organization serves the same function as the student council and as the faculty when it meets as a committee of the whole. It may appoint a number of committees that can serve a useful purpose and that give further opportunities for participation.[15]

The whole organization is strengthened and participation is appreciably increased, however, if the homeroom group [16] in the school is made the unit of participation for the parent organization. If a drive is made to organize the fifty or sixty parents and guardians whose children are grouped in the same homeroom at school, it is likely that a larger percentage of the adults of the community will be reached than are in the habit of attending general parent-teacher meetings. In these groups, the curriculum of a given group of learners can be studied realistically, and here there seems to be most promise that parents may actually participate in curriculum development.

There is much to learn concerning the best ways to encourage and guide this participation, but it appears that the process is greatly facilitated by such a development in parent organization as the "room group." Whether or not the participation of non-parents can be secured more easily through this organizational form remains to be seen. Some gain could probably be made by encouraging parents to invite to membership in the room group friends, relatives, and neighbors who would have a somewhat close interest in the problems the group would be considering.

If the parent-teacher organization can provide that the parent chairman of such room groups become part of the executive council of the large association, really functional relationships are established and lines of communication are set up among the

[15] In Bronxville, N.Y., for example, the Parent-Teacher Association usually has the following committees at work: program, recreation, health, cafeteria, library, student-aid, clothing-exchange, adult-education, motion-picture, public-relations, membership, senior-high-school, junior-high-school, and elementary-school.

[16] This term is used here in an inclusive sense to signify the group of learners, at either the elementary or the secondary level, for whose guidance one teacher is primarily responsible.

small groups as well as between the small groups and the large.

As a result of an organization which provides a legitimate rôle for teachers, learners, and school patrons, interpersonal relationships have every opportunity of being improved. Criticism can be put upon a constructive basis. The members of the various groups can come to know one another as persons. Mutual respect can grow as a result of coming to appreciate the contributions each group and individual can make.

Constructive Social Purpose That Is the Group's Own Purpose

The rôle of organization can be weak or strong, malevolent or benevolent, depending upon the use made of it. Organization is used variously according to the purposes of those who help a group to become organized. Sometimes people are called together to be told something, to have a certain idea or project *sold* to them. Sometimes a group is asked to give counsel to some person in power. They know that this advice may be accepted or summarily rejected. Sometimes organization is used to further the group's own education and to help the group to serve itself and the community. In this last case, the group participation may be limited to discussion, which is unfortunate, or it may extend to decision-making, which is more desirable. Needless to say, there is small benefit from the standpoint of morale if the group that goes to the work of arriving at a co-operative decision cannot rest assured that its decisions will be honored. To engage in genuine group thinking, drawing on all available wisdom, in full knowledge that the resulting decision will be used is the highest type of group experience and one that will make a most significant contribution to security, growth, and accomplishment.[17]

Such uses of organization are all legitimate although not all equally effective from the standpoint of the growth of the group and the quality of its accomplishment. There are malevolent uses of organization also. Certain of the pressure groups

[17] See Kilpatrick's description of this process quoted in Chapter **VI**, "Leadership," p. 158.

of our nation fall in this category. They misuse propaganda and will even resort to violence to gain their ends. Yet not all pressure groups are harmful. With our present limited conceptions of community organization, the only way to counteract the work of antisocial groups is to organize other groups to look after wider interests of the community. We have here one of the difficulties in community organization—how to foster some forms of association and discourage others.

A promising solution seems to be to find a type of community organization that will serve the same function that Dewey's good state does and which he describes as follows: [18]

It is quite true that most states, after they have been brought into being, react upon the primary groupings. When a state is a good state, when the officers of the public genuinely serve the public interests, this desirable effect is of great importance. It renders the desirable associations solider and more coherent; indirectly it clarifies their aims and purges their activities. It places a discount upon injurious groupings and renders their tenure of life precarious. In performing these services, it gives the members of valued associations greater liberty and security: it relieves them of hampering conditions which if they had to cope with personally would absorb their energies in mere negative struggle against evils. It enables individual members to count with reasonable certainty upon what others will do, and thus facilitates mutually helpful coöperation. It creates respect for others and for one's self. A measure of the goodness of a state is the degree in which it relieves individuals from the waste of negative struggle and needless conflict and confers upon him positive assurance and reënforcement in what he undertakes. This is a great service.

Far-sighted community leadership should look to wider community organization to absorb the pressures of special interest groups and to facilitate the process of controlling social change.

Constructive and Purposeful Organization—Implications for Curriculum Change

From the standpoint of desirable organization, a city-wide approach to curriculum change reveals another serious weak-

[18] John Dewey, *The Public and Its Problems* (New York, Henry Holt and Company, Inc., 1927).

ness. It fails to generate the motivating power that results from a working group's setting of its own goals. The problems attacked are not those peculiar to a group of teachers, students, and patrons in a given section of the city and are not, therefore, those most in need of solution in that area. Either the selection of problems is made by the central staff or it is the result of compromise. For, if the selection is left to the representative curriculum council, a choice must necessarily be made from among the problems offered as pertinent by various council members. There is no guarantee that the resulting selection will represent a problem of any great moment to the majority of the individual schools—it is merely a problem in which common interest could be found.

On the other hand, if the individual school is made the unit of participation, teachers, learners, and community adults may all have an opportunity to share in appropriate ways in selection of problems to be worked on. They may all take part in a fact-finding survey and then plan together in what ways the school curriculum may best contribute to the solution of problems uncovered. Or participation of learners and patrons in planning the curriculum may be less direct. They may merely by their behavior, their way of living, reveal to an alert faculty needs which the school curriculum should meet. Even though the faculty makes the initial study of the situation, however, constructive participation of the other groups must be enlisted. Otherwise the principle of self-set goals is violated.

Continuity of Problem-Solving

The most deplorable result of the loose nature of community organization at present is that problems abound, many persons recognize them, yet responsibility for attacking them belongs to no one in particular. Even if some socially minded group or individual makes an attempt at solving a problem, the effort is soon lost to view and forgotten. The work is seldom followed up so that gains may be maintained.

The community coördinating council is the best answer yet found for ensuring continuity of attention to community problems selected for attack. Experience with community councils has revealed five desirable functions of such an organization: [19]

1. To meet urgent, current community needs, whether they be war, floods, delinquency, beautification, or any other.
2. To help organizations work together on the community activities of common interest.
3. To use local and distant resources as effectively as possible in meeting community problems. The council inventories local resources in health, recreation, leadership, money, space facilities, business opportunities, and other areas; as well as finding and using the advice and personnel of colleges, successful councils, state governmental bureaus, service clubs, and others.
4. To define the nature of the neglected areas of community life and plan suggested solutions.
5. To indirectly stimulate the member organizations through routine participation in the council, to a continuous self-evaluation of their own activities as a community group.

The accompanying diagram shows well the organization of a typical community council, that of Glencoe, Illinois.

The coördinating council can be no stronger than its constituent groups, however. If they represent only a minority of the community population, it is evident that many community problems, perhaps the most serious ones, will continue to be overlooked.

Continuity of Problem-Solving—Implications for Curriculum Change

As is true in the community so in schools: one of the commonest faults of group action is the spottiness of attack on curriculum problems. A problem arises; a committee is appointed to solve it. The committee studies, reports, and is dissolved. Action recommended by the committee may be taken and the report may be filed. But there is no one responsible for follow-up; no group is charged with responsibility to make continuous study in the area in which the problem arose. Two or more years later, the problem recurs. A new committee studies it, usually without knowledge of the work of the previous com-

[19] "The Community Council in Defense," p. 7.

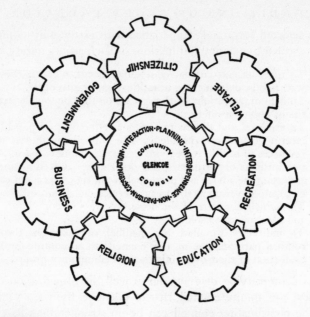

BUSINESS
  Chamber of Commerce
  Rotary Club

RELIGION
  First Church of Christ, Scientist
  Glencoe Union Church
  Lutheran Church
  North Shore Congregational Israel
  North Shore Methodist Episcopal
  St. Elisabeth's Church
  St. Paul's A.M.E. Church

GOVERNMENT
  Caucus Plan
  Library Board
  Park Board
  Village Board

WELFARE
  Arden Shore
  Infant Welfare
  Relief and Aid

EDUCATION
  Board of Education
  Parent-Teacher Association
  Glencoe Public Schools

RECREATION
  Boy Scouts
  Girl Scouts
  Glencoe Amateur Players
  Playground Committee
  Threshold Players
  Garden Club of Glencoe, Shokie
  Garden Club of Glencoe, Founders
  Masonic Lodge No. 983
  New Trier Sunday Evening Club
  Woman's Library Club

CITIZENSHIP
  American Legion
  D.A.R.
  League of Women Voters
  Glencoe Historical Society

ORGANIZATION OF A COMMUNITY COUNCIL

From Koopman, Miel, and Misner, *Democracy in School Administration* (New York, D. Appleton–Century Co., Inc., 1943), p. 301.

mittee. And so it goes. The procedure is wasteful in the extreme.

To overcome this weakness in group action, it is suggested that a small number of functional, standing committees be appointed to assume responsibility for continuous study in a given area of the school program. For example, it has been found in several schools that suitable standing committees for a faculty organization would be one on the curriculum, which would deal with all problems relating to the experiences of students and would further student organization and participation in curriculum development; one on teacher affairs, which would be concerned with professional growth and problems of the faculty; and one on community relations to take special responsibility for coöperation with the adults of the community, organized or unorganized, and for furthering adult organization. For any problem that might arise, there would be, under such a plan, an existing group ready to assume responsibility for it. In fact, standing committees should be engaged in such continuous study of their area of responsibility that problems are anticipated before they assume serious proportions. If a special committee is needed to handle some matter, a subcommittee could be appointed to report to the parent committee, which would be responsible for follow-up work after the subcommittee had discharged its special assignment. With such adequate provision for continuous planning, emergencies that cannot be cared for by existing machinery should seldom arise.

Provision for Necessary Coördination Among Groups

The need for social invention in the realm of community organization is great, particularly at the point of coördination. The observation has been made that the day of isolationism in organizations is past. Councils of social agencies as well as all-community coördinating councils are common.[20] Within large

[20] A biennial summary (mimeographed) of community coördinating council activities at Dowagiac, Michigan, lists twenty-three community needs to which attention had been given. These needs were adult education, community seal, city improvement, rural economy, delinquency, public discussion, music, rural education, underfed children, clinical services,

cities coördination has been tried on the block and neighborhood basis. One is beginning to hear of coöperation between school and stage and among radio station, school, and museum. Such efforts should be extended. We have only to note the divisions and cleavages that are still frequent among community groups to realize the need for further efforts at coördination. Whatever discoveries are made, it is certain they must follow the principle that organization should provide within itself for coördination.

Coördination—Implications for Curriculum Change

Coördination within the school is a more simple problem than at the community level. Yet even here it is difficult, especially in larger cities, and coördination of efforts of the school and of other community agencies presents special problems.

From the standpoint of coördinating efforts the traditional organization of larger school systems has been particularly weak. Caswell has given a good description of the typical situation: [21]

. . . the school curriculum has been a battleground of special interests—forming alliances, making plans, developing programs, each interest with relatively little concern or regard for the others except as its own field is advanced. . . . The program and administration of our schools as organized facilitates the operation of these special interest groups. Programs of supervision have made it easily possible for supervisors in specialized areas to work without regard for the total educational program, methods of curriculum development have assumed as a basis of organization the independence of specialized areas, and the most widely employed methods of teaching have contributed to the same end. The condition which has grown up in practical school situations frequently makes impossible the development of a unified and well-balanced educational program. In one large city, for example, there were at one time fifty-seven separate and distinct supervisory agencies dealing directly with instruction in the individual schools of the city. Programs were projected by

youth hazards, jobs for young and old, charity funds, entertainment, economy, medical equipment, date clearance, youth coöperation, books, church coöperation, health, recreation, welfare.

[21] H. L. Caswell, "The Function of the Curriculum Director," *Curriculum Journal*, Vol. IX, Oct., 1938, pp. 245–249.

these groups with little knowledge and almost no concern for or understanding of the larger educational program. One group after another descended on the schools with its enthusiasm and program. . . . The disintegrating effect of this procedure on the instructional program may well be imagined.

If the individual school is made the primary action agency in curriculum development, many of these difficulties resulting from faulty organization can be avoided. Instead of the old arrangement whereby each teacher served ten or more masters, specialists can be brought into a service relationship to the teachers and principal of a given school.

If widespread participation in curriculum-building is to be encouraged through the medium of the autonomous individual school, coördination at many points will be needed. Within the school's faculty organization itself there will be need for coördination among the basic committees. This may be provided by the faculty serving as a committee of the whole or by a coördinating committee of some kind on which the chairmen or other representatives of the basic committees will serve as a matter of course. The student council serves as the coördinating agency for the student organization, while the executive council is the coördinating agency of the organization of community adults.

Coördination Among Schools. Coördination among schools is also highly desirable, not for purposes of securing uniformity but to quicken the pace of curriculum change through exchange of experience and dispersion of practice, as well as to come to certain working agreements. These agreements should be such as to facilitate coöperation among schools, to reduce as much as possible and desirable the spread in policies and procedures which results from the "broken front" approach to curriculum development, to attack problems that the system as a whole may have in common (such as articulation between levels of the school), and, in general, to further group solidarity throughout the school system.

A curriculum council of some sort can facilitate the exchange of curriculum records among schools. It can supplement the efforts of individual schools to evaluate their results by instituting and servicing certain evaluative studies for the system as a whole. A central council can also keep watch that spread in practice does not become greater than teachers, patrons, and learners can tolerate. In case of need, it can engineer the fashioning of broad working agreements among schools.

An agreement that school staffs may find it convenient to hold in common for the system as a whole has to do with the use of manuscript writing in the elementary grades. It may be desirable to agree whether or not children shall be asked to make the transition to cursive writing, and, if so, at what approximate grade level the change shall be made. Or the teachers may wish to agree that children will be placed in appropriate class groups without regard to academic achievement, necessitating the willingness of all to adjust curriculum experiences to the varying abilities of the children even at the secondary level.

Another service that can be rendered by a curriculum council is to provide for inter-school and inter-level teacher participation on projects that concern them. Many times teachers find it profitable to work with teachers in similar positions in other schools on matters of common concern. Again teachers from the elementary and secondary school find value in attacking common problems.

A final service that can be rendered by a central council is to provide in various ways for in-service education of the professional personnel. Such a council should take responsibility for only those activities which are more effectively provided for the system as a whole. For example, it may organize workshops, provide for the publication of various kinds of curriculum materials, plan and engineer conferences or institutes of different kinds, and plan for use of experts who may be secured from within or from outside the school system.

In order to function effectively, such a council should not be too large, yet it should include at least one representative from each school as well as appropriate members of the central staff. If the size of the school system would make it impossible to follow the latter principle without creating an unwieldy council, it is suggested that the system be divided into districts of reasonable size. A senior high school with its contributing junior high and elementary schools would in most cases make a natural and functional grouping.

In addition to the central curriculum council, it is often helpful to include in organizational plans at the city or district level, a council composed of all specialists (health, library, the arts, general curriculum, and others) in order that they may meet to plan and better coördinate their services to teachers and principals and to faculty groups. The curriculum director is the logical choice for chairman of this service council as coördination of special services is a suitable responsibility for him to assume.

City parent-teacher councils also have some usefulness as coördinating agencies, although community coördinating councils which coördinate efforts of all organized groups in the community are probably preferable. In such a group, the school can take its proper place in the larger setting of community education and the efforts of all groups that are directed toward this end can thus be made more efficient.

In concluding this discussion of the rôle of organization in effecting curriculum change, it may be well to give special emphasis to two points. First, the plan which makes the individual school the unit of participation multiplies the amount of experimentation carried on within a school system and therefore increases the chances of social invention.[22] This is merely

[22] In Kansas City, Mo., individual school faculties under the leadership of their principals are trying a variety of approaches to curriculum improvement. One group of three elementary schools is coöperating with the secondary school in their district in promoting the work of a community coördinating council for community improvement. Another elementary school is making much use of parents in extending to children opportunities for participation in the management of the school. A group of high-school teachers has voluntarily banded together under the leadership of a counselor to study ways of improving opportunities for gifted students to realize their potentialities. And so it goes.

In Denver, Col., individual schools are experimenting with various ways of making a transition from the platoon organization which still exists in some of the schools. One school is making a special study of how to use the staff in order to give a maximum of service to the children

one way of applying the principle of heterogeneity which is discussed in later pages of this chapter.

A second point that should be stressed is that, while some of the details of organization here suggested may seem to resemble those in current use in many school systems (the central curriculum council, for example), there is a vast difference if the usual hierarchy of a school system is turned upside down. In a school system where primary responsibility for innovation resides with the central office staff and where the major objective is to secure uniformity, a central council is very different from what it is if variety is encouraged through placing responsibility with the individual school faculties.

GROUP SOLIDARITY

That group solidarity is an essential condition for effective group endeavor is obvious. Membership in a group that is having success experiences reduces the loneliness of human beings. It reduces the sense of frustration that the individual feels in a period of extremely rapid change like the present. For, as Margaret Mead says,[23] "It is a bleak and lonely business looking into the future, modeling one's life on an undrawn blueprint."

---

and yet relieve teachers for desk work, planning, home calls, and so on.

In Philadelphia individual teachers were invited one year to make an attempt during the year to use the community in some way in their teaching. It was suggested that they might make a study of some aspect of community life and find some way of bringing the community into the school and the children out into the community so that both might learn and both might serve. The response was amazing. Excellent accounts of unusually realistic educational experiences poured in. The most suggestive of the curriculum records thus obtained go to make up a body of illustrations that should help and stimulate other teachers. By giving teachers freedom to be different, the realm of choice for all teachers is enlarged and enriched.

For a detailed account of the way in which heterogeneity has been allowed to operate as a factor in the program of curriculum development in the state of Maine, see Appendix C, pp. 212 ff., an account by William H. Burton.

[23] Margaret Mead, *And Keep Your Powder Dry* (New York, William Morrow and Company, Inc., copyright 1942 by Margaret Mead), p. 74. By permission of the Company.

It has been observed that it is easier to change the ideologies of groups than of individuals. It is well known also that problems can be solved by the application of group power that could never have been touched by individuals working singly. The value of strong social cement is so apparent that we need not labor the point further. Let us, instead, turn directly to consideration of various ways of achieving such solidarity.

There are many methods of promoting unity within groups —some sound, some unsound. As a general rule, the easy, short-cut routes to solidarity are the least desirable both from the standpoint of permanence of the unity achieved and from the standpoint of the effect on the individuals composing the group in question. In all choices of means we should keep in mind that we desire to guarantee security, growth in socialization, and satisfying and satisfactory accomplishment for the individuals concerned.

Lippitt suggests that group solidarity may have either external or internal sources of strength but that the resulting unity will vary according to its source. He writes: [24]

Whether the group's interpersonal unity is derived from mutual resistance to external pressures or from spontaneous inner sources of cohesion is a fact of considerable importance both in determining the extent to which the group will resist disrupting forces and persist in its efforts toward goal attainment, and in determining what channelization the tension resulting from group frustration will take.

Examples of unity derived from resistance to external pressure might be those secured from use of fear and hatred of others. Such motives are unsound. Racial, religious, and economic antagonisms may serve to unite certain groups within the culture, but they cause such cleavages in the culture as a whole that the net result is most destructive. A desirable type of group solidarity does not preclude but rather fosters feelings of unity with larger and more remote groups.

[24] Ronald Lippitt in Goodwin Watson, Ed., *Civilian Morale* (New York, Reynal & Hitchcock, 1942), p. 131.

Another source of solidarity that might be called external is leadership. Lippitt's experiments at Iowa University have demonstrated the character of group structure resulting from three types of leadership: autocratic, laissez-faire, and democratic.[25] Groups with laissez-faire leadership show more signs of frustration than do groups under either autocratic or democratic leadership. A laissez-faire policy on the part of the group leader cannot be depended upon to produce strong group loyalty.

The apparent group solidarity resulting from dependence on a dominating leader disintegrates rapidly, Lippitt found, when the leader's direction is withdrawn. Groups under democratic leadership are little affected by the withdrawal of leaders, which seems to indicate morale of high order. In addition, such groups produce more socially constructive suggestions on practices and policies than do groups under other types of leadership. Democratic leadership capitalizes upon inner sources of strength and thus produces a sounder type of unity.

In helping to build this sounder type of solidarity the leader may draw heavily upon the cohesive force of common values and purposes in ways which have already been discussed. He may take account of the fact that solidarity grows out of group action as well as out of group planning. He may use organization in creative ways for increasing unity. In this connection, Lynd gives support to the principle, elaborated in the earlier discussion, that organization should be based upon units where there is a large sense of common membership. He declares: [26]

Human beings crave big, aggregating symbols on a culture-wide scale, but they also crave localized and highly personalized meanings. Human loyalties are largely built of an infinite number of shared purposes in commonplace daily acts.

The general point of view taken here with regard to group solidarity may be expressed in these words of Childs,[27] "We must not *force* unity; we must *find* it."

[25] *Ibid.*
[26] Robert Lynd, *op. cit.*, p. 86.
[27] John L. Childs, class lecture.

Group Solidarity—Implications for Curriculum Change

The problem of achieving solidarity in schools has been over-simplified. Educational leadership in the past has counted too heavily upon the mere fact of teachers' working together in the same building or school system for the same apparent purpose to build staff unity. An occasional parent-teacher meeting and school assembly have been thought enough to promote solidarity among school patrons and learners. Reference has already been made to the weakness of the method of representation for building a common philosophy and fostering curriculum change.

One of the first responsibilities of educational leadership should be to promote pride and joy in the work people do around a school. It is probable that a strong sense of responsibility results more from enjoyment of a job than from a sense of duty. It is a great weakness not to be proud of what one is doing, not to want credit for it. There should be no cause for apologetic attitudes on the part of teachers, learners, or patrons. The daily work of all these persons should be dramatized by viewing it frequently in its broad perspective, stopping to take stock every so often so that groups may have the pleasure of saying, "This, this, and this have we accomplished; what shall we do next?"

Opportunities should be provided for all individuals to make their unique contributions to the whole educational enterprise, opportunities to be followed by generous recognition and praise for accomplishment. There should be enough routine in daily work to give security but there should be enough flexibility to make the teaching-learning process somewhat exciting and adventurous. Promotion of social good times for all participants in the process of curriculum change is another important way of increasing solidarity. Finally, a "we" feeling may be engendered by giving different individuals opportunities to interpret the school program to others: children to parents, parents to other parents, teachers to the Woman's Club or to teachers from another community.

A special responsibility of educational leadership toward

teachers is to help them to become real members of the community. This can probably best be brought about, in an official way, through provision of opportunities to participate in joint enterprises, opportunities which are facilitated by the type of school and community organization advocated earlier in this chapter.

Solidarity between school and home can also be built around the values for which Lynd believes the home stands: [28] "sympathy, understanding, neutrality, gentleness, treating persons as persons, coöperation rather than aggression." It is easy to see that the school values these same things.

The organizational scheme which is built around the individual school as a unit has both advantages and disadvantages when judged by its effect on group solidarity. It is a comparatively simple matter to build strong group feeling among the teachers, learners, and school patrons belonging to an individual school. This very fact may operate to make group solidarity in a city school system less possible. It is true that there is a tendency for a school that has moved rather far ahead of the procession to develop an unconscious attitude of superiority, while resentment of the success of others is a frequent defense mechanism of those who have achieved rather less. Thus professional jealousy and community rivalries may be encouraged.

In facing this possibility, it is well to recognize the fact that such antagonisms were prevalent long before individual school autonomy was thought of. Furthermore such results are not inevitable. Certain means of promoting unity have already been suggested—teacher coöperation on inter-school and inter-level projects, the central curriculum council and the community coördinating council, workshops for teachers (which might well be opened to community adults also), and educational conferences (in which patrons as well as educators from different schools may join).

It may be well to examine present practices which foster disunity, such as inter-school contests of various kinds. It may be possible to realize the values claimed for such activities in ways

[28] Lynd, *op. cit.*, p. 95.

that will not promote the solidarity of the smaller group at the expense of wider community solidarity. For one thing, it seems certain that there should be further exploration of such promising practices as exchange of assembly programs, inter-school festivals on a non-competitive basis, all-city bands, orchestras, choruses, and verse choirs, inter-school conferences on problems of student government, inter-school visitation by groups of children, and many more. Inter-school visitation might also have value for groups of school patrons. We may assume that it should be common practice as far as educators are concerned.

For groups of learners, teachers, and other adults to work together to render some kind of community service is an additional means of achieving group solidarity. Invention of other ways of promoting solidarity assuredly is called for. Such invention is facilitated in the presence of good organizational forms.

Educational leaders have the further responsibility of extending group solidarity, through organization and other means, to the area, state, regional, and national levels. All who are concerned with education will get support, courage, and vision from a growing realization of their common cause with teachers, learners, and patrons in other communities. That this wider solidarity is important for curriculum change was discovered by Saylor in his study in certain counties in Virginia. He found isolation a retarding factor: [29]

. . . this factor of isolation—in some states amounting to no more than sheer distance from the cultural and educational centers of the state—is something that must be faced by state curriculum directors and educational officials.

HETEROGENEITY

Another factor conditioning effective group endeavor is the way in which heterogeneity is utilized. The relationship between heterogeneity and group solidarity is apparently paradoxical. On the one hand there is the point of view expressed by

[29] Galen Saylor, *Factors Associated with Participation in Coöperative Programs of Curriculum Development* (New York, Bureau of Publications, Teachers College, Columbia University, 1941), p. 237.

Park and Thomas, who state: [30] "It is evidently important that the people who compose a community and share in the common life should have a sufficient body of common memories to understand one another." On the other hand there is little stimulus to change in a group containing too few differences. Urwick has described well the results to be expected in proportion as groups are homogeneous or heterogeneous: [31]

The least stimulating group is usually one which is most homogeneous. . . . The tendency to innovation, to the formation of new social aims and impulses, is largely conditioned by the comparative homogeneity or heterogeneity of grouping. . . . We may safely assert, then, that the process by which social change takes place is closely connected with the two opposite processes of imitation and criticism of ideas; imitation predominating undisturbed as a conserving influence in proportion as the group is homogeneous; critical selection predominating as an innovating factor in proportion as the group is heterogeneous, or as close contact with other groups increases.

It would appear that a relatively heterogeneous group has two advantages over one that is more or less homogeneous: (1) a heterogeneous group is bound to have more evidence of need for change, for, because of differences in needs felt and facts possessed by the members of the group, more problems will come to the group's attention; and (2) a heterogeneous group is more likely to arrive at solutions that contribute to the welfare of all for the reason that different biases will tend to counteract one another. The common denominator reached as a result is likely to serve the interests of the total group.

Integrating Extreme Differences

It is true that groups may contain such wide differences that to find common bonds is extremely difficult. Some are inclined to believe that there are limits to the differences that can be tolerated if group effectiveness is to be maintained. There is a

[30] Quoted in Kimball Young, Ed., *Source Book for Social Psychology* (New York, F. S. Crofts & Co., 1927), p. 50.

[31] E. J. Urwick, *A Philosophy of Social Progress* (London, Methuen and Company, Ltd., 1920), p. 107.

strong possibility, however, that extremes are most difficult to tolerate in cases where only the extremes are present; for example, monopoly capital and labor. Those same extremes might be able to contribute usefully to the solution of a problem being attacked by a group representing a fuller range of experience and interests. At least this seems to be an hypothesis worth testing.

There is nothing really incompatible about valuing a condition of group solidarity and at the same time believing that heterogeneity of a certain amount and kind is a desirable group characteristic. One of the most concise statements of the amount and quality of heterogeneity desirable comes from Lewin: [32] "Productivity depends upon the number of diversified abilities and needs that can be integrated into an organized, unified endeavor." This is characterized as "diversity within unity."

Thus group solidarity and heterogeneity are not mutually exclusive. Diversity within unity is possible. But it requires nice judgment to determine in each actual situation the point beyond which diversity cannot go without destroying desirable unity. The remainder of this chapter is devoted to the problem of building and maintaining solidarity while yet utilizing heterogeneity. In the nature of the case, it will be impossible to give exact prescriptions. It is possible, however, to point out the kinds of decisions that may have to be made and to present certain suggestions for consideration as those decisions are made.

The problem of achieving diversity within unity has two aspects: (1) that of determining the proper rôle of the individual in group process and (2) that of determining the proper rôle of minority groups. Let us examine these two phases of the problem in turn.

The Rôle of the Individual

The status of the individual in a group has everything to do with his security, his growth, and his contribution to joint achievement. We have already discussed briefly the interrelationship of the process of individuation with the process of

[32] *Civilian Morale*, p. 57.

socialization.[33] Follett contributes to the expansion of this theory the statement: [34]

> We need a technique of human relations based on the preservation of the integrity of the individual. Of late years we have heard too much of the collective life as an aim in itself. . . . What we care about is the *productive* life, and the first test of the productive power of the collective life is its nourishment of the individual. The second test is whether the contribution of individuals can be fruitfully united.

We have the fact of human differences to deal with. We should value them as sources of innovation. We should learn how most wisely to "nourish" and "fruitfully unite" those differences in order that they may be productive.

This has implications for the values and goals of the individuals making up a group. It is agreed that centering upon some guiding principles is essential to group solidarity. Yet, it is only realistic to expect that various persons will conceive the end differently. Some may envision a human being socialized beyond the point that others in their present state of development can conceive. Ideas as to the good life differ with the experience of people. That very difference in vision is a requisite for progress.

There are bound to be differences also in the steps taken toward the goal. In other words, there may be much variety in the immediate and specific goals of different individuals. This, again, is a development we must expect and value. Better ways are found out of wide and wise experimentation. Wisdom in experimentation depends upon the controlling purpose of the experimenters coupled with the intelligence they apply to the situation. Thus, we value unity in general purpose, diversity in ways of achieving that purpose. If conditions are right, ways found best will spread and further the unity of the group. If conditions are right the best ways of today will endure only so long as there is nothing better to replace them.

Implications for organization are that the freedom of choice given to an individual and the degree of responsibility he is

---

[33] See pp. 24–25.
[34] Mary P. Follett, *Creative Experience* (New York, Longmans, Green & Co., 1924), p. xiii.

encouraged to take should be adjusted to his ability at a given time. The organization should provide so many opportunities for participation in different capacities that each individual can be a contributing member at all times no matter what his aptitudes.

It is well to recognize that there are differences that cannot be tolerated. Antisocial behavior on the part of some individuals makes it impossible for other individuals to play their rôles creatively. The organization must protect the group from noncontributive and destructive individuals, while these persons are being helped to find a more productive rôle.

The Rôle of the Individual—Implications for Curriculum Change

If difference is fruitful for change, the first consideration of leaders in education should be to secure a desirable amount and kind of heterogeneity. As far as teachers are concerned, this will mean a change in employment policies in many instances. Instead of giving preference to products of local teacher-educating institutions and to people who come from the home town, conscious effort will be made to employ products of various institutions, persons from different states and regions. It would be well also to balance faculties as to age and sex, even in the elementary school. Persons of different kinds of ability and interests should be sought. Persons of different race and creed, persons of foreign birth should be considered valuable additions to a teaching group if their other qualifications are satisfactory.

A word of caution, however. It is unwise to bring into a staff persons who will seem to the rest of the teachers and to the learners and community adults to be extreme, to be "freaks" as it were, merely because of the limited contacts which the members of the receiving group have had. The principle of heterogeneity must be applied gradually as groups show readiness. It would not be wise, either, to bring into the group persons whose social and educational philosophy is known to be reactionary. It is enough of a problem to build unity of value and purpose out of the diverse elements to be found in any school and community without deliberately adding to the difficulty. In other words, differences *to be sought after* should be productive ones.

Standardization Incompatible with Heterogeneity. The principle of heterogeneity has implications also for the ways in which individual teachers are treated on the job. The emphasis on standardization in schools has caused deplorable social waste. In a futile attempt to prevent any teacher from falling below an arbitrary standard of performance, detailed instructions have been issued which limit the exercise of whatever creative ability a given teacher may possess. Even in the schools where teachers were expected to follow uniform directions they have not really done so—they could not, differing from one another in every way as they do. Since there usually is more than one way to reach a goal, it would seem better to help each teacher to develop his own best procedures. Naturally, these procedures would be based upon the best available educational thought. It is the responsibility of those who give or take freedom to make use of the best thinking of the time. The resulting discoveries will give the group as a whole a wider range of choice.

The faculty will still be a team working together and in various relationships with learners and school patrons. We have no desire that teachers turn into a group of prima donnas, each vying with the other to see who can learn and hoard the greatest number of secrets to success. Differences have little value unless shared. The responsibility for a good school must remain a collective responsibility of teachers, principal, learners, and community adults, utilizing all possible resources including members of the central staff. Each teacher must expect that some of his planning *for* his children will be done coöperatively with the faculty and community adults of his school and that, also, some of his planning *with* his children will be submitted to the wider authority of the group of co-workers responsible for that particular school. These are necessary steps for achieving and maintaining desirable unity and for supplementing the relatively limited vision and ability of the individual.

Heterogeneity and Common Values and Goals. All the operations sketched above are assumed to take place within the framework of broad and continually refined agreements as to philosophy and goals. Application of the principle of heterogeneity raises a problem at this point. The problem is the amount of difference in educational philosophy that can be tolerated within a school and school system. Is it justifiable, in the interests of capitalizing upon the values that come from the factor of heterogeneity, to require children to make difficult hourly, daily, or yearly adjustments from authoritarian to democratic to laissez-faire teacher leadership as they proceed from grade to grade, from level to level of the school system, or from one subject teacher to another?

It has already been indicated that it is best deliberately to select teachers whose philosophy of education and life is "desirable." In the case of teachers who are already on the staff, there can be no short cuts. However desirable it might be that they begin to operate at once on the basis of a common philosophy, the achievement of such a condition must be a gradual process if the desire is for a genuine conversion that will be reflected in practice. If earlier advice is to be relied upon, it will probably pay dividends if educational leaders bend their efforts toward helping teachers as quickly as possible to learn what it means to be consistently democratic in their dealings with children. Meanwhile, it would be the better part of wisdom to use good judgment about the kind of children who are placed with certain teachers. With a little care it is usually possible to protect individual children from the necessity of adjustments that are more difficult than they can reasonably be expected to make.

The Volunteering Principle. Still another choice which the principle of heterogeneity imposes is that having to do with volunteering for participation in curriculum development. This is not an easy question nor one that can be answered arbitrarily. In general, it may be said that the volunteering principle does not promote balance. Some persons volunteer for too many things, some not at all. Many volunteer for posts that have least promise of promoting their growth. A desirable combination of the volunteering principle with planned experiences in participation can possibly be arrived at. It may well be that every teacher should be expected to assume as part of his responsibility for curriculum development, three kinds of assignment in the school: (1) his regular teaching assignment; (2) an assignment to one of the basic faculty committees; and (3) an assignment as faculty adviser to one of the student committees. Membership in a parent room group would be automatic for each home-room teacher.[35] Each teacher might indicate his preferences as to committees on which he will serve. Appointments could be made in the light of these choices by the faculty coördinating committee in the case of faculty committees and by the faculty curriculum committee in the case of advisers to the student committees. With regard to participation in inter-school and inter-level committees the volunteering principle might well be used or it might be combined with elections by the faculty from among those willing to serve. Membership on the central curriculum council should be elective. Decision would have to be made as to whether attendance at all-city educational conferences should be voluntary or required. For workshops it seems almost certain that attendance should be voluntary, but local circumstances might make a difference.

In order to make the best use of individual differences and of readiness for change as exhibited by some persons, some administrators believe it wise to invite "key" teachers to experiment with new ways. The effect of such procedures on group solidarity must be closely watched. Professional jealousies should not be needlessly aroused. It is unfair both to the group and to the individual concerned to fasten on him the label of "teacher's pet." It would seem preferable to make experimentation open to anyone, subject to the limitations of group agreement at the building level. Freedom to experiment is an essential element in the development of creativity in teachers.

Transfers of Teachers and Principals. The plan of introducing new elements into static situations by the transfer of teachers and principals is a defensible one provided the integrity of the individual involved is respected and the effect on the solidarity of the group from which the person is transferred is studied.

[35] See the definition of this term, p. 71.

Transfers should be employed frequently enough to make them appear not at all unusual and frequently enough to keep faculty groups alive. Teachers should be free to suggest transfers for themselves also.

In giving thought to the rôle of the individual, his need for leisure and recreation and his right to a private life should not be overlooked. We should aim at a working day of reasonable length which has in it time for coöperative work on curriculum-building.

Further Implications of the Principle of Heterogeneity

Two further implications of the principle of heterogeneity may be worth thinking about. One is the matter of the composition of the local board of education. The heterogeneity of its membership should be increased considerably if support for curriculum change is to be expected from that quarter. A board composed of men representing only business and the professions is not likely to be aware of certain needs the school may be failing to serve.

The second is the matter of grouping children in schools. Attempts to group children homogeneously still continue, grouping by chronological age being popular at present. Perhaps it is time for the desire for homogeneity to be abandoned and for more experimentation to be done with forming groups heterogeneous in character, in which children may have the benefit of wider contacts, yet in which diversity is controlled to the extent that group solidarity is readily achieved.[36]

The Rôle of Minority Groups

People have, in this country, unusual opportunities to work with and through heterogeneous cultural groups. The potentialities of those human resources have not been well enough recognized. In fact, there has not been sufficient value placed on minority groups in general. As in the case of individuals, differences

[36] For an adequate presentation of the arguments in favor of heterogeneous grouping in schools, see Viola Theman, "Continuous Progress in Schools," *Childhood Education*, Vol. XVIII, Sept., 1941, pp. 21–23.

which such groups represent could make a contribution to social change. Yet differences and conflict are shunned. Follett says,[37] "Difference is always a challenge. We should never avoid it." She goes on to admit that not all differences can be integrated. "But it is certain," she continues, "that there are fewer irreconcilable activities than we at present think."

Taba has given a good explanation of the creative rôle that conflict, which grows out of difference, can play: [38]

There is a difference between the conception of conflict as sustaining the activity and between conflict as a starting point of activity; conflict, in other words, transforming itself into a new synthesis, into a new harmony. Conflict and the succeeding integration on a new level are two moments of the same process.

If we are to make creative use of the differences which cultural and other minorities present, we must come to value conflict as a starting point in change but learn to convert it into the new harmony of which Taba speaks.

The Rôle of Minority Groups—Implications for Curriculum Change

The school faculty itself may be thought of as a minority group in a community. It is a group which, because of the great ability and educational advantage it possesses in the aggregate, may, if it will, serve as a leavening agent in the community. The school faculty should study how it may best serve that function.

On the other hand, one problem which a faculty as a minority group may present to the community is that of holding up different standards to the children from those common in the community. Not enough is known about the effect on children of the pull of different standards. The effect is undoubtedly devastating for some. This is a problem that can merely be recognized in this volume but not solved. It may be that the school should change its standards in some matters—"correct" English usage and "worth-while" books, for example. Educators would do

---

[37] Follett, op. cit., pp. 162–163.
[38] Hilda Taba, Dynamics of Education (New York, Harcourt, Brace and Company, 1932), p. 61.

well to examine critically all standards they hold for children. They might make a group study of such a work as Warner and Lunt's *The Social Life of a Modern Community* in order to gain more understanding of the standards and habit patterns of the various social classes from "upper-upper" to "lower-lower" that are to be found in every American community.[39] It may help such a faculty group to be more intelligent in the application of standards in school if they come to realize the extent to which they tend to be governed in all their acts by middle-class mores and if they learn what that implies for all their dealings with children and parents of every class. The long-time need is to discover the best possible methods for helping all persons to improve their values and goals without undue strain on individuals.

Dealing with Minority Groups Within a School Faculty. The school faculty must also be prepared to deal with minority groups within the teaching staff itself. Frequently the teachers' union presents a problem in a school system. Ideally, it might be supposed, the functional organization of a school and school system should provide sufficient opportunities for participation and sufficient security to the participants so that additional organization would be unnecessary. This may some day be a more frequent state of affairs than it is at present. Meanwhile, if educators are realistic they will study the reasons for the existence of such minority organizations, help them to find a useful rôle, and make it unnecessary for them to operate continually upon the level of conflict. Need for a teachers' union is sometimes dictated by political considerations in the community which seemingly make it necessary for teachers to seek the support offered by another well-organized group in the community, such as the labor union. Correction of conditions giving rise to this need will have to await better community organization.

If the need for a teachers' union arises out of faulty internal

---

[39] William L. Warner and Paul S. Lunt, *The Social Life of a Modern Community* (New Haven, Conn., Yale University Press, 1941). See also William L. Warner, Robert J. Havighurst, and Martin B. Loeb, *Who Shall Be Educated?* (New York, Harper & Brothers, 1944).

organization and management of the school, the union may be expected to lose its function as that organization and management are improved. At present, many teachers' unions are serving to call attention to the desirability of certain curriculum changes, and they are themselves making needed studies. The union in one city, for instance, is inquiring into the platoon system which has a firm grip on the elementary schools there.

It is a different matter when teachers form minority organizations that widen cleavages. In one large school system, teachers are organized by creeds, Jewish, Catholic, and Protestant. Such groupings of teachers are indefensible and are evidence of what results when better organization is lacking.

SUMMARY

In this chapter it has been observed that accomplishment cannot be expected without organization for channeling and regularizing individual contributions to the process of curriculum change. The proper organization under proper leadership will make creative use of differences while building ever greater unity of purpose and endeavor. In the chapter that follows study is made of some of the social inventions available for achieving control over social change. Also it is suggested at what points in group process there is need for further invention.

CHAPTER V

Social Invention

"I'd like to see this school run more efficiently but that wouldn't be democratic." So speak in substance a group of sincere but confused school administrators. "I'd like to see this school run more democratically but that wouldn't be efficient." So speak a second group of equally sincere and equally confused school heads. Both groups seem to assume that they must make a choice between democracy and efficiency.

There are two causes for the confusion that makes democracy synonymous with inefficiency. The first is the *conception of efficiency* that is held. This cause is rather easily removed. It is usually not impossible to convince a person who honestly wishes to be democratic that democracy *can* provide a higher type of efficiency than any resulting from authoritarian régimes. As already pointed out democratic efficiency is sourced in purposeful activity, planning, flexibility of arrangements, and self-discipline.[1]

That democracy *does not more frequently demonstrate its potential efficiency* is the second cause of confusion. This cause is more difficult of removal. For one thing, the techniques for making democracy work that have been discovered and tested are comparatively few. In the second place, the number of persons who have any degree of control over the known techniques is, relatively speaking, small indeed. In the third place, people tend constantly to limit experimentation by a priori judgments that such and such procedure is "not democratic."

It is the belief of the writer that the range of possible democratic procedures has by no means been exhausted and that in-

[1] See p. 26.

vention and discovery in this realm is sorely needed. Pearl Buck counts it as one of the strengths of the Chinese people that they can reject tradition without rejecting a principle, that they can keep steadfast to an end but approach that end by changing means.[2] In our short national life, we in this country have come to accept all too narrow a range of techniques as the full repertory of democracy. We are inclined to pre-judge anything outside that range as undemocratic.

In a recent book devoted entirely to the thesis that "new methods of democratic, free, and co-operative living have to be worked out," De Huszar makes a distinction between a "talk-democracy" and a "do-democracy." [3] A talk-democracy, he points out, has developed too little in the category of the *how*. A dynamic, do-democracy will require that Americans transfer some of their interest in a technological know-how to a know-how in the social fields.

While this book in its entirety is concerned with the process of curriculum change as a special form of deliberate social change and is thus primarily a "how" book, the present chapter deals with points at which further social invention or more attention to existing inventions would be desirable. We shall attempt to take stock of inventions already at hand and awaiting more extensive use and development, and we shall try to draw together the needs for new invention that seem to exist. Topics around which the discussion is organized are (1) discovering the proper relationship between knowledge and desires and beliefs, (2) studying the rôle of communication, (3) discovering the best uses of the expert, (4) practicing and extending techniques of group action, and (5) building constructive social power.[4]

[2] Pearl Buck, *American Unity and Asia* (New York, The John Day Company, 1942), pp. 79–80.

[3] George B. de Huszar, *Practical Applications of Democracy* (New York, Harper & Brothers, 1945), pp. 10–11.

[4] In connection with social change, Karl Mannheim places much importance on what he calls the "will to plan." In this he shares the concern expressed in Chapter II that human beings shall value deliberate or planned social change. His suggestions with regard to what shall be planned are exceedingly fruitful. For one thing he suggests that planning can "take into account the unexplored territory between institutions." This aspect

RELATIONSHIP OF KNOWLEDGE, DESIRES, AND BELIEFS

People who would educate others commonly fall into the error of assuming that dissemination of knowledge is the chief problem with which one has to deal in paving the way for desired social change. Much as one would like to see the method of intelligence prevail in this world, he will, if realistic, admit that up to now knowledge has not made its fullest contribution to social change. Gates and others point out man's proclivity for unscientific behavior: [5]

Once a person has taken a stand he may persist in it quite tenaciously in spite of subsequent contradictory evidence. . . . In matters involving his own prestige he may not only reject information that is unfavorable but he may also seek information to confirm his bias. . . . In studies of adults as well as of children it has been found that there is little correlation between the intensity of partisanship or feeling and the amount of information possessed.

Todd has expressed somewhat the same idea in picturesque language. And he sees this tendency to believe what one desires as a serious limitation to progress.[6]

Ideas always come swaddled in feelings. We recognize that reason in men is only at the very tip of their iceberg of mental life: they live by habit, impulse, illusion . . . they easily compel a satisfactory harmony between belief and gratification of desire. . . . This is the lead in humanity's wings.

---

of planning was dealt with in connection with the discussion of *organization* in Chapter IV. Mannheim suggests also "planned criticism," a matter taken up under the heading of *dissatisfaction* in Chapter III. Other suggestions as to what shall be planned are treated in this chapter under the somewhat different headings listed above. These are "planned persuasion" (topics 1 and 2), "planned specialization" (topic 3), "planned interdependent thinking" (topic 4), and "planned strategy" (topic 5); see also the succeeding chapter on leadership. In *Man and Society in an Age of Reconstruction* (New York, Harcourt, Brace and Company, 1940), pp. 109–261 *passim*.

[5] Arthur I. Gates and others, *Educational Psychology* (New York, The Macmillan Company, 1942), p. 204.

[6] Arthur J. Todd, *Theories of Social Progress* (New York, The Macmillan Company, 1922), pp. 472–473. By permission of the publishers.

Lund produces scientific evidence for this point of view. He reports the following results of an interesting study of the relationships among beliefs, desires, and "evidence": [7]

The correlation between belief and desire was +.88 . . . between belief and "evidence" +.42, between "evidence" and desire, —.03.

From this he concludes (1) that "emotional factors are significant determinants of belief"; (2) that there is a "marked tendency to idealize the rational principle and to conceive of it as the most valid and important of belief determinants, notwithstanding the fact that non-rational factors appear to outweigh it so largely in conditioning our belief-attitudes . . ."; and (3) that "beliefs, once formed, are not willingly relinquished." He believes therefore that the side of the question first presented and the first influence brought to bear are most effective in determining beliefs, so much so as to suggest the "law of primacy in persuasion."

If desire and belief are of such importance in influencing the decisions of people, it is evident that the problem of fostering the method of intelligence is a broader one than is usually conceived. Even so apparently simple a matter as dissemination of knowledge requires much more psychological insight than we have heretofore assumed to be necessary.

Prescott makes a strong statement with regard to the proper rôle of affective experiences in the process of social change: [8]

World political developments, new devices for swaying the emotions of entire nations simultaneously, emphasis on blind mass fervor, impatience with the scientific approach to national problems, all have driven home the lesson that the job of education is not done when knowledge is disseminated and increased. If the scholar, concerned with his primary business of knowledge, fails to deal with the whole man, particularly with the control of passion and the guidance of desire, he may properly be charged with contributory

[7] F. H. Lund, "The Psychology of Belief," *Journal of Abnormal and Social Psychology*, XX: 193-195, 1925-1926. Quoted in Kimball Young, Ed., *Source Book for Social Psychology* (New York, F. S. Crofts & Co., 1927), p. 283.

[8] Daniel A. Prescott, *Emotion and the Educative Process* (Washington, D.C., American Council on Education, 1938), p. vii.

negligence when the democracy becomes either a mob or a regimented army, when freedom to learn or to teach disappear, when the neglected emotions submerge the life of reason, and so force recognition of their claim to a share in the lives of man.

Todd, too, suggests that education of desires is essential: [9]

The kernel of the whole matter is that desires are open to suggestion, to molding, to pruning, and educating . . . since desire is multiform . . . education of the will means educating to desire rightly, to choose between conflicting desires, to arrange the various types of desires . . . according to definite standards of value, to be determined by their bearing on real development.

We do not know too well how to educate the desires of people. This is an area in which much experimentation is required. We are certain only of profitable directions of effort, which are the replacement of empty verbalization with generalization upon actual experience and the use of many media for presenting ideas. The former point has already been touched upon in the chapter on motivation; the latter is elaborated in later pages where communication is discussed.

A device that might be tried is one used by Lynd in his volume, *Knowledge for What?* where he lists twenty ambivalences of the American people. Some representative ambivalences as seen by this sociologist follow: [10]

Individualism, "the survival of the fittest," is the law of nature and the secret of America's greatness; and restrictions on individual freedom are un-American and kill initiative. *But:* No man should live for himself alone; for people ought to be loyal and stand together and work for common purposes.

Life would not be tolerable if we did not believe in progress and know that things are getting better. We should, therefore, welcome new things. *But:* The old, tried fundamentals are best; and it is a mistake for busybodies to try to change things too fast or to upset the fundamentals.

Education is a fine thing. *But:* It is the practical men who get things done.

[9] Todd, *op. cit.*, pp. 480–481.
[10] Robert Lynd, *Knowledge for What?* (Princeton, N.J. Princeton University Press, 1939), pp. 60–62.

Analysis and discussion of such a list of ambivalences with a group of people might start them reflecting upon the illogical nature of some of their desires. This would be a first step in re-educating those desires.

Dewey's analysis of the difficulty involved in promoting the method of intelligence implies another possible line of action, that of raising doubts in people's minds: [11]

The undisciplined mind is averse to suspense and intellectual hesitation; it is prone to assertion. It likes things undisturbed, settled, and treats them as such without due warrant. Familiarity, common repute, and congeniality to desire are readily made measuring rods of truth. Ignorance gives way to opinionated and current error—a greater foe to learning than ignorance itself. A Socrates is thus led to declare that consciousness of ignorance is the beginning of effective love of wisdom, and a Descartes to say that science is born of doubting.

Using Knowledge to Widen the Area of Choice. In suggesting the importance of creating doubt and consciousness of ignorance, Dewey is suggesting the great service which knowledge can render, namely that of increasing the range of choice in many areas.

It is at this point that the cultural anthropologist has a particularly valuable contribution to make. In the words of Linton: [12]

A knowledge of other cultures and societies cannot fail to give the educator perspective on the values of his own. I have heard more than once that it gives him too much perspective and that the inevitable result of realizing the relativity of values and the variety of successful patterns functioning in different cultures is a passive attitude of "some do and some don't." I can hardly imagine this happening in the case of any individual who had a strong drive toward bettering society. It seems to me that the knowledge of what other societies had done would be more likely to fill him with hopes of what our own can do.

[11] John Dewey, *Democracy and Education* (New York, The Macmillan Company, 1916), p. 222. By permission of the publishers.

[12] Ralph Linton, "Potential Contributions of Cultural Anthropology to Teacher Education," *Culture and Personality* (Washington, D.C., American Council on Education, 1941), p. 13.

Cultural anthropology can serve the useful purpose of enabling persons to stand off, as it were, and view elements in their own culture that they would not otherwise think of questioning. This technique would seem to be especially effective with relation to mores and attitudes that are more or less highly charged with emotion. This may be at the bottom of Ruth Benedict's declaration [13] that "social thinking at the present time has no more important task than that of taking adequate account of cultural relativity."

There is reason to believe that people are affected also by awareness that other persons have discovered better ways of doing things than they themselves have. As long as no one knew much about child care, mothers could go about their other duties with little thought of the baby. The mere knowledge that someone knows a great deal about nutrition and health measures for infants now causes mothers to feel concern. Of this Lynd observes: [14]

People's susceptibility to strain in a given case varies inversely with the following ratio:

$$\frac{\text{what they can do about it}}{\text{what they know about what } anybody \text{ can do about it}}$$

While such situations are a source of strain, they also give basis for hope that people are becoming increasingly susceptible to new knowledge. People will still make judgments in terms of values they hold, but there is more likelihood that wise decisions will ensue if those choices are made in as wide a context as possible. While it is agreed that preparation for social change must consist of more than mere spreading of knowledge, it would be foolhardy to overlook this avenue of improvement. *Valued* knowledge has an important rôle to play. As Max Lerner says, just because we recognize the rôle of the irrational it does not mean that we should glorify it. Lerner [15] believes that the prin-

[13] Ruth Benedict, *Patterns of Culture* (Boston, Houghton Mifflin Company, 1934).
[14] Lynd, *op. cit.*, p. 112.
[15] Max Lerner, *Ideas Are Weapons* (New York, The Viking Press, 1939), p. 7.

cipal task of our age may be that of "finding a resolution between the necessary rôle of the irrational and the demands of social rationality."

Knowledge, Desires, and Beliefs—Implications for Curriculum Change

Teachers are a more highly literate group than the average of the population and somehow we expect them to be in the vanguard of curriculum change. Yet Mort and Cornell found, in their study of adaptations in the schools of Pennsylvania, that in the schools which had not made the adaptations being studied, the teachers were usually "in a position of neutrality with reference to them." They add: [16]

In a great number of cases the teachers are actually unaware of the conditions and problems demanding the change and the various adjustments which schools in other places have undertaken to meet these demands.

This is an unfortunate state of affairs. The problem of education of desire and belief, of increasing the power of the rational at the expense of the irrational is not easily solved and the help of teachers is needed.

Some useful leads as to how teachers may be helped to see the need for change may be secured from study of the results obtained by Mort and Cornell [17] when 2,416 Pennsylvania teachers were asked the question: "Where did you get ideas for changes you have made or would like to make?" These were the replies:

Item	No. of Teachers Indicating Item
Professional literature	506
Teaching experience	445
Observation of other schools in system	288
College or university	233
Study of pupil needs and interests	195
Contact with other teachers in system	176

[16] Paul R. Mort and Francis G. Cornell, *American Schools in Transition* (New York, Bureau of Publications, Teachers College, Columbia University, 1941), p. 206.

[17] *Ibid.*, p. 264.

	No. of Teachers
Item	*Indicating Item*

Summer school	162
General literature	133
Conventions, conferences, institutes, other professional meetings	120
Original ideas	111
Special courses	96
Extension work	86
Experimentation	64
Other public school systems	51
Teachers colleges	49
Lectures	46
Principal	43
Study of children's interests	38
Superintendent	38
College or university professors	36
Suggestions of students	36
Local supervisors	35
Contacts with educational leaders	34
Examination of newer school books	33
Faculty meetings	33
Common sense	29
Study of industrial changes or social trends	28
Study of life itself	26
Demonstration schools	21
Contacts with people in professions, politics, industry and the like	21
Work of private experimental schools	21
Training schools	20
Travel	20
Demonstrations by outstanding teachers in system	19
Research	17
Trends in education	16
Parents or adults of community	16
Local administrative bulletins	16
Community affairs	13
Radio programs	11
Social contacts	11
Normal school	9
Experience in business or industry	9
School surveys	8
Home life	7
Teacher study groups	7
Interest in professional advancement	7
Visits to museums, libraries, art exhibits, and the like	5
Original research or professional study other than college	4
Desire for increase in salary	3
Introspection	2

Such results would have more value if they could be matched with information regarding the degree to which the various items mentioned had entered into the experience of the teachers reporting. It is interesting to note the relatively wide influence of professional literature. This would indicate the desirability of an adequate collection of professional literature and curriculum materials in each school. It is interesting to note also the tribute paid to actual experience in the classroom, to observation of other schools in the system, and to contact with other teachers. The influence of other school systems might have been more extensive if provision for visitation out of the local community were more common.

Study of pupil needs and interests is near the top of the list. School surveys have perhaps not been given full trial in the case of the teachers studied. Administrative and supervisory officers with their faculty meetings and their bulletins do not come off too well in this study. Note that the supervisors fall slightly below students as a source of suggestions. Yet all these could be powerful influences in the in-service education of teachers if techniques were improved. Workshops are not mentioned specifically. Teacher study groups apparently have not yielded much in this instance.

Many of the items on this list and other ways of increasing the rationality of the basis upon which teachers operate should be explored. Special thought should be given also to the suitability of some of these suggestions for use in helping community adults to see the need for curriculum changes. In studying the items for this purpose, it should be remembered that teachers have the advantage of familiarity with the special vocabulary of professional education. With them, too, organized education has fewer competing interests than is true of those whose vocation is not involved. However, a thoughtfully stocked and conveniently arranged parent library might be one implication of this study for community adults. Another might be that each teacher who is given a day to visit the schools in another community might take a group of parents along. Teachers might even be given short leaves to visit schools in another part of the country.

Promoting Desire for Curriculum Change. The suggestion made in Chapter III that teachers and school patrons engage in studies of human development and of social problems as manifested at the local community level is appropriate for the purpose under discussion. Study of cultural anthropology would seem to be rewarding for both groups, but ways of making the study have appeal and value would have to be explored. Study of a cultural minority group in the local community and study of the background from which they have come might be a promising approach. It has already been suggested that community adults be encouraged to participate in workshops with teachers and that they be invited to participate in educational conferences held in the community. Selected patrons may also be taken to state, regional, and national conferences, although the benefits will remain small unless ways are found of sharing them with others. Something better than the typical convention report should be invented.

Lynd's scheme of helping people to see their ambivalences [18] might also be applied to curriculum development. Teachers and parents might receive benefit from working out and discussing together their own ambivalences with regard to their children and the school program. For example, adults want children who show initiative, *but* they want obedience to authority; they believe individual differences should be respected, *but* they want long division taught in the fourth grade.

If individual school faculties and other professional groups really put their minds to it, they will be able to discover many new means of widening not only their own horizons but those of the adults with whom they wish to coöperate.

MAKING COMMUNICATION SERVE SOCIAL CHANGE

The difficulty of helping knowledge to play its full rôle in hastening social change points to the fact that much more *social* invention is needed in the field of communication. We have the mechanical means of communicating quickly and easily with

[18] See p. 103.

numbers of persons and at distances more or less great. One of our problems is to use these mechanical means to facilitate the spread of knowledge as a part of the process of bringing social change under greater social control. The other problem is to learn more of the art of communication among persons in actual contact with one another. Accordingly the discussion in this section deals with (1) the problem of making constructive use of technical inventions in the communications field, and (2) the problem of capitalizing upon opportunities for face-to-face communication.

Making Constructive Use of Technical Inventions

Effective communication with persons at a distance requires creative use of our modern inventions for that purpose. The effect of these inventions has been to draw groups closer together and to step up the rate of change through the resulting sharing of differences. The disadvantages of isolation are thereby removed. Modern inventions make it possible for all persons to come in contact with the best social thinking of the time. Social documents appear in many forms—the dance, painting, drama, photography, music, and literature. Through modern means of communication we can bring these social documents to the attention of millions if we will.

If available means of communication are to be used for a constructive social purpose, there must be development in two directions: (1) an increasing amount of social control of the great opinion-forming agencies—press, radio, and motion picture; and (2) further experimentation with different media as a means of establishing communication with persons of varying intelligence, interests, and experience.

Studying Sources of Information. As a first step in promoting this dual development, it would be well to make a study of the sources of information at present available to the people of the community and to attempt to discover what persons are reached by various kinds of information. For example, many facts should be known about each and every newspaper that serves the community, including labor papers and those in foreign languages.

Knowledge of the kind and quality of information carried and of circulation data gives only one side of the picture. To supplement it, studies should be made of what newspapers are taken by representative families and what parts of those papers are actually read. Similar facts should be known regarding magazines and pamphlets.

In the case of radio, the national, local, and regional programs available should be taken into account with special attention given to informational programs. Again it is important to know what programs are listened to.

Not only the use of public library facilities but those of rental libraries as well should be known. Sales of different kinds of books through book stores and book clubs will yield additional information that is of value in sizing up the problem of making communication serve social change.

In connection with movies there is value in knowing audience reaction to various kinds of pictures and shorts. The successful use of documentary films should also be noted.

The number of exhibits and performances in the realm of painting, sculpture, dramatics, dance, and music should be studied along with audience figures and reactions.

The nature of the subjects treated in lectures, sermons, and discussions, as well as the size and nature of the audiences and their appraisal of them, should be taken into account.

The availability and use of classes for adults should be known, nor should posters, signs, and exhibits of various kinds be overlooked in any survey of community sources of information. Topics discussed in conversations would also yield some interesting data. The ways in which people express their interests and values are most revealing.

Several interesting analyses of these findings could be made. One analysis might be in terms of what facts are true for various community groups. Another might be in terms of materials used. What source is used most frequently? What is the content covered? Is it accurate, adequate, and understandable? Are there important areas not covered? The comparative use of a verbal and a non-verbal approach might also be studied.

All this study would be futile, however, were the data not used to bring about changes in persons—in the level of public opinion and participation in civic enterprises and in concern for information as shown by increased participation in discussion groups, increased use of the library, improvement in informational quality of movies, newspapers, and magazines patronized, and improvement in quality of conversations.[18a]

If communication is to help to produce desirable social change, it is essential that the integrity of all parties be maintained. With so many means of rapid and easy communication at hand, there is great temptation in our culture to use them to take advantage of others. Lynd shows how commercial control of most of our means of communication has worked out. "Learning to live by new ways," he declares,[19] "is left up to the individual in those cases where it is not commercially profitable to somebody to 'educate' him." Furthermore, he continues,[20] if it is "to the private interest of any person to oppose cultural change, our institutions allow, if they do not actually encourage, him to do so to the limits of his resources. This anarchistic philosophy tends to reduce change of a non-commercial sort to a trickling minimum."

Studying the Uses of Propaganda. The use of channels of communication in the public interest is important for deliberate social change. To achieve such use is a problem, for it means that people must learn how to deal with propaganda. As a result of the work of certain individuals and groups a healthy skepticism has been developed with respect to some kinds of propaganda. Unfortunately, there has not been an even development in this regard. On the one hand, skepticism has become so great that groups operating in the public interest have difficulty securing attention to and confidence in their attempts to inform people. On the other hand the public continues to be extremely

[18a] The foregoing suggestions for studying sources of information are based on a mimeographed document, "What Happens When Who Knows What?" prepared by Ralph Spence for use at a conference on communication held at Teachers College, Columbia University, in April, 1943.

[19] Lynd, *op. cit.,* p. 75.

[20] *Ibid,* pp. 110–111.

gullible with respect to certain other types of propaganda. The continued enormous sale of patent medicines is proof of the latter point.

Everyone agrees that propaganda has its good and its bad uses. Since it is likely that the stream of false propaganda will not dry up, it seems the better part of wisdom to try in every way possible to counteract its influence with the greatest possible amount of good propaganda, that is, propaganda that is in the public interest. Those who would do this well might ponder the advice of Jones in this matter: [21]

Actual deceit of the public is very dangerous, however, and using its various devices, propaganda succeeds best when it formulates propositions that people are already prepared to believe, but do not know how to state for themselves. Propaganda can thus give one side in a controversial issue the advantage of the feeling of confidence through easy verbalization. A propagandist will succeed only if he recognizes that the most he can do is divert an existing flow of water. If he tries to make the water flow uphill, or if there is no water to begin with, he is bound to fail.

If, in this connection, we remember Lund's suggestion that there may be a law of "primacy in persuasion," [22] we have some useful hints as to constructive ways of combating propaganda that is undesirable from the standpoint of the common welfare.

In addition to learning how to make good use of propaganda, efforts must be continued to help an increasing number of people to distinguish between good and bad propaganda. This will help us to take an important step forward in directing social change. Constructive use of our channels of communication will come to be valued more and more highly; destructive uses will prove less and less effective.

Constructive Use of Technical Inventions—Implications for Curriculum Change

While educators do not have a profit motive for making questionable uses of techniques of communication, interest in an in-

[21] Alfred Winslow Jones, *Life, Liberty, and Property* (Philadelphia, J. B. Lippincott, 1941), p. 187.
[22] See p. 102.

stitution sometimes works to the same end. Educators have been known to employ somewhat shoddy techniques at times in communicating with their constituents. Often this is done with the intention of counteracting propaganda against the schools, frequently to save a good school program from being scrapped at the insistence of certain pressure groups. If such tactics become necessary, it is unfortunate, for whatever seems to be gained at the time is likely to be lost in the long run in public confidence in the integrity of the school officials. It is much better, if possible, to forestall emergencies by continuous attention to sound measures of communication. Says a bulletin of a state education association,[23] "Public education deserves a better fate than to be advertised like a beauty contest."

Good advice seems to be: Follow the law of primacy in persuasion. Get "good" propaganda before the public first. Use honest facts and reasonable methods. "Divert the existing flow of water." Have a planned program of interpretation.

Communication Through the Written Word. The medium most commonly employed by educators is the written word. Even here techniques should be vastly improved. A great deal remains to be learned in the field of educational journalism. If the press is to be utilized, educators must learn to respect deadlines and rules for interesting and acceptable copy. In all publications intended for the public, photographic and other graphic illustrations should be liberally employed and a truly readable style sought for. It should be possible to learn how to make news stories of progress in curriculum development that may hope to share the limelight with accounts of the latest athletic contest at the local high school. Some of these stories may well be based on developments of national interest, but even these should be given a local slant of some kind. In acquiring reporting skill the help of an experienced journalist might well be sought.

Parents can sometimes do a better job of writing for other parents than educators can. In Bronxville, New York, the citizens have appreciated a weekly column in the local newspaper

[23] "A Cooperative Study of Community Relations," Bulletin No. 24 (Lansing, Mich., Michigan Education Association, 1932), p. 3.

in which a parent answers questions concerning the school program sent in by other parents.

In Glencoe, Illinois, a member of the board of education has taken over the responsibility of preparing a printed leaflet for school patrons. In addition to a brief lead article on a topic such as "discipline," the leaflet gives brief news items concerning the school and action taken by the board of education.

The bulletin for school patrons can be used by the staff of the schools to present a picture of modern schools in action. Explanations of the value of various types of activities that have come into favor since the days when the oldsters went to school can be built upon well-written descriptions of actual curriculum experiences of their own children in the local schools.

A bulletin for school patrons takes on extra interest and value if the contributors are many and varied. Parents and teachers can write of ways in which the home can facilitate the program of the school. The secretary of the parent-teacher organization can furnish periodic reports of the activities of that body. The librarian can report on special library activities, circulation figures, and other items of interest. Community leaders can contribute accounts of coöperative community enterprises in the form of both progress reports and final reports. The head engineer may well write of the condition of the school plant, explaining the need for repairs and expansions to care for various school and community groups. The head of the custodial staff may write of the qualifications for that work and of the importance to the school as a whole that persons of high caliber fill such positions. Needs in the way of additional personnel, equipment and supplies can be presented by the school superintendent or principal along with pertinent data on school finance and child accounting. Much of this information would be equally valuable for the teaching staff. Some school heads place such bulletins in the waiting rooms of doctors and dentists.

If such a bulletin is used in common for a city school system it may well be supplemented by special communications or circulars to care for matters of more local interest. For example, one school faculty found it desirable to issue a written appeal to parents to study what was happening to their children over the weekends to cause them to come to school on Monday mornings at once fatigued and over-stimulated. Questions regarding school hours, appropriate clothing for different seasons, homework, and the like can be dealt with also.

Sometimes it is desirable to prepare special bulletins giving a complete picture of the program of a school for use by study groups and individual families. The values that accrue to a faculty that works coöperatively on the preparation of such a document should not be overlooked.[24]

A handbook for parents filled with specific answers to the kinds of questions frequently asked regarding the school curriculum has been found to be a useful medium of communication in some communities.[25]

The school newspaper, written, edited, and published by the children, should not be overlooked as a means of interpreting the school to community adults into whose hands they frequently fall. If such papers are exchanged regularly with other schools, they may be a means of spreading news of curriculum innovations.

If filled with brief, well-written, useful items that do not duplicate the contributions of educational periodicals, the house organ can be an important means of communication among the members of a teaching staff. Such publications can be most effective in helping to build a feeling of common membership in a significant enterprise. It is highly desirable that the editorial board of a school's house organ contain some classroom teachers.

A second important use of the written word in facilitating the process of curriculum change as far as teachers are concerned comes under the heading of curriculum materials. As educational leaders have come to see how prescriptive and detailed courses of study tend to stifle initiative and hamper the development of

[24] Examples of such bulletins are *The High School in Review*, prepared by the faculty of the Mt. Pleasant, Mich., High School in 1942; and *Environmental Guide for Wholesome Education*, created by the Roslyn Heights, Long Island, faculty in 1944–1945.

[25] See *Handbook for Parents* (Richmond, Virginia State Board of Education, 1941).

creative teachers, they have turned their attention to types of curriculum materials that give help and guidance to teachers in their planning for and with children yet which do not cripple them or make them overly dependent on the thinking of others. Of this development Hopkins, Stratemeyer, and Woodring write: [26]

An examination of the material submitted and of the letters written to the committee by interested persons in the cooperating school systems, lead (sic) to the following observations:

The older type courses of study as a source of material to guide teaching are being displaced by special bulletins on aspects of the teaching-learning problems in the various schools. Many superintendents wrote that they did not expect again to issue general courses of study as they had in the past. Instead, individual schools would work on their own problems with the advice and counsel of other persons within or outside of the system. The newer and more liberal practices or suggestions for such practice seemed to be found in the general and special bulletins rather than in the courses of study.

Among the materials that have promise are the following:

1. Curriculum records—descriptive accounts of actual curriculum experiences of children showing how the activity originated, steps taken in developing it, successes and failures, materials found useful, values received, etc.
2. Resource units—a wealth of suggestions for possible use in guiding the study of a group of learners along some line of general interest and value.
3. Teaching aids—specific bulletins giving help to teachers along special lines such as conducting discussions, encouraging creative writing, planning successful excursions, making use of certain visual aids, and so on.
4. Policies and procedures—brief statements of instructional policies and the procedures necessary for carrying them out as agreed upon by faculty groups.
5. Materials on child development—summaries of findings in the

[26] From the introduction to "List of Outstanding Teaching and Learning Materials" prepared by L. Thomas Hopkins, Florence Stratemeyer, and Maxie N. Woodring for the Department of Supervision and Curriculum Development, National Education Association (Washington, D.C., 1945).

field of child development that will help teachers to plan and work more wisely with children.

6. Bulletins on community resources—names, addresses, and telephone numbers of persons with whom to make contact in making arrangements for use of people and institutions in the instructional process, along with suggestions for making best use of each resource listed.

Curriculum materials of these types should be developed cooperatively with teacher help or by specialists to whom they assign the job. They should be prepared in response to expressed needs of groups of teachers to ensure optimum use.

Radio and Motion Picture. With the radio and motion picture as means of disseminating information to the public, educators are much less familiar. In many cases they are naïve, not realizing the expertness required for getting proper effects with these media. As with educational journalism, much remains to be learned before school radio programs and films of school activities will function as they might in the cause of curriculum change. It is encouraging, however, that school systems in increasing numbers are experimenting with the production of films, film strips, and slides depicting school activities.[27] Until the time comes when a school can employ or develop qualified educators who are expert in these fields, the aid of certain members of the community who have special ability in radio and film might well be enlisted.

Along with exploration of the use of radio and recordings to enlist the coöperation of the public in the process of curriculum change, there has been experimentation in a few school systems with the use of these media with teacher groups. In places where it is impossible, because of the size of the group or difficulties of transportation, to assemble all of a teaching group, teachers' meetings have been conducted by radio with listening groups assembled in each individual school. In Cleveland when a survey of social studies teaching had been completed the results were broadcast over the school station for the benefit of all teachers. In Philadelphia some use has been made of recordings of discus-

[27] Greenwich, Conn., for example, has been making a special study of the most effective use of a technicolor film developed in the schools there.

sions of a selected topic by a group of teachers. These and other uses of radio, recordings, and film for facilitating curriculum change should be explored more extensively in the near future.[28]

A last word about modern means of communication has to do with the two-way microphone system, to install which many an administrator has strained the school budget. This device may properly be used to give learners experiences with broadcasting and to bring to classrooms desired radio programs. It should not be used for listening in on unsuspecting teachers, constantly interrupting teaching plans, or consistently replacing face-to-face communication with announcements from the principal's office.

Capitalizing upon Opportunities for Face-to-Face Communication

The foregoing discussion of constructive uses of technical inventions in the communications field necessarily has looked upon communication as a one-way process, a disseminating of information. Cherrington shows the challenge inherent in this one-way emphasis: [29]

. . . means available for shaping and controlling public opinion have been strengthened and modernized, while the means for expressing this opinion and giving it contact with government processes have remained primitive or at least medieval. It is a challenge to American inventive ingenuity to devise ways for curing democracy of inarticulation.

Ways of curing democracy of inarticulation must indeed be found. We must supplement dissemination of information with

[28] For films that are useful in helping teachers and other adults better to understand modern schools and modern theories of child development see "Films Interpreting Children and Youth" (Washington, D.C., the Association for Childhood Education, the Department of Supervision and Curriculum Development of the National Education Association, and the National Association of Supervision of Student Teaching, Mimeographed, 1945). A committee of the Department is at present engaged in a study of what further films are needed for the purpose of interpreting children and youth. Their recommendations will be submitted to appropriate persons engaged in film production.

[29] Paul T. Cherrington, "Our Freedoms and Our Opinions," *Public Opinion Quarterly*, Winter, 1942, p. 617.

a sharing of information, a process in which all parties concerned are active. The solution of the problem probably consists of multiplying contacts and coöperation at the local level where face-to-face contacts are possible. This highlights the rôle of organization in furthering free-flowing interpersonal relationships, a matter already touched upon.

In face-to-face situations there is opportunity of search for ways of helping minds to meet. There must be sharing and pooling of ideas, harmonizing of conflicting beliefs, desires, and values, and arriving at common purposes and goals. Sometimes this process is best facilitated by careful definition of terms; at other times it is preferable to make new definitions of familiar terms or to abandon them altogether in favor of new terms. The growth of exact, scientific terms has been one of the phenomena of our modern world, a development that has necessarily paced the development of science itself. We need a similar development in the social sciences, to the extent of discovering in some cases entirely new categories of thinking.

On some occasions and for some purposes non-verbal methods of communication may serve better for establishing real communication than verbal ones. Enjoying music, looking at photographs, dancing, eating together, playing games all will serve the purpose. Communication is not just talking.

Face-to-Face Communication—Implications for Curriculum Change

The provision for participation of community adults in a functional organization is probably the best way of curing school patrons of inarticulation. In all parent-teacher conferences and meetings there should be give and take, exchange of information. The parent knows some things about his children that the school cannot know. There must be regular opportunities for constructive criticism and suggestion. Curriculum development should be undertaken as a partnership.

It must be expected that many parents will be tongue-tied at first, especially in a group of any size. Most adults of the present generation were not given opportunities to learn discussion techniques when they were in school. This means that teachers, principals, and other leaders of groups will have to develop much skill at drawing people out. They will have to invent ways of getting talk going and of engaging the participation of a large percentage of the group.

The Room Group as a Means of Face-to-Face Communication. The strength of the room-group organization of parents [30] lies in the fact that it brings many more persons face to face than would otherwise come into relationship with one another. In such a small and intimate group, that shares so many problems in common, it is easier to free people of inhibitions and to secure lively participation in group discussion.

One young man who was teaching third grade "across the tracks" in a small midwestern town had great success with a Fathers' Club which he organized. Before long fathers of his own children were asking if they might bring friends and neighbors to the monthly meetings. A mimeographed directory of members, giving nicknames, occupation, and hobbies and interests, did much to make a group of diffident men feel important and respected. After a number of informal talks among themselves about the importance of treating their children as people and other matters of value to these particular fathers, the club was ready to take over the April meeting of the parent-teacher association. They mustered a very creditable panel from among the members. Under the leadership of the teacher the panel discussed the topic, "Shall We Leave the Job to Mother?" Following the program all in attendance were invited to partake of a fish supper which the men had planned and prepared all by themselves. The indirect effects of this fathers' club on the children—through improved family relationships and increased self-respect on the part of the parents—could not be measured. Adults were changed because the teacher established genuine communication with these men whose own schooling had been meager.

The room group of parents may also be the medium for carrying out further steps in a planned program of interpretation to complement the use of press, radio, and film. A useful program

---

[30] See p. 71, where this development in parent organization is described.

of interpretation for parents grouped according to interest in children of a certain age might be somewhat as follows: The parents of entering kindergarten children may be invited to come together early in the term or before school opens if possible. The teacher and others can let them know some of the things they may expect from the school. Ways in which they may help their children get ready to enter school may be suggested. Educators should also find out what the parents would like the school to do for their children.

Parents of first grade children should be helped to understand modern methods of helping children learn to read, and their coöperation should be enlisted. In such technical matters the educational personnel usually are the experts, and their judgment should be respected.[31] As children go on through school, their parents can be carried along with them, being prepared for changes in schools that have occurred all along the line since their day and being given chances to share in planning better experiences for the children. Parents as well as children should be helped when transfers from level to level of the school are imminent.

This is only the briefest sketch of a constructive program of communication. Many details should be added and developments of many other sorts planned for.

Other Innovations in Face-to-Face Communication. Other ways of promoting face-to-face communication are being tried in some schools. For the usual written report to parents many schools are substituting parent-teacher conferences and are finding them most rewarding for both parties. Parents are beginning to entertain teachers as friends, not just as teachers of their children, and teachers are reciprocating. One superintendent of schools has made fireside discussion groups in people's homes an institution in his community.

Wishing to have certain new departures in the education of

[31] It would be dangerous to assume that the professional personnel in education is at all times in advance of lay opinion. Members of the two groups should work together in such a way that all may learn freely from one another and that the best thinking of which any individual is capable receives serious consideration by the group.

the mentally handicapped meet with a friendly reception from the public, the supervisor of this branch of education in a section of a large city used a novel method of communication. She gave a tea one Sunday afternoon to enable the minister and other community leaders to meet a new director. She had her guests listen to two brief talks, one on the psychology of the subnormal child and the other on new methods of teaching such children. Thus she enlisted valuable aid in interpreting the new program to the parents.

Teachers, too, value face-to-face contacts above written communication from supervisors and administrative heads. The truth of this statement is borne out by a small study by Van Antwerp [32] which revealed the fact that supervisory bulletins are regarded by teachers as the least helpful of four supervisory techniques employed with them. The techniques preferred were supervisory visits, individual conferences with the supervisor, and group meetings with the supervisor, all of which allow for face-to-face communication.

If more attention is paid to ways in which ideas can be communicated most effectively, a great obstacle to social change can be considerably reduced.

THE EXPERT

Specialization in its present form is a modern phenomenon, resulting from developments in our technology. It is useless to expect the problem to be solved by the disappearance of the expert. The more complex our culture becomes, the more need we have for all kinds of specialization.

Yet, the expert presents a problem which we are only on the way to solving. The problem results partly from the halo surrounding the specialist. A man is outstanding as a military commander; people begin to talk of him as presidential material. Another man wins renown as a poet and author of

[32] Harriet Van Antwerp, "Teachers' Evaluation of the Effectiveness of Supervisory Activities," *Educational Method*, Vol. XV, May, 1936, pp. 441-447.

children's books; when he turns to writing of professional education, his work is consumed with reverence by numbers of people. The worst of it is that the expert is frequently only too glad to lend himself to this game. Frequently, the more fame a man acquires for some particular specialty, the more readily he fancies himself qualified to speak authoritatively on other questions, particularly education.

But there is another side to the problem. While the layman is eager to accept the pronouncements of the expert on all sorts of questions outside his realm of specialization, he is singularly loathe to accept his advice in the field where he is well qualified to offer it. Urwick has sketched the process in penetrating fashion: [33]

Sometimes . . . the verdict of the expert is allowed to be decisive especially in matters about which we are both nervous and ignorant, such as the national health. But in this case it is to be noted that we do not simply accept the dictation of the expert, but incorporate his conclusions (with some of his reasons for them) in our own thought-system, so converting ourselves into quasi-experts. But . . . the guidance of the expert is seldom allowed to decide the question authoritatively in any matter which touches the conduct of our life as a whole. We accept his "science" only to mix it in a distorted form with our own ignorance, and so make the judgment really our own. And the basis of knowledge which we may claim to have secured thus becomes a basis of knowledge confused with ignorance, and made still more insecure by the fact that we are quite certain to have selected some facts and rejected others, under the sway of our ingrained prejudices.

That we are still a nation of people who love to prescribe for themselves is only too true. The great misunderstanding of the increasingly important rôle of the expert in our national affairs is manifested in current complaints against bureaucracy. To some, government bureaus are a device invented by the New Deal to assassinate democracy. A saner view is presented by Merriam: [34]

[33] E. J. Urwick, *A Philosophy of Social Progress* (London, Methuen and Company, Ltd., 1920), pp. 227–228.
[34] Charles Merriam, *The New Democracy and the New Despotism* (New York, McGraw-Hill Book Company, Inc., 1939), p. 124.

More revolutionary than the changes precipitated by violent overturn accompanied by blood and fire is the quiet revolution going on in the nature of public administration, in the transition from arbitrary and rigid inflexibility to modern personnel with scientific equipment, with objective determination of standards and their application. No war has been fought to establish better administration. Technology, science, training have quietly taken their places in branch after branch of the public service as doctors, engineers, teachers, welfare workers, technicians in industry, agriculture, labor, geology, botany, chemistry, etc., have filtered into administration. Partisan and personal administration still survive over great areas of service and will not disappear at once, but they are on their way out; and when they have gone they will not be missed.

From this it would appear that we can hope for ever better use of experts as the public comes to understand and value the trend of which Merriam speaks. It is apparent that the services of the expert are needed. It must be recognized also that we should be searching continually for better ways of using our experts. Indeed, this may be the central problem in the matter of directing social change in the years ahead.

Three Directions of Improvement

Specialization Must Be Broadly Based. Endeavors to improve the use made of the expert may well take three directions. First, we may insist that all specialization be based on a broad understanding of our culture as a whole. As L. Moholy-Nagy, an artist, has well said: [35] "We need specialists with a universal approach to human activities and a sense of the relationships of these activities."

Moholy-Nagy's idea received reënforcement from an unexpected quarter during World War II. Major Lawrence Weinberger, a brain surgeon with the armed forces in Italy, was quoted as follows: [36]

Before the war I listened to my friends talking about social questions and politics and fascism and I thought they were getting pretty excited. Now I know they weren't.

[35] L. Moholy-Nagy, "Fundamentals of Design: Bauhaus Education," *Art Education Today* (New York, Bureau of Publications, Teachers College, Columbia University, 1939), p. 21.
[36] *Chicago Sun*, May 7, 1944.

Doctors are supposed to make sick people well and leave politics to the politicians, but to hell with that. If we're going to come out of this war with anything we say we are fighting for, everybody's got to take some interest and assume some responsibility. We've got to find a method whereby the average American is identified with other people. Old-fashioned ruthless individualism is what makes fascists.

Lynd [37] proposes a way in which our specialists who have already completed their formal education may build for themselves a broad base of operation by collaborating on research and thus pooling their specialties. His suggestion is that "the several disciplines, as we now know them, would be supplemented and in part replaced by a series of specific problem-areas on which workers with all types of relevant specialized training and technique would be coöperatively engaged."

If Lynd's analysis is correct that the new function of the learned man is "to increase rather than to preserve knowledge, to undermine rather than to stabilize custom and social authority," it behooves us to find ways to increase the prestige of ideas coming from experts out of their specialized study and experimentation.

Proper Place for the Expert Must Be Found. A second line of endeavor may be to help the expert to find his proper place in the democratic process. Like the democratic leader, the expert in a democracy is, properly, a servant of the people. It is the people who, by appropriate democratic processes, determine the policies which they wish carried out. At this point experts of all kinds receive assignments from the group. The specialists can and should use all kinds of imagination and daring in carrying out their assignments. In fact, it would be most short-sighted of the large group to limit the usefulness of its experts in any way, especially by the device of defining their tasks within narrow limits. There must be much room for creativity if progress is to result. A final safeguard in a democracy lies in the fact that the results must undergo critical evaluation by the people; they must meet both operational tests and

[37] Lynd, *op. cit.*, p. 166 ff.

the tests imposed by the over-arching values of the group.

Many persons see an opportunity in this process for one of the most important of the expert's contributions, that of demonstration. Prescott,[38] for example, believes that the broad education of public opinion is not very feasible "except by the process of demonstrating the superiority of new arrangements and methodologies." The developments for which the Tennessee Valley Authority [39] has been responsible are a favorite example of demonstration by experts of the way in which social enterprise may work. The results have been submitted to the public for appraisal. So long as opportunity for disapproval is guaranteed equally with opportunity for approval, this process is a democratic one. The method of demonstration has proved so successful that it would seem wise to extend its use, particularly as a means of educating beliefs and desires. It is especially important that such methods be explored as a means of facilitating the acceptance of the *social* inventions of experts.

Conceptions of the Expert Must Be Expanded. A third line of endeavor in a search for ways of improving the value of experts to a democratic society might be to expand our conception of the expert. Experts are not alone scientists and technicians of various sorts. We have need for experts in public administration, in coördination, and in human relationships of all kinds. Merriam sees emerging a new type of expertness which he calls that of "executive" leader: [40]

In close connection with public administration may be observed the emergence of the modern type of executive who combines the direction of public administration with leadership—a phenomenon of business, labor, and government alike. . . .

The growth of the modern "executive" in many different social groups is not due merely to the desire of some persons for undue authority, but to the general appreciation of the facility with which the executive may take an over-all view of a set of complicated and conflicting situations which have brought him to the fore. . . . In a period of extraordinary division of labor of all sort, and of ex-

[38] Prescott, *op. cit.*, p. 137.

[39] For a splendid account of this project see David Lilienthal, *T.V.A.—Democracy on the March* (New York, Harper & Brothers, 1944).

[40] Merriam, *op. cit.*, p. 125.

treme rapidity of change, the overhead view of the general coordinator has become of unusual significance, and to this may be attributed the rise of the persons who fill this function in the modern social process.

That there are dangers in the possession of such authority is evident. What is not always equally evident, although equally important, is that there are greater dangers in lack of such power, in inability to act in critical situations. Inaction may ruin a state as well as a man.

The times demand that we should not only develop more expertness in this and similar directions, but that we should pay the same respect to expertness in political and social fields that we do to our specialists in the fields of physical and natural science.

The Expert—Implications for Curriculum Change

In the case of the professional personnel we are dealing with a group in which each member must be considered an expert in the matter of curriculum change. There are merely differences in degree and kind of expertness. The specialization of the classroom teacher consists of knowing children well at a particular stage of development. Administrators have or should have specialized in coördination and the science and art of human relations. Various other forms of expertness that are to be found in most schools are well known, although not all are accorded the proper respect—that of the engineer, for example, or of the secretary.

The problem in schools is the same as that in the general culture, the broadening of the specialist's point of view, helping him to find his proper place, and expanding the conception of the expert. The school has an additional problem, one shared by the local community, that of developing needed expertness.

The Point of View of the Specialist Should Be Broadened. As has just been indicated, every professional educator is actually a specialist. Therefore, the principle that the point of view of the specialist should be broadened must be applied to every member of the staff. Carrying out the suggestions already made with regard to functional internal organization and coöperative study programs would contribute much to this end. In fact, the entire program of in-service education, if properly conceived, will have the effect of giving a broader view of the educational picture to every participant.

In the case of community adults one encounters frequently the phenomenon of the expert in natural science, medicine, or law who thinks of himself as an expert in education because he went through college. There is no one way of broadening the point of view of such persons. Many opportunities for regularized participation in curriculum development should help. Contact with teachers in joint enterprises should increase respect for their particular form of specialization.

The Expert Should Be Helped to Find His Proper Rôle. In this section we shall consider as experts in schools only those persons who are so considered by the teachers: general and special supervisors, specialists in art, music, health, and so on.

A whole book could be written on the problems in this area alone—of the over-specialization which makes of health education and physical education fields wide apart, that makes the second grade teacher feel incapable of teaching a third grade, that makes a school principal feel qualified to check on attendance but not to give leadership in curriculum development.

Improved organization has already been suggested as one solution for the problem that results from the division of supervision into subject areas in the elementary school. The suggestion that general supervisors replace many of the special subject supervisors does not imply discarding special talent. All the expertness which special teachers and supervisors possess is needed; we have merely to learn better ways of utilizing their talent. A desirable trend in the elementary school seems to be to place experts in the arts and sciences, health and library in charge of well-equipped centers in each individual school. There these individuals may become an integral part of the unit group in curriculum development. Their specialization thus can be made available to members of the community also if proper attention is given to scheduling their time.

The principal should become coördinator of curriculum development for the individual building. He and his staff should be able to call on the help of experts in curriculum development, the arts, psychiatry, and so on, who are at the service of all teachers and faculty groups in a city or district. The device of a service council for coördinating the efforts of this group has already been suggested.

At the secondary level the picture is complicated by greater specialization of personnel in school subjects. As the trend continues toward the core curriculum and other means of reducing excessive departmentalization, there will be need for vocational realignment of some teachers. This presents a difficult problem which can be solved well only if the necessary decisions and adjustments are made coöperatively.

The whole matter of use of experts from outside the school awaits extensive development. Schools have not begun to make use of the expertness that resides in various members of the community. The state education department, teachers colleges in the area, and other sources outside the community have not been used to their utmost, although lessons about the use of consultant service are being learned. The leaven of an outside point of view is essential for introducing ideas that might be long in originating in a local community.

A consultant brought into a western state had the following suggestions for ways in which he could serve the centers of the state: [41]

1. Acting as a resource leader for a day's conference of representatives of the region on ways of promoting school-community relationships.
2. Addressing faculties of colleges and universities concerning the need for a vital and significant social education for teachers.
3. Discussing with faculties of individual schools or school systems the place of community-school projects in the curriculum.
4. Sitting down with the planning group of the center and making suggestions relative to the improvement of activities already underway.

[41] "Final Report, Colorado Statewide Commission on Teacher Education to Colorado Education Association" (Mimeographed), p. 17.

5. Sharing with a group, large or small, his own experiences in school-community relations.
6. Suggesting the general directions which a given center might follow in its future planning.

This consultant happened to be particularly sensitive to the need for vital community-school projects in the curriculum and believed that he could best serve the function of stimulating thinking along those lines. Teacher reactions to his visit were mixed. Three typical ones are offered as evidence that discovering the most useful rôle for the outside expert is a problem:

Teacher A: The talks by Dr. M. were interesting and well given, but I don't feel that they will be of much value to us in this community. We are aware of our problems and he did not solve them for us.

Teacher B: The talks given by Dr. M. were educational and inspiring; but they were very different from what I had expected and also a little disappointing. I had assumed help would be given on specific teacher-problems.

Teacher C: Although no specific plans have been made to follow up any of the suggestions which the consultant gave, the thinking of many of his listeners went around a curve as a result of what he had to say.

Two of these reactions reveal the frequent desire of teachers for immediate, specific solutions for their problems. In planning the use of the outside expert, the stage of development of those who may expect to benefit from his service should be taken into account. There is increasing recognition of the value of the outside expert who has "specialized" in being a general consultant. Often this person can render the best service by helping school faculties and other working groups in a community to learn useful techniques of group problem-solving. Such a consultant should be an expert in social processes with particular reference to curriculum change.

The best strategy in the use of all experts who are outside a given situation would seem to be to find the point at which the group wants help, find the person most likely to be able to furnish that help, find out under what conditions the expert feels he can do his best work, and then clear the way for him to be his most effective self. For the expert of great repute, ways should be sought to reduce the suspicion people tend to have of the great. Having teachers and community adults meet the person socially is one way of helping them to discover his human qualities.

Conceptions of the Expert Must Be Expanded. It has already been stated that teachers, engineers, and secretaries should be regarded as experts in their own right. If the expertness of teachers is respected, they will be treated less often as clerks. Their valuable time will be protected by the employment of clerical assistance to care for the more routine aspects of their jobs. It is important that teachers be looked upon as experts by community adults also in order that their effectiveness as leavening agents in the community may be fully felt.

The expertness of community adults should be discovered and utilized to supplement the abilities of the teaching staff. Talent surveys may be made or ability uncovered in the course of a process of coöperative curriculum development in which there is extensive participation by community adults. No library or art center in a school should remain locked, no lunchroom go unused for lack of funds to employ expert help. Persons in the community with special ability along such lines can usually be found to operate such a center until necessary ability has been developed in others or until the usefulness of the service has been so clearly demonstrated that it comes to receive public financial support.

In the Glencoe, Illinois, public schools a great deal of use has been made of the time and talent that parents are able to contribute. Parent participation in school activities has included accompanying children on excursions, helping with gardening and other hobbies, taking charge of the costume room, tutoring, serving as hostesses, giving assistance in the school library and in the arts and crafts laboratory, showing films, telling stories, giving travel talks, giving musical entertainment in the form of solos or ensembles, and teaching sewing, knitting, and other such arts. Many parents indicate willingness to be on call at any time. Others designate given days when they will give regular service. Most schools can uncover some such aid if they will take the trouble to make a plan for surveying the adult group concerned with the school.

Needed Expertness Should Be Developed. All members of the professional staff as well as learners and community adults can and should develop expertness as needed to supplement that available from recognized specialists. Some of the needs that frequently arise have already been indicated. If a trained librarian is not available in an elementary school, a teacher and children can take over the responsibility if given proper assistance. Teachers and learners can find out how to operate projectors and apply paint to furniture. With the help of the local garden club, they may landscape the grounds and make a rock garden. All elementary teachers can gain more skill in guiding some of the art and music experiences of their children if specialists in those fields will devote some of their attention to helping teachers develop ability along those lines instead of spending all of their time teaching children.[42]

Besides developing more ability at coördination of curriculum development the school principal may make a special study of some area such as evaluation, reading, or health education. This principal can then serve as a consultant to the teachers in other buildings as well as in his own. Teachers can specialize and be used in the same way. Some teachers may become experts in photography and be invaluable in the interpretation of the school's program to the public. Such methods of extending expertness are especially valuable in smaller school systems. The effect on the personalities of those who come thus to be highly valued by other people is most wholesome.

[42] At the Whittier Elementary School in Denver, Col., programs of "special" teachers have been staggered in order that each may devote one after-school period per week to helping "room" teachers as individuals or in groups to develop more expertness in particular areas. To lighten the load of the room teachers to the point where they may find it reasonable to add an after-school period to their day, arrangements have been made whereby each such teacher has ninety minutes per week during regular school hours when he is freed of the responsibility of being with a group of children.

Group action in itself is a social invention of great moment. Everyone who has had satisfying experiences with it must feel with Sumner that "the interaction defies our analysis." [43] The products of effective group action offer overwhelming proof that the whole is greater than the sum of its parts. Follett [44] speaks of the "plus value" which can be obtained if groups will persist past the point of compromise to the reaching of a consensus and uses this intriguing expression: "the mystery moment which leads from the existing to the new." It is these mystery moments which make group process exciting to those who have a part in it.

While it is impossible to analyze the many intangibles that go to make group action possible, certain it is that a prerequisite to the action is a *meeting* of people for the purpose of securing a meeting of minds. For a meeting to achieve such success it is essential that *discussion techniques* receive careful attention. A third requisite to efficient group action is *division of labor;* a fourth is *record-keeping.* Many other topics could be discussed under the heading of group action—organization, communication, and the like—but since they have been treated elsewhere in this volume, the present section on group action will be restricted to the four topics aforementioned.

The Meeting as an Instrument for Group Action

The meeting is such a commonplace in American life that sometimes it is not recognized as a social invention of importance. Too often it is believed that the mere fact that a group is meeting is evidence that democracy is being nourished. As a matter of fact, there are rules for a successful meeting just as there are for anything else. Good meetings do not just happen.

The first thing to be clear about is the purpose of the meeting. If the aim is to stir emotions and create a desire for change

---

[43] W. G. Sumner, *Folkways* (Boston, Ginn and Company, 1906), p. 118.
[44] Mary P. Follett, *Creative Experience* (New York, Longmans, Green & Co., 1924), pp. xiv–xv.

or to bring a large number of people into contact with advanced social thinking, an address or lecture is justified. One should not expect too much in the way of group action as a result of such a meeting although a discussion period following the talk will likely move the group one step further toward action.

The participatory type of meeting has much more promise from the standpoint of group action. For most effective participation the small working group is recommended.

For sizable groups it is preferable to use the small group conference plan in order that more persons may be talking at the same time. This means merely that the large group is broken into groups of from eight to ten or fifteen persons, all of whom may be discussing the same question or different phases of a common problem. It is also possible to plan in such a way that there is overlapping of topics under discussion without complete duplication from group to group. This provides the necessary coverage while retaining the advantage of giving to the large group the benefit of differences in approach to the same problem on the part of two or three of the small groups.

It is sometimes desirable to hold large forum discussions as a further means of encouraging participation leading to group action. It is probably wisest to make use of a combination of these types of meeting over a period of time in most situations.

Assuring Satisfactory Physical Arrangements. After the purpose and probable size of the meeting are known, perhaps the first thing to be taken into account in planning a meeting is the physical arrangements. Surroundings should be as comfortable as possible. De Huszar makes a great point also of the circle rather than the rectangle as the "formation of democratic togetherness." He writes: [45]

A committee which meets around a rectangular table, with a gavel-wielding chairman at the end, has two strikes on it before it starts. Such an arrangement is spiritually authoritarian; it impedes spontaneity, it blocks the reaching of a genuine consensus. It somewhat improves the situation to have the leader in the middle, as is Jesus in Leonardo da Vinci's "The Last Supper," which pictures one of

[45] De Huszar, *op. cit.*, p. 30.

the most potent small groups ever assembled. It is still better to have a round table that is really round. The symbolic and psychological importance of meeting around a circular table is enormous.

Worse even than the rectangular committee table is the ordinary assembly room wherein chairs are arranged in rows, screwed to the floor, either physically or figuratively, with a raised platform in front for the speaker, leader or chairman. We are so accustomed to this arrangement that we do not realize what an antisocial symbol of authoritarianism it is.

While forum techniques can be improved to the point where a high quality of group thinking can take place in the typical assembly hall, de Huszar is certainly right when he stresses the psychological effect of a simple thing like the seating arrangements for a meeting.

If any kind of group planning is to be done, it is almost essential that there be a blackboard in the room. That is one reason why schools make such good community meeting places if, indeed, their furniture is movable.

Giving Attention to the Psychological Environment. Attention should be given also to the psychological environment. Do members of the group know one another? If not, time spent in introductions is not wasted. If the group is very large it is still possible to take some account of who is in attendance. The chairman may take a quick poll to see how many there are present who are housewives or have attended a forum before or have lived in the community all of their lives or come from another state or have had direct experience with an aspect of the problem to be discussed. In the case of a fairly small working group often it is a good idea to encourage each person in introducing himself to state his particular interest in the problem. In this way, special ability or unusual experience is revealed early in the meeting. Some kind of participation at the beginning of the meeting, even to the extent of raising one's hand in answer to a question, and some knowledge of the composition of the group serves to hasten the welding of the group into unity.

Another psychological factor to be taken into account is the likelihood that members of the group are unusually fatigued or operating under great tension for any reason. If so, the length of the meeting may be adjusted or a brief recess provided at the half-way point. A bit of humor may be introduced to provide a good laugh. It never comes amiss to secure as relaxed and informal an atmosphere as possible right from the start.

Meetings—Implications for Curriculum Change

Meetings of those concerned with the program of the school may follow any of the patterns discussed—they may be listening meetings or they may be participatory ones; they may involve small working groups or they may be large forums. Naturally all that has been said regarding physical arrangements for a meeting and the setting of a relaxed and friendly atmosphere applies here.[46]

In planning faculty meetings it is especially important to find a sufficient period of time to allow for good group thinking that is not at the same time appended to a long working day from which teachers come too fatigued to give or get the most. Some of the schemes that have been tried by various schools are: a brief meeting every morning before school; a longer meeting before school once a week with children reporting somewhat later that day; early dismissal once a week to allow for at least half of the meeting to take place on school time; dinner meetings; Saturday morning meetings once a month in cases where teachers themselves see this as the best time for their professional study together. Each school faculty can, of course, best work out its own plan.

Many schools are providing for teacher-administrator planned conferences for a few days before school opens in the fall. The best of these employ a combination of meeting types with plenty of time allowed for group work on curriculum plans for the coming year.

The small-group conference plan is especially appropriate for the individual school faculty with its standing committees

[46] For accounts of actual meetings of various types, see "Excerpts from Professional Logs," Appendix A, p. 195.

as well as for large central curriculum councils. In the case of the latter it is sometimes advisable to shuffle the membership of the small groups in successive meetings and to give to different members the opportunity of serving as chairman of a small group.

Discussion Techniques

Discussion techniques are employed at all stages of the social process, from the time when purposes are agreed upon and plans are made until the results of individual and group action are evaluated and new plans are formulated in the light of that evaluation. Urwick shows the function of discussion in this way: [47]

Only by long-continued discussion can any proposal be brought into connexion with the deeper instincts and impulses, the needs and wants, the desires and aims, the life-values and estimates, of individuals and groups or the society as a whole.

Discussion serves to bring new facts, ideas, beliefs, and attitudes into people's environment. It exposes prejudices and puts them in a position to be examined. It thus has the power to change moods. Discussion should never be allowed to degenerate into mere debate. Debate serves largely the purpose of making each disputant cling more firmly to his original position. The purpose of discussion should be to integrate differences.

In the case of huge forum discussions, a useful technique for breaking the ice is for the chairman to present the topic with brief comments on its possible implications, then to ask the group to spend the next three minutes talking with their immediate neighbors about it. This usually causes a lively forum discussion to begin at once when the group has been called to order again.

Techniques of Decision Making. Lewin emphasizes the rôle of decision for making discussion productive. He points out that group discussion is one excellent means of clarifying issues and bringing about motivation. But he goes on to show how

[47] Urwick, *op. cit.,* p. 229.

controlled experiments have revealed that a discussion without decision does not lead to a parallel increase in production. "There are indications," he writes,[48] "that, even if the discussion leads to the *general* decision of raising production without setting *definite* production goals to be reached in a definite time, the effect is much less marked. . . . Discussions without decisions do not make for efficient democracy." The process of decision-making is divided by De Huszar into three parts: (*a*) definition of the problem, *what* it is; (*b*) deciding *how* to deal with it; and (*c*) deciding *who* should do what.[49]

Follett has further advice for facilitating discussion when issues are complex. Referring to "the mistake we often see in discussion of not breaking the question up into its various parts," she says: [50]

. . . either the disputants are discussing a vague and nonexistent whole, or else they are discussing different parts of the question without knowing that they are doing so. This is a frequent and fatal error. The disputants must first agree to differentiate the question into its parts and then to take them up one by one.

Good discussion techniques are not easily described. So much of what accounts for the difference between effective, democratic techniques and poor techniques is quite intangible. A few definite suggestions for group planning can be offered, however: [51]

1. Give full opportunity for every member of the group to contribute every suggestion that occurs to him.
2. Keep the gathering of suggestions as a phase in the discussion process separate from the evaluation of the suggestions. (This usually ensures a more impersonal discussion of the suggested solutions.)

[48] Kurt Lewin, "The Dynamics of Group Action," *Educational Leadership*, Vol. I, Jan., 1944, pp. 195–200.
[49] De Huszar, *op. cit.*, p. 37.
[50] Follett, *op. cit.*, p. 166.
[51] For a valuable list of suggestions for participating in group discussion turn to Appendix D, p. 219. Here J. Cecil Parker has brought together from a number of sources practical aids to both the leader and the participant in the discussion process. This list is most pertinent for the type of discussion which has as its aim to clarify views on some subject.

3. Allow plenty of time for pooling of facts and harmonizing of conflicting values.
4. Before final votes are taken use straw votes to uncover minority opinion early in the process. In this step allow each voter to register as many choices as he wishes.
5. Seek for a consensus by allowing full discussion of the minority view before entertaining formal motions.
6. If after adequate discussion the group is still fairly evenly divided as to the proper course of action on a given matter, consider whether or not a decision really must be made at the time. Often it is better to postpone making the decision until further study can be made by all parties.
7. If a decision of some sort must be made, have it understood that the decision is a trial one whose results will be carefully reviewed in order that the large minority will coöperate as wholeheartedly as possible.

Division of Labor

Division of labor is a requirement not only from the standpoint of saving time and energy, but also from the standpoint of utilizing special abilities residing in members of the group. The utilization of special abilities was touched upon in connection with the treatment of the expert. To be really useful, however, one's conception of specialization and expertness must be one that can be applied to every individual in a group. The kind of expertness frequently needed in many of the less spectacular group endeavors can be developed as persons fulfill functions assigned to them by the group.

A common form of division of labor is the appointment of committees. In order to make sure that labor is actually divided by this device, committees should conform to the following specifications:

1. All committees should be functional. There is too much essential work to be done to permit the luxury of honorary and useless committees. The purpose of each committee should be clear to the group that authorizes its appointment and to each member of the committee accepting the responsibility that goes with membership.
2. To ensure continuous attention to major, persistent problem areas, standing committees are desirable. Sub-committees may

be appointed to care for certain problems needing special attention over a relatively short period of time. Such sub-committees should report to the parent committee and be disbanded when they have served their usefulness.

3. While matters of major policy should be decided by the group as a whole, committees must be given power to act in matters of procedure if the time of the large group is to be saved.

Record-Keeping

Closely allied to the problem of perfecting means of dividing labor efficiently is the problem of discovering useful types of records of thinking and action by large and small groups within an organization.

At every meeting in which the group is striving for some type of accomplishment, it is well to have a secretary to keep a record of discussion and decisions. The secretary may be used periodically throughout the meeting to summarize and help keep the group on the right track. In addition, a "board" secretary is useful during periods when lists of suggested plans or solutions are being gathered preparatory to making a decision. Having the suggestions recorded on the blackboard helps the group to think more clearly.

Record-keeping is a technique of such value in the process of directing social change that new forms of records and better ways of exchanging records among various working groups should be sought. The typical minutes of business meetings are scarcely adequate for this purpose.

A record form that has proved especially useful contains the following items:

Name of group
Meeting place, date, hours
Members present (names)
Members absent (names)
Problems discussed
Suggestions made
Problems to be referred to other committees
Decisions reached
Plans for next meeting

The advantage of such a form is that the record is quickly and easily reviewed by participants in the meeting and by other members of the organization who wish to keep in touch with developments in the particular group reporting. Such a report also may serve as a working plan for the succeeding meeting of the group. Note that this type of record includes the decision reached by the group, summaries of discussion leading to decisions, and plans for a future meeting. Such records are essential for maintaining continuity of planning, avoiding the waste of repeating discussions already held, and keeping all members of the group in touch with the work done by individuals and committees.

Records of group accomplishments should also be made. The mere fact that records are being kept often increases the significance of the activity for the participants. Furthermore, records of all kinds afford a basis for evaluation of group progress whether they be streamlined minutes of meetings of small working groups or whether they be periodic reports of progress or summaries of agreements reached.

Techniques of Group Action—Implications for Curriculum Change

In the case of discussion techniques, special application to the process of curriculum change is unnecessary. They are techniques that, as far as we know, can function in much the same general way in groups of different types.

The material on division of labor presented in this chapter is more or less a summary of principles implied throughout the discussion of organization. In trying to overcome the drawbacks inherent in curriculum committees whose members each represent a number of individual schools, Philadelphia teachers and central office staff have together made several useful discoveries. In reporting to the groups they represent they have learned that they must give to others the ideas they have gained from their stimulating contacts with other committee members and with consultants. Merely to return with emotional reactions such as, "It was a thrilling meeting," "The speaker was wonderful," or "I am getting so much out of my committee work" is not conducive to coöperation from those who had to stay behind to teach while a few had a "day off."

It has been learned also that it is futile to urge blanket coöperation with the committee on arithmetic or the committee studying health education practices. Invitations should be issued for specific participation in well-outlined projects. When several committees are working simultaneously on different aspects of the curriculum, care must be taken also that the same teachers are not "expected" to coöperate intensively on several ventures all at the same time. Use of the voluntary principle serves to obviate this difficulty.

Finally, the central committees in Philadelphia have learned that they must guard against appearing to have secrets that the rank and file may not share until some future date. No final reports or products of committee work should come as a complete surprise to those for whom the committee has been working.

A few specific suggestions may be made also regarding record-keeping as a part of the process of curriculum change. The first is that groups should avoid keeping too many records; all that are kept should be functional. The best judges of what is useful are the participants in the process. For example, teachers should help decide what curriculum records will be valuable aids in further curriculum-planning.

A second suggestion is that careful records be kept of agreements reached by the group, with enough recording of discussion to indicate the reasons for reaching the decisions. Every working group should have a secretary for this purpose. Every so often decisions should be compiled and discussed in order to dramatize progress and ensure frequent review of decisions. One school faculty keeps a policy book that is continuously revised and added to.

It is especially important that records of meetings be exchanged with other working groups. Every teacher should receive a copy of the report of each meeting of a standing committee in advance of the faculty meeting where such reports are scheduled for consideration. Minutes of individual school faculty meetings should be exchanged among buildings in order to keep each faculty group in constant touch with the thinking and the activities of other groups facing similar problems. Curriculum directors, supervisors, and the superintendent of schools all should be kept on the mailing list for all major products of committees and faculty groups. This is a simple and easy way to keep these individuals constantly informed of developments throughout the system. Needless to say, all persons giving special service to a school should not only be made a part of its on-going planning but should also receive copies of all reports whether or not they seem to have direct bearing on the individual's area of specialization. It is in these seemingly small ways that experts are enabled to broaden their approach to educational problems.

As curriculum-planning becomes more and more flexible, a third type of record will become increasingly necessary. This is the cumulative record of group experiences of each class of children going through the school. In one elementary school, a loose-leaf notebook goes along with each group of children as they pass from one teacher to another. Each year the teacher in charge adds the class roll for that year; a compilation of test results, health findings, and similar data; a list of excursions taken by the children as well as other major group experiences, such as plays, adults with whom they have come in contact, and so on. Major group interests followed in science or social studies during the year are recorded, and, if children have been divided into reading groups, the books read by each group during the year are listed. In short, the notebook contains the information about a group of children needed for wise planning with and for them during the new year. Such a group record is both a summary of and a supplement to individual cumulative records.

A fourth type of record that some teachers find useful is a daily log of major events in the classroom and of significant items relating to individual children. Such a log makes for wiser planning throughout the year.

CONSTRUCTIVE SOCIAL POWER

The most active and relentless obstacle to deliberate social change is the present distribution of social power in American communities and in our national life. This power has varying bases, but much of it is economic. With the economic power which great monopoly corporations have achieved goes enormous political power which operates at the local, state, national, and international level. This power is maintained partly through monopolistic control over opinion-forming instruments which give full expression to the propaganda of selfish interest groups. In the face of this tremendous power the ordinary citizen feels virtually helpless, a state which leads to the two conditions of apathy and skepticism referred to earlier.

Another source of social power is that which a small, well-organized minority can always achieve over a large, unformed majority. When this power is not well integrated into pursuit of the larger purpose of improved community living, it operates in the form of undesirable pressure groups which can counteract the constructive efforts of other groups. Often, however, the groups which wield so much social power and block desirable social change are composed of well-intentioned citizens who believe sincerely that they are upholding American traditions. The numerous patriotic societies in our culture are examples of groups of the latter type.

A third type of social power which is frequent in American communities is that which certain individuals with unusual leadership ability can acquire. Some persons seem always to be able to develop a large following for whatever they put their minds to. Unfortunately, this power frequently resides in neurotic individuals who find it easy to discover personal grievances and who delight in wielding their power to correct their grievances in a militant manner.

Finding Power in Coöperative Action

Fortunately for the course of future events, there is a fourth kind of power, the strength of which we are only dimly aware.

That is the kind of power that might be marshaled if people were to acquire effective ways of directing and controlling social change. That is the kind of power that would rest in persons united and motivated by common values and goals, organized for effective coöperation, and possessed of techniques for effective group action.

Follett offers substantiation of this belief: [52]

What is the central problem of social relations? It is the question of power. . . . But our task is not to learn where to place power; it is how to develop power. Genuine power can only be grown, it will slip from every arbitrary hand that grasps it; for genuine power is not coercive control, but coactive control. Coercive power is the curse of the universe; coactive power, the enrichment and advancement of every human soul.

The struggle to transfer power from the hands of less constructive groups into the hands of an organized and articulate public will demand the best that can be produced by way of social invention and the widest possible application of social findings. The building of constructive and broadly based social power is the major task involved in achieving control over social change.

Social Power—Implications for Curriculum Change

The effect upon the school curriculum of economic power groups and of other groups and individuals wielding social power in the community is better realized by some educators than others. Those who have been burned at the stake for refusing to remove textbooks disapproved by the advertising industry, for insisting upon the right to discuss controversial issues in the classroom, and for failing to "coöperate" when asked to sponsor an essay or poster contest for a local patriotic society know well what power means. There are good grounds for belief that the present wave of attack on modern educational theory by press and radio is the result of a realization on the part of economic power groups that modern curriculum trends constitute a threat to special privilege in this country.

[52] Follett, *op. cit.*, p. xii.

If effective curriculum change is to be produced, educators will have to depend upon two lines of endeavor. One is the general one of helping people of all ages to become organized for effective social action, to determine what they want to accomplish, and to learn the techniques necessary for that accomplishment. Suggestions for increasing the success of such efforts have been given throughout this work.

The second line of endeavor that seems indicated is study of the power-equation in the community. Groups and individuals exercising power or capable of doing so should be located—both those that are contributive to desirable curriculum change and those that have detrimental effect. Every effort should be made to utilize actual or potential social power that is constructive to turn the efforts of other individuals or groups into productive channels if possible; if that is impossible, to cancel out their effectiveness.

Specifically, it will be well to study the motivations of various groups and individuals. Find out to what threats they are sensitive. Learn what groups tend to block what kind of thing and what agencies can be counted on for support of an improved school program. Discover what kind of projects the women of the community are active on. Study whether or not it is true that men are more likely to exert undesirable pressure on the school curriculum and that women are more likely to play a constructive rôle if active at all. Find out from year to year the nature of the national program on which local branches of various organizations are operating.

The task of integrating the power of different individuals and groups into a constructive force for curriculum change will be facilitated by information of the sort indicated in the preceding paragraph. It is on the basis of such information that prediction can be made and constructive action taken to forestall unfortunate requests. An example of this strategy was the action taken in one state at the time when war seemed imminent for this country. Knowing that patriotic groups would be making all sorts of ill-conceived suggestions in heat of war, the state department of public instruction called together during the summer a large representative group of educators and lay persons. This group mapped out a number of desirable curriculum emphases which were suggested to local schools in the state for consideration in the fall. This move was successful in heading off the developments that appeared in many other states where such precautions were not taken.

SUMMARY

Some, not all, of democracy's techniques have been discussed in this and previous chapters. There is need to invent, test, and prove a great many more. One of the most dangerous restrictions on the effectiveness of groups is the assumption that the limit of social invention has been reached; that existing democratic forms are sacred—not to be added to nor subtracted from. Yet, we in this country certainly have not arrived at the best ways of choosing our representatives in government; we have not discovered final answers in the field of public administration; and our knowledge of techniques in the field of human relations is slender. In the matter of all democratic techniques we cannot afford to be anything but experimental. Some persons believe that experimentation with new social forms may be done with smaller social risk within the organization of the school. It is worth considering that the school may well be democracy's proving ground.

CHAPTER VI

Leadership

If any factor may be considered crucial to the success of man's efforts to control change, it is the quality of the leadership present in a given situation. With proper leadership the members of the group can be helped to have experiences that will affect the nature and intensity of their motivations. Conditions favoring group endeavor can be produced or interfered with, depending upon the type of leadership involved. Good leadership can help to bring to bear on the solution of problems the best available wisdom; malevolent leadership can deprive groups of access to information. Weak leadership can be worse than useless because it can occupy strategic positions which should be filled with effective leadership, producing a type of frustration in the group that is torture for persons with vision and ability.

The question that must be answered in this chapter is, "What is good and proper leadership for the purpose under discussion —the achieving of deliberate social change?" Two conflicting theories with regard to leadership are current. Let us examine them to discover which seems most likely to guarantee for all participants in the process desirable security, growth, and accomplishment.

LEADERSHIP BY AN ÉLITE

One theory of leadership, we find, is based upon the premise that the majority of people are not wise enough to govern themselves; they are born to be followers. Only a chosen few, the élite, are gifted with powers of leadership. Rocco, an Italian Fascist, expresses the idea thus: [1]

Fascism insists that the government be entrusted to men capable of rising above their own private interests and of realizing the aspirations of the social collectivity, considered in its unity and in its relation to the past and future. . . . [Fascism] proclaims that the great mass of citizens is not a suitable advocate of social interests for the reason that the capacity to ignore individual private interest in favor of the higher demands of society and of history is a very rare gift and the privilege of the chosen few.

According to democratic theory, there are two basic fallacies in this point of view. One is the difficulty of finding an adequate basis on which to select the élite. Merriam [2] has developed this point at length, showing that first one criterion of selection after another has had to be abandoned as inadequate. Birth, seniority, property, occupation, arms, and intelligence are among the criteria that have been found wanting.

A second difficulty with Rocco's position is that experience has shown how ill founded is faith in the ability of man, once he has acquired power over other men, to ignore individual private interest or interests. In sum, as Lerner has observed, [3] "There is no élite that is not subject to the same irrationalism as the people ruled."

It would be unnecessary to answer Fascist arguments for rule by an élite were it not for the fact that there are so many people in this country who, though professing to be democratic, actually have serious reservations about the wisdom of majority rule. These persons range all the way from those who would have deprived men and women on W.P.A. rolls of the right to vote, and who now uphold the poll tax, to the individuals who, when they get opportunities to exercise leadership, adopt the paternalistic attitude that they know best.

[1] Alfredo Rocco, "The Political Doctrine of Fascism," in Donald O. Wagner, Ed., *Social Reformers* (New York, The Macmillan Company, 1934), p. 654. By permission of the publishers.

[2] Charles Merriam, *The New Democracy and the New Despotism* (New York, McGraw-Hill Book Company, 1939), p. 29 ff.

[3] Max Lerner, *Ideas Are Weapons* (New York, The Viking Press, 1939), p. 11.

Leadership by an Élite—Implications for Curriculum Change

Believers in leadership by an élite are found all too commonly in our schools. Representatives of this school of thought are much concerned with maintaining their authority and with securing proper respect for their position. An extreme example is offered by the elementary-school principal who, for instance, will not permit the teachers to make calls on the office telephone (the only one in the building). If this administrator asks for a report to be handed in at nine o'clock in the morning, she not only flies into a rage if a teacher fails to get hers in on time, but she also refuses to accept a report five minutes early. Only once has this principal been known to admit an error and that was when she insisted, over the protests of a teacher, that a group of children use a certain door as an exit during a fire drill. The principal was new in the building then, and she did not know that the door in question led only into a supply closet.[4]

Not all administrators are as unreasonable as the woman just described, but many operate on an, often unconscious, assumption that they are superior beings. When they do so, they are inevitably led to make the same type of mistakes our unbending autocrat did, even though they may be more subtle in their attempts to secure "coöperation." They exhibit in countless ways lack of confidence in the teachers "under" them. They prepare courses of study for teachers to follow, giving minute directions. They select the textbooks and other materials to be used. They decide when the curriculum needs revision, what revision is needed, and how it shall be done.

If they decide to appear more "democratic," they may appoint some committees, but even then they are quite likely to direct every move that is made or even to step in and do the work themselves in their impatience for accomplishment. They may ask teachers to decide how a problem shall be handled and then refuse to abide by the decision if it happens not to coincide

[4] To learn how one group of teachers dealt with a similar situation, turn to Appendix A, 3, pp. 198–199.

with a prejudgment of theirs. Such leaders are likely to approve of time clocks for teachers. They are inclined to be thoughtless about interrupting teachers' work with children when it suits their convenience, thus revealing what they actually believe to be the relative importance of the teaching and the administrative function.

Characteristics of "Badministrators"

Such leaders might well be dubbed "badministrators." They are likely to see nothing wrong in marking teachers by means of a rating scale in order to determine the distribution of salary increments. They are frequently unwilling to allow teachers to attend educational conferences during school time, although they find it easy and natural for themselves to attend. They act on the assumption that only they are qualified to speak before the Woman's Club and to take other responsibility for interpreting the schools to the public. They are likely to take all the credit for school activities that meet with public favor and to place on other shoulders the blame for anything that receives criticism. These badministrators have the particularly annoying habit of presuming to make public statements about what "the teachers think" without having used adequate means to determine teacher opinion on the matter in question. They "know" their teachers are well satisfied and are "sure" their teachers will be "glad" to work on this or that "interesting" experiment.

False Assumptions of Superiority. At no period in American education would practices such as those outlined in preceding paragraphs be justified. They are not designed to help people to grow more able, but merely to obviate the most egregious results of incompetence. The assumption on which these authoritarian practices are based—that the administrative staff of a school contains the most capable persons associated with the enterprise—is ill founded also—ill founded on three counts. First of all, it ignores the fact that the competence of teachers has been greatly improved since the early days of American education. If we admit, as we must, that the preparation of today's teachers still leaves much to be desired, it is only fair to recognize that the preparation of those in the administrative and supervisory groups also leaves room for improvement. Even so, the ability of all these groups has been increased to such an extent that our permanent school personnel now represents a more intelligent and more highly educated group than the mean of the population as a whole. There is much competence upon which to build in all educational groups. This fact should be borne in mind at all times by those who would set themselves up as an educational élite.

A second error made in assuming the superiority of administrative and supervisory groups is that of overestimating the soundness of the principles used in selecting administrative and supervisory leadership. Everyone knows that such choices are frequently made on the basis of very inadequate criteria. Sometimes the "best" classroom teachers are chosen, without thought of their potentialities for developing the other types of competence required in the new position. The loss of an excellent classroom teacher can hardly be compensated for by the creation of a mediocre principal or supervisor, which is often, though not, of course, always the result of selecting solely on the basis of unusual competence in the classroom.

Just as often the mediocre or poor performer is chosen for promotion because he has desired it enough to pull all the proper strings and has sold his soul on enough occasions to demonstrate that he is sufficiently "safe" to be entrusted with a little power. It appears that in many instances selection of administrators and supervisors is made on too questionable a basis to allow one to make a sweeping assumption that all such persons are inherently superior to all those in the "ranks."

The assumption of superiority is proved false on a third count also—the fact of increasing specialization in education. More and more we are coming to realize that the ability to guide in an artistic and scientific way the educational destinies of twenty or thirty or forty third-grade children requires a competence that all too few superintendents of schools or even curriculum directors, supervisors, and principals can be presumed to possess. While the educational administrator is developing competence in other directions than classroom teaching, his colleagues who remain in the classroom may well be increasing their skill in their line of work.

All in all, the situation usually is that there are some highly competent people, and some less competent, in both teacher and administrative groups. It can happen as easily as not that extremely able classroom teachers are subjected to indignity and frustration through the antics of a mediocre and, therefore, often insecure and defensive status leader.

One of the most telling effects of an acceptance of the élite principle of leadership by administrators and supervisors is the attitude toward in-service education which such a theory engenders. Such persons think always in terms of educating others, of "making" others grow. It sometimes does not occur to them that they, too, must keep on growing. Even though they may be most capable individuals, the nature of the educational task in these days is such that competence is maintained on a high level only if one is ever learning, changing, and growing as circumstances alter.

Further Applications of the Élite Theory

The theory of an élite works in other ways in education also. It affects relations with both community adults and learners. One superintendent of schools in a suburban city was bemoaning the fact that a great many of the men in his community worked in the metropolis and that, therefore, at Rotary Club he made contact with only a comparatively small handful of local merchants, bankers, and professional people. "Why, in ———," he exclaimed, naming a city where he had been superintendent of schools previously, "when I attended Rotary Club, I reached practically all the men in the community."

Unwittingly this man had revealed in his remark fundamental acceptance of the élite theory. His many counterparts in American education believe they have a program of community education when they in some way secure the cooperation of the "key" people in the locality. (Even the "key" people, however, are not always considered to be capable of

contribution to curriculum improvement.) Principals and
teachers often become infected with this attitude. In how many
communities is it not considered a promotion to be assigned to
a school on the correct side of the railroad tracks where one
may hobnob a bit with all those of the upper class who have
not sent their children to a private school? This attitude often
leads to the premature "promotion" of a principal who has been
exerting unusual leadership in a section of the community
where such leadership was badly needed. The promotion may
be judged premature because the principal in question has not
yet had sufficient time to help others to build the leadership
ability that will guarantee that gains made will not be sacri-
ficed by his removal from the situation. From the standpoint of
fostering desirable curriculum change, this application of the
élite principle is costly in the extreme.

In the case of learners, acceptance of the theory of an élite
has led to a number of curious practices. Special classes are
set up for gifted children in order to prepare them to be the
leaders of tomorrow; opportunity rooms are provided to remove from the environment of these coming leaders those dul-
lards who might retard their progress.[5] Certain private schools
base their whole case for survival on the grounds that they are
educating the group that is destined to lead the nation. On the
other hand, the principal of a vocational school prides himself
that he turns out an excellent type of employee from his school
because he teaches his boys to follow his favorite bit of advice:
"Keep your ears open and your mouth shut." In this man's
opinion two days a week of social studies are ample for a boy
who is going to be a mechanic, while his English requirements
are met when he has learned to fill out application forms.

On a wider scale the élite theory works to excuse the uneven support of schools as between rural and urban areas, North
and South, and negro and white groups.

[5] There is no intention here of implying that equality of opportunity
means identity of opportunity. The criticism is leveled at some of the
practices employed in attempting to provide appropriate educational opportunities for various types of children.

Élite Leadership—a Sterile Concept

If we apply to the process of curriculum change some of the principles derived from our study of directed social change, it is quite clear that the theory of an élite is a sterile concept for educational leadership. The strongest indictment against such leadership is its failure to promote desirable growth on the part of the group being led. It is true that security of a kind is ensured for certain individuals. Some persons apparently enjoy playing the rôle of follower. They find their security in a release from responsibility. If a "superior" makes a certain decision and if the results are not successful, it gives many a teacher a comfortable feeling to be able to say to himself: "My principal wanted me to use this new method. I knew all the time it would not work. The parents really can't blame me if their children do not learn."

Some persons in schools actually go so far as to revel in a rôle of servility. It may be that they delight in abasing themselves before a beloved leader. It may be that they hold the traditional awe for certain positions in the school system and take it for granted that they should "respect" the persons who hold those positions.

The security that rests in release from responsibility for thinking for oneself, for showing initiative and taking an active part in the process of improving the product of one's efforts is a vicious type of security. Those who go too far in humbling themselves before others are likely to become neurotic if not psychopathic. Others play the servile rôle willingly because they can in turn exact servility from others, a principal from teachers, teachers from children. For all persons reduced to this rôle, the result is a deplorable lack of confidence in one's own powers, which is exactly the opposite from the desired effect of a security that allows for growth.

Accomplishment of a kind is assured also under the theory of leadership by an élite. But accomplishment is more limited than it need be if the powers of all the group are freely utilized at all stages of the process from the conception of the goal toward which efforts will be directed through the steps of planning and working to reach the goal.

It would seem that the élite theory of leadership has little to offer in the way of guaranteeing a process of deliberate social change that meets the criteria we have selected. Let us turn, then, to a second theory of leadership now current to determine whether it possesses more desirable qualifications for our purpose.

DEMOCRATIC LEADERSHIP

Proponents of the opposing theory of leadership have much less faith in an élite than does Rocco, but they have much more faith in the people as a whole. Believers in democratic leadership have an entirely different conception of authority from that held by those who pin their faith on an élite. With the believers in an élite, authority is something one *begins* with; with the believers in democracy it is something one *ends* with. With the élite group, authority resides in persons by virtue of positions they hold; the view of the democratic group is that authority is distilled anew as persons in different capacities learn to work together and as responsibility of various kinds is placed on different shoulders. The democratic theory is that, in the last analysis authority resides in the group, although it is delegated as occasion demands. The recognized leaders of the group are thus relieved of the necessity for "maintaining" and demonstrating their authority. Such persons can cease their struggles for jurisdiction and power and concentrate instead on offering a maximum of service. This should have a beneficial effect upon the human relations round about them.

Consistent with the democratic view of authority, the theory of democratic leadership consists of two parts. One has to do with the rôle of the so-called "status" leader—the president of an organization, the chairman of a committee, the principal of a school, the teacher in a class, and so on. The other has to do with what is referred to as "shared" or "emerging" leadership. The two are so closely intertwined that it is difficult to separate

them even for purposes of discussion. Perhaps it will be easier
to understand the unique functions of the democratic "status"
leader if we first examine the concept of "shared" leadership.

Shared Leadership

Kilpatrick has given a classic description of the way in
which leadership is shared or emerges from a group situation: [6]

Many seem to think of leadership as if it were only or primarily
fixed in advance, either by appointment or election or by special
ability and preparation. On this basis, those proceed to divide people into two fixed groups, leaders and followers. Such a view seems
inadequate, quite denied by observable facts. Actual leadership as
we see it comes mostly by emergence out of a social situation. A
number of people talk freely about a matter of common concern.
A proposes a plan of action. B successfully voices objection and
criticism. C then proposes a modified plan. D, E, and F criticize certain features of this plan. The group at this point divides, seemingly
unable to agree. G then comes forward with a new plan that combines the desired features and avoids the evils feared. The group
agree. Here A, B, C, D, E, F, and G were successively leaders of the
group. And each such act of leadership emerged out of the situation
as it then appeared. This is democratic leadership and its success
depends on—nay exactly is—an on-going process of education inherent in the situation.

Shared leadership works in other ways than as a feature of
the process of group thinking. If the status leadership is truly
evocative, the group will be organized for working in such a
way that suitable opportunities for leadership will arise for
every member of the group. Individuals and small groups may
and should be entrusted with the responsibility of carrying into
action policies and plans made by the group.

All this does not mean that one should never be a follower.
It does mean that persons should become capable of alternately
exercising leadership and serving under the leadership of another. Only thus will individuals develop their utmost power
and become truly socialized. Whether one is serving temporar-
ily as a leader or a follower, he should be aware of the problems

[6] William H. Kilpatrick in Samuel Everett, Ed., *The Community School*
(New York, D. Appleton–Century Company, Inc., 1938), p. 20.

facing the group. While he is acting in the capacity of follower, he should accept the leadership of another and coöperate actively. We have Lewin's authority for the soundness of
this idea: [7]

Establishing democracy in a group implies an active education: The
democratic follower has to learn to play a role which implies,
among other points, a fair share of responsibility toward the group
and a sensitivity to other people's feelings. . . .

What holds for the education of democratic followers holds true
also for the education of democratic leaders. In fact, it seems to be
the same process through which persons learn to play either of these
roles and it seems that *both roles must be learned if either one is to
to be played well.* [Italics mine. A. M.]

Functions of Democratic Status Leaders

Even though we have a situation in which leadership is widely
shared, there still seems to be a place for the status leader. This
term does not imply that every person with leadership status
is a good leader, but it does imply that there are important functions for persons who are placed in "leadership" positions in a
group. The Iowa experiments already referred to [8] have revealed the weakness of laissez-faire leadership, which is practically equivalent to no leadership at all. Group work seems
to be facilitated by the presence of status leadership of the right
kind. If elected or appointed leaders are to play their proper
part in the process of deliberate social change, they must take
special responsibility for the security, growth, and accomplishment of all participants in the process. Accordingly, appropriate functions for status leaders will be somewhat as follows:
(1) improving the human relations within the group; (2) furnishing expertness along certain lines; (3) generating leadership in others; and (4) coördinating the efforts of others.

Setting a Desirable Tone for Human Relations. If the status
leader is to set a desirable tone for the human relations within a
group, it will be necessary for him to have a deep understand-

ing and appreciation of people in general and of the particular persons with whom he is dealing. He will also have to have a great respect for the unique contributions which it is possible for each group member to make under favorable circumstances. His example in interpersonal relationships will have a strong influence on all of the group. Confidence, ease, poise, kindness, and thoughtfulness are just as contagious as are fear, insecurity, excitability, irritability, and callousness. Teachers are quick to sense these qualities in their leaders. Note this entry in a professional log:

Our principal is beginning to get much better cooperation now than at first because he is much more relaxed and does not become excited over the least little thing.

It is particularly important for the leader to recognize and help the group to make allowances for differences in temperament and tempo on the part of various individuals. It takes patience and reasonableness on the part of all persons in the group to reach a deliberate consensus. Since few leaders have the opportunity to handpick their groups and since most groups contain their full quota of impatient and even irrational souls, it is necessary to learn how to cope with variations in temperament while yet helping all to acquire behavior patterns more congenial to group process.

The sensitive leader will also search for ways of enabling the more slow-spoken in the group to have access to the floor along with those who are quick to speak forth. For some minds more than others it is essential that the discussion be summarized and pointed up frequently.

For understanding all people and allowing sufficient time for growth it might be well to ponder such a fact as the following: It takes between three and four weeks for an adult to learn the simple operation of turning a light on at the new location of the switch.[9]

Helping People to Learn Techniques of Coöperation. The status leader, more than anyone else, is responsible for helping

[9] John Franklin Donnelly, "It Takes Time to Learn," *Journal of the National Education Association*, Vol. XXX, Nov., 1941, p. 233.

others to learn techniques necessary for a high level of coöperation. Good intentions and an attitude of understanding and helpfulness are important attributes in status leaders and other members of coöperating groups, but they are not enough. There are too many groups expending a great deal of energy yet accomplishing little of significance. There is so much to be done by way of improving conditions in local communities, states, the nation, and the world that we must expect groups coöperating to effect social change to produce noticeable results. It is the status leader who is often able to help people to learn to plan and work together to reach goals they set for themselves. This leader must possess unusual expertness in techniques of group action. He will also be expected to be especially well equipped in certain specialized lines useful to the group. Insight into financial problems, special executive ability, skill in human relations, unusual background in the social sciences, ability to lead discussions, knowledge of statistical methods, skill in survey techniques, understanding of curriculum trends —expertness in one or more of these on the part of the leader will prove valuable to the group.

Helping to Develop Further Leadership. Perhaps the chief obligation of the status leader, if he is to play a rôle that is consistent with democratic theory, is that he be concerned primarily with developing power, responsibility, and leadership ability in others. This ability to generate more leadership does not come naturally to man. The temptation of those who have "natural" leadership ability is to be concerned only with keeping a following. Like all democratic techniques, evocative leadership is an art that has to be cultivated with all the help that the science of human development can offer.

If social change is to be controlled, it is essential that more leadership ability be generated in this way, for it is common knowledge that there is great lack of dependable leadership in our communities, large and small. There is much potential ability going untapped. We cannot afford the social waste of large stores of undeveloped leadership. We can and should "grow" democratic leaders. The best way in which to do so is to give more and more persons opportunities to exercise leadership. Leadership training institutes have been found helpful for making early attempts at exercising leadership more successful than they would otherwise be.

Serving as a Coördinator. Coördination of efforts of individuals and groups is an increasingly necessary function in a society which grows ever more complex and in which specialization is growing so rapidly. The ability to serve as a coördinator presupposes a good understanding of the rôle of organization and of ways of making organization functional. It also presupposes ability to help a group with strategy and timing of efforts. The maintenance of a balance between gradualism and rapidity of change is the special responsibility of the status leader who is usually in a favored position for seeing the situation whole and can help the group judge when it should move forward.

Democratic Leadership—Implications for Curriculum Change

In the preceding section it was pointed out that there are two parts to the theory of democratic leadership. There is in the theory a concept of shared or emerging leadership, which connotes for each individual involved a dual rôle of leader and follower, played as the occasion warrants. Kilpatrick has shown in his description of the process of group thinking how those rôles alternate.[10] Another example may be the supervisor of music who now conducts a workshop for interested teachers and, on another occasion, meets with a committee, whose chairman happens to be one of the workshop group, to make plans for improving the induction of new teachers into the school system.

The other part of the theory of democratic leadership is based on the need for status leaders who are qualified to fulfill certain functions. Five such functions were discussed. Their implications for leadership in curriculum change will now be treated in turn.

[10] See p. 158.

Improving Human Relations in and Around a School

It is not putting the matter too strongly to say that leadership in improving human relations can be exercised only by one who has a growing understanding of people. For the educational leader, this means coming to understand teachers both as professional workers and as people. In the same way, it means coming to understand community adults and learners as people.

Teachers Must Be Understood as Professional Workers. A person's work life is of utmost importance. His vocation colors his desires and beliefs—it determines his basic interests. This is as true of the professional educator as of anyone else. Prall [11] has invented a term, "the teacher culture," for the rather peculiar environment in which the educator moves. This teacher culture has both favorable and unfavorable characteristics. There is strength on which to build resulting from the closeness of association within the teacher culture, the similarity of interest and purpose, the very real and common desire to see a better school. Yet there is, as we have shown, much dependence upon persons in authority. There is also much resentment and frustration on the part of the more spirited. The teacher culture has its full quotas of both apathetic individuals and of skeptics.

A second weakness of the teacher culture is lack of information and lack of consistency on the part of its members in matters of economics, politics, and social problems of the day. As a result of his well-known study for the John Dewey Society, Hartmann was prompted to declare: [12]

Teachers tend to be well informed in the field of conventionalized and historical knowledge and relatively weak in their grasp of vital contemporary issues . . . where the "growing edge" of cultural change is concerned the unsatisfactory character of teachers' information about public problems is most poignantly displayed.

[11] Charles E. Prall with C. Leslie Cushman, *Teacher Education in Service* (Washington, D.C., American Council on Education, 1944), p. 277.

[12] George Hartmann, *Teacher and Society*, First Yearbook of the John Dewey Society (New York, D. Appleton–Century Company, Inc., 1937), p. 210.

This study substantiates the declaration made earlier in this chapter that administrators are not necessarily superior to teachers: [13]

The evidence available does not indicate any notable difference in broader social attitudes between classroom teachers and their administrative colleagues. . . . Apart from the fact that the teachers were somewhat more conservative than the administrators in their social philosophy and a bit more progressive in their educational sympathies, the results for the two types of educational service ran almost perfectly parallel.

The administrator who would make full use of Hartmann's conclusions might well move in two directions. First, he might study ways of helping all members of the teacher culture to become better informed with regard to the realities of the current social scene and to develop strong social consciences. Second, he might utilize forces outside the teacher culture in promoting curriculum change. In this connection Todd [14] has given us a succinct reminder that "the school, speaking by and large, has never of its own motion added a single subject to its curriculum. Social pressure has always forced it to adjust." This accounts in large measure for the mode of curriculum change by accretion rather than by wise anticipation of changing human needs.

A third, rather common, characteristic of the teacher culture is its peculiar remoteness from the stream of community life. More than the members of most professions, educators in the past seem to have exhibited a well-marked type of institutional behavior. The community and the teachers themselves have operated on the assumption that here was a group apart, a state of affairs that has caused dismay among those who desire to hasten the arrival of realistic community education.

All these characteristics of the teacher culture should be comprehended by those charged with special leadership within that culture, for otherwise it is impossible fully to know and

[13] *Ibid.*, p. 228.
[14] Arthur J. Todd, *Theories of Social Progress* (New York, The Macmillan Company, 1922), p. 514.

understand teachers and other fellow educators to say nothing
of oneself. Without this understanding, it is impossible to build
upon the real strengths of the teacher culture and to plan experiences that will ensure necessary growth in overcoming
weaknesses present. Experiences that will increase the self-
respect and social understanding of teachers and experiences
that will make them actual members of the community require
forethought and planning in the light of data obtained in the
community in question.

If teachers are to be understood as professional workers,
studies of teacher load should be made periodically and in good
faith. Also teachers should be given regularized opportunities
for suggesting desired changes in their schedules and in their
class and extra-class assignments. A simple staff information
blank can be worked out to provide such an opportunity for
expression of teacher wishes at least once each semester or
school year. Planned interviews may also be used for studying
teachers in their professional rôles.

Teachers Must Be Understood and Dealt with as People.
While it is important to have an analysis of the teacher culture
and of its effect on individual personalities within it, that alone
is not equipment enough for fulfilling the leadership function
in a school system. Each member of the professional personnel
should be known and valued as a person in his own right. This
means that he should be known as a totality, not just as an institutional cog.[15]

There are several ways of going about a study of the individuals with whom one is associated. First, it is helpful to
learn all one can about principles of human development. This
includes an understanding that the best modern conceptions
of the learning process apply to adults equally as much as to
children. This includes also an understanding of personality
development and of principles of mental hygiene.

Burgess suggests a useful outline for "the study of the per-

[15] Hazel A. Kier, Intermediate Supervisor in Kansas City, Kansas, has
prepared a description of her plan for inducting new teachers, a plan that
takes into account their personal living. See Appendix E, p. 222.

son." As he indicates, this outline includes aspects of behavior for which no standardized technique of measurement has been accepted. This perhaps increases its value for the school administrator, for the outline should be employed only as a guide to informal study of persons. The outline runs as follows: [16]

1. Participation
    a. Extent of membership in groups (ratio to total number open to the individual)
    b. Intimacy of membership (fraction of total time devoted to this social world)
    c. Rôle in groups
2. Character (stabilized or unstabilized)
3. Personal behavior pattern
    a. Objective or direct (equable, enthusiastic, frank, aggressive)
    b. Introspective or indirect (imaginative, sensitive, secretive, inhibited)
    c. Psychopathic or perverse (eccentric, egocentric, emotionally unstable, psychic inferior)
4. Social type (practical or Philistine, Liberal or Bohemian)
5. Idealistic or religious
6. Philosophy of life

Now it would be most unfortunate were administrators to confine their efforts at study of individuals to a cold process of classifying them according to various types. Walter Lippmann, in discussing how prone we are to reduce everything to stereotypes and to form blanket judgments, makes this astute observation: [17]

Those whom we love and admire most are the men and women whose consciousness is peopled thickly with persons rather than with types, who know us rather than the classification into which we might fit.

Study Teachers in Many Ways. Study such as Burgess suggests should be supplemented with other means of coming to

[16] E. W. Burgess, "The Delinquent as a Person," *American Journal of Sociology*, 1922–23, XXVIII: 665–68, 671–73 (The University of Chicago Press). Quoted in Kimball Young, Ed., *Source Book of Social Psychology* (New York, F. S. Crofts & Co., 1927), p. 409.

[17] Walter Lippmann, *Public Opinion* (New York, Harcourt, Brace and Company, 1922), pp. 88–89.

understand colleagues as people. There are dozens of homely devices for coming to know the home situation, the family background, the joys and hopes, the anxieties and sorrows of teachers. How such information can be utilized to good effect in counseling teachers is well illustrated in Stephen Corey's series, "The Importance of People," carried in recent issues of an educational periodical.[18] The hopeful part is, as Burgess says,[19] that "mentality, affectivity, temperament, and will are not uninfluenced by social experience. They are all more or less profoundly modified by education and social contacts."

The value of study is the guidance it gives in planning experiences that will promote growth. One important means of influencing the experiences of teachers that frequently is overlooked is placement in the most promising working situation. The assignment of a teacher to a faculty group should, whenever possible, take into account the personality, special strengths, and needs of that teacher, of the principal to whose leadership he is consigned, and of the faculty and community group with whom he will be working. This calls for careful placement of new teachers and for the judicious use of transfers to other teaching situations in the case of those already in the system.

Find New Adventures for Teachers. Another way of influencing the experiences of teachers that has received too little attention is to give teachers carefully selected opportunities for new adventures in the school system—chances to do broadcasting, perhaps, or to specialize in educational photography, or to assist with leadership institutes for labor unions and other community groups—all these in addition to the more usual conferences, workshops, opportunities for visitation of other teachers, and other means employed to promote in-service growth of personnel.

It might be well also to experiment with appropriate cumulative records for each teacher. These should include information, both of a personal and a professional nature, that will be

[18] *Educational Leadership*, 1943–1944.
[19] Burgess, *op. cit.*, p. 411.

useful to those responsible for the guidance of teachers.[20] For teachers presenting unusual personality problems detailed case studies might be made by qualified individuals. Fenton in a recent book has included several excellent examples.[21] If persons with severe difficulties can be helped and saved for the teaching profession without endangering the interests of the learners, such study will prevent much social waste. If it is discovered that an individual should not really be teaching at all, the study made will enable responsible officials to help that person make the necessary adjustment to a new vocation.

One word of warning should be issued at this point. The relationship between an administrator and a teacher is not analogous to the relationship between teacher and pupil, as is frequently assumed. The former relationship is a peer relationship, one in which, as we have shown, different kinds and amounts of competence and maturity are present in both parties. This means that the task of leadership is all the more delicate and requires the utmost understanding of past experiences and present motivations. As Prescott says,[22] it is necessary to "understand what an individual is trying to get out of life and why he thinks that certain behavior is the road to optimum conditions for him." It is only when fortified with such information that the administrator can help individuals to find satisfaction in new kinds of behavior.

Community Adults and Learners Should Be Understood and Dealt with as People. In preceding paragraphs, attention was turned exclusively to the professional personnel as a key factor in curriculum change. Now, changing teachers and changing schools are not wholly identical processes. Two other groups must be taken into account—learners and community adults.

Much of what has been said with regard to studying and

[20] For a description of such a cumulative record developed coöperatively in the J. J. Smallwood Elementary School in Norfolk, Va., under the leadership of Margaret L. Gordon, turn to Appendix F, p. 228.

[21] Norman Fenton, *Mental Hygiene in School Practice* (Stanford University, Cal., Stanford University Press, 1943).

[22] Daniel A. Prescott, *Emotion and the Educative Process* (Washington, D.C., American Council on Education, 1938), p. 80.

trying to understand teachers as people is equally applicable here. It is helpful to understand general principles of human development and mental hygiene in order to be able to determine the motivations of people and the kinds of experiences they need if they are to become contributive. For this understanding to be completely useful, it must be applied to the study of particular individuals and their specific needs. Just as in the case of learners, so with adults, the best way to study individuals is to observe behavior. From the standpoint of the *process* of curriculum change, it is essential to discover answers to some such questions as these:

1. Where is this city on a scale of localism—cosmopolitanism? [23]
2. Who are its leaders? Why?
3. What natural communities exist within this city?
4. Who are the leaders in these smaller districts? Why?
5. What do the inhabitants of each of these districts feel about their position in the community as a whole?
6. What particular understandings and lacks of understanding, what abilities and what needs and desires are revealed by different learners in the various districts?
7. What understandings, abilities, needs, and desires are revealed by various adults with whom educational leaders come in contact?
8. How can such contacts with community adults be extended?
9. What are particular community stereotypes of schools and teachers in the various districts?

On the basis of answers discovered to these and similar questions, plans can be made for improving relationships among all concerned with the school.

Leaders Must Have Realistic Faith in Human Potentialities. In addition to achieving a growing understanding of people, a second requisite to improving human relations is that leaders must have realistic faith in human potentialities. Faith in other

[23] Carle C. Zimmerman, *The Changing Community* (New York, Harper & Brothers, 1938), pp. 107–109, discusses the characteristics of the community falling toward the end of the scale marked localism. Fear of change, nationalism, and antipathy for strangers all are mentioned. In the more cosmopolitan community, the author points out, much unassimilated growth can be expected and heterogeneity is extreme.

persons may be adopted a priori as a value to be operated on because the experience of so many people has been that such faith pays dividends in terms of human growth. Urwick's testimony is: [24]

We all tend to act up or down to the standard which is confidently expected of us; it is therefore hardly possible to have too much faith in the potential goodness of any one.

While Urwick's statement may be accepted intellectually as a valid one, it is only out of a study of people and out of observation of their responses to demonstrations of faith in their ability, actual or latent, that faith in them will become a genuine, deeply held value for an administrator. Real progress toward a better curriculum will not be made until all persons concerned with curriculum improvement are treated with respect, until it is demonstrated in countless ways that their opinions are valued.

Faith in human potentialities must be a realistic faith, however. All evidence points to the fact that human beings are not equal in their potentialities. The process of individuation to which one is committed when he accepts *democratic* socialization as his means and end requires recognition of the great human differences that exist. It requires that each individual be helped to have experiences that will be most fruitful for growth toward his full potentialities while yet allowing the business of the group to move forward as expeditiously as possible. Since most persons are far from reaching the maximum of their capacities in most respects and since we know too little of what those maximum potentialities may be for any individual or for the human race as a whole, the better course for the educational leader to take is to help groups lay their plans in the light both of present abilities and concerns and of promising lines of future growth for each individual and the group.

In recognizing that human beings differ in their potentialities it is particularly important that the status leader not assume

[24] E. J. Urwick, *A Philosophy of Social Progress* (London, Methuen and Company, Ltd., 1920), p. 119.

that his own potentialities are, because of his position, automatically higher than those of all others in the group. In fact, it occurs frequently that one or several teachers who are expected to follow the leadership of a given supervisory officer may actually be in advance of that officer in educational thinking. It is disconcerting, for example, for the elementary teacher who has gone beyond "unit" teaching to be asked by a visiting supervisor, "What is your unit? I do not seem to observe that a unit is going on in this room." It should be equally disconcerting to the high-school art teacher to be required to give a final examination in his courses. A supervisory officer may or may not be aware of the fact that he is "behind the times" or at least behind some of the teachers. The only safe course is to create a situation in which a teacher is not forced to set his ideas by the supervisor's educational clock, a situation in which, rather, there is room for many ideas and where there is a cordial welcome and an honest consideration for a new idea no matter what its source. It is particularly important that the superintendent, principal, or curriculum specialist be able to entertain suggestions not as criticisms levelled at them personally but as evidence of constructive interest.

The intention here is not to imply that there is anything automatic in the process of human development. If a school situation is tangled with conflicts, if a great deal of social power resides in somewhat unprofessional, unethical, and ruthless individuals, the "faith" cure will not clear matters as if by magic. But, within all groups and within all individuals there are many conflicting tendencies. The rôle of the leader is to throw the weight of circumstances in the direction of helping the constructive tendencies to win out. Various ways in which this may be done in schools have been described in foregoing chapters where participation through functional organization in group enterprises has been discussed. The chief principle upon which all recommendations rest is that enunciated by Linton to the effect that behavior is the easiest of all culture elements to modify. At all times the status leader should keep in mind that beliefs and desires are affected by *doing things in new ways*.

The Educational Leader's Obligation to Furnish Expertness

Perhaps the most essential area of specialization for the leader in curriculum development is the social setting of the curriculum. No one is qualified to exert leadership in the American school of today if he is not a student of American civilization in the fullest sense. It is out of insights and appreciations with respect to the past, present, and future of our country that the educational leader derives his values, his concepts of the broad purpose of education, his sense of direction that guides him in the selection of every goal and every technique for reaching that goal. All educators should possess this qualification, but its lack in the status leaders in our schools is a luxury our society cannot afford. Educational leadership can rise no higher than its vision. If that vision is poverty-stricken, the school curriculum will be barren indeed.[25]

The great need for expertness in techniques of group action on the part of every status leader in education has already been referred to and need only be reëmphasized here. The day of directed and controlled social change will surely be hastened as more persons become skilled in democracy's techniques. These techniques should be practiced and learned by pupils in school under the guidance of teachers and administrators who consider them as part of their special equipment. These techniques must at the same time be practiced and learned by a growing number of community adults organized for working together. Special ability in demonstrating and guiding the use of these techniques is one important type of expertness which professional educators should contribute to community living. One has only to visit a typical business meeting conducted by adults to discover the urgency of the need.

In addition to expertness in social science and in techniques of group action which should be cultivated in all members of the administrative, supervisory, and teaching groups, each status

[25] In the selected bibliography at the end of this study is a group of books especially useful for helping one round out his background of understandings with regard to the American scene and its wider setting.

leader in education should have his own specialized functions to perform. The following analysis is merely suggestive of types of specialization required in most school systems.

The superintendent of schools may well specialize in such matters as school finance, school architecture, selection of personnel, induction of principals, school-board relations, community organization, teacher personnel problems, and the like. Yet, like all other agents in the school, his major interest and responsibility should be an improved school curriculum. All of his activities from budget-making to dealing with teachers' unions and sitting on the central curriculum council should be carried on in such a way as to facilitate the process of curriculum change. The school superintendent should make himself as familiar as possible with principles of child development, modern theories of learning, modern curriculum trends, and the reasons for them. He should utilize every opportunity to *learn from* teachers, principals, supervisors, curriculum directors, parents, and children. He must attain the broadest possible view of the curriculum and of means of improving it if he is to operate at all wisely. In no other way can he derive skill as a coördinator and strategist. Yet, he must at all times form judgments and act in coöperation with others, for education in our modern communities is too complex an undertaking to be encompassed by one brain.

The school principal, too, must have a broad view of the curriculum and must feel that his chief function is to furnish leadership in curriculum development in the individual school unit. He, too, should be a specialist in coördination, strategy, and organization. If assistance can be supplied the principal, he should be relieved of matters of routine that can be handled by clerks and assistants and should concentrate his efforts on the larger aspects of the principal's job. He may well specialize also in some area of the curriculum such as evaluation or reading, as suggested earlier.

In the case of *supervisors* of all kinds, the special function to be served is to offer consultant service to individual principals and teachers, to individual school faculties, and to working committees of various kinds. Such consultants will be invaluable for staffing local workshops for teachers and community adults. Consultants in the various arts will continue to be of value both for the elementary and the secondary levels of the school. Changes in the organization of the elementary school and in views as to the interrelatedness of the various parts of the elementary-school curriculum make the contributions of the "general" supervisor more valuable in most cases than that of the "subject" supervisor. Supervisors of penmanship, geography, arithmetic, and similar subjects will probably find it increasingly difficult to be of service in an integrated elementary program.

Development of an integrated program proceeds more slowly at the secondary level. Needed specialization in the secondary school can likely be furnished by the special subject teachers, rendering the employment of special supervisors unnecessary. If need is felt for consultants in such broad fields as language arts, social studies, mathematics, and science, it would appear wise to develop persons capable of serving both the elementary and secondary teachers in a given school system or subdivision of the school system. As already pointed out, teachers and principals may develop expertness in such fields and make their special knowledge available to others.

The curriculum director will naturally be a curriculum specialist, which means that he will have more than average knowledge of the social scene, of principles of child development and of learning theories. He, too, must be a coördinator and a strategist and a specialist in the uses of organization. He can serve a useful function by coördinating the services of the school psychologist, doctor, nurse, and specialists in the arts and crafts, music, library, and other fields. He should also assume special responsibility for coördinating the efforts of those engaged in the preparation of curriculum materials. Possession of the ability to edit such materials would stand this officer in good stead.

He must have unusual ability in human relations and a genuine appreciation for the fact that effective curriculum change means change in people. It is his special function to help all other educational workers from teacher to superintendent of schools to see the curriculum implications of various proposals and decisions. The curriculum director must, then, learn all he can of school finance, school architecture, and other matters often believed to be in the province of the school superintendent. In fact, the curriculum director may well supply the needed link between the functions of administration and instruction in schools until such time as the ridiculous nature of this separation becomes apparent to numbers of educators.

Caswell advocates a place for the curriculum director in the administrative organization of the school and gives good reason for his belief in this arrangement: [26]

[The task of the curriculum director] is far greater than that of writing courses of study or preparing units of work, and carries significant implications for the place of the curriculum director in the administrative organization of a school and the nature of his duties. He must be in a position administratively to work with all groups affecting instruction. He must work cooperatively, depending upon the modification of viewpoints as a means of progress and thus must be in position to lead in development of an in-service educational program for workers in the school system. He must be in position to coordinate supervision and to relate it to the evolving program. He must have opportunity to bring the findings of guidance workers to bear on the revision of the curriculum.

All of the aforementioned agents should develop skill in the techniques of coöperative or self-surveys of the school. Fact-finding should be a constant activity in the process of curriculum change and certain persons in the school system must be prepared to give leadership in this enterprise. Surveys of textbooks now in use, age-grade surveys, surveys of maps and other equipment available for teachers' use are examples of simple beginnings that may be made in securing data upon which to work out policies of purchase, of promotion, and so on.

Expertness Must Be Integrated. The integration of the various types of expertness on the part of different status leaders in a school system into a unified whole can be accomplished best if all specialization is broadly based. If individual specialists are well informed regarding the general educational program into which their contribution is to be fitted and if they are more concerned with contributing the authority of their expertness for what it is worth to the group than with exercising a personal authority that tradition has associated with the title they hold, their special abilities and knowledge can be of real value in effecting vital curriculum change.

The central office staff of a large school system faces a puzzling problem of how to be most effective. The printed page is a comparatively cold and insensitive medium. Speeches to large groups are somewhat better for conveying enthusiasm and point of view and for giving the teaching group an opportunity to learn something of the personality of the officer in question, but they are not enough. Face-to-face contact with all teachers in small problem-centered groups, the ideal situation, is an impossibility.

It seems that members of the central staff in large cities must recognize that, from the standpoint of number of school units, teachers, and pupils, their situation is comparable to that of the educational officials in some entire states. They would do well to try to operate as do the best representatives of state departments of education who encourage wisest use of our national tradition of local control and operation of schools.

Relationships of Central Staff to Teachers and Learners. If they are to render maximum service, it is of first importance that individual specialists and status leaders in central offices see clearly their relationship and responsibility to teachers and learners. To promote improved relationships, the typical hierarchical arrangement in a school system must give way to flexible and democratic arrangements whereby services flow to the children through the faculty group in charge. The accompanying diagram shows rather well the type of relationship advocated.

In implementing this concept a passage from Prall and Cushman will be useful. These students of in-service education of

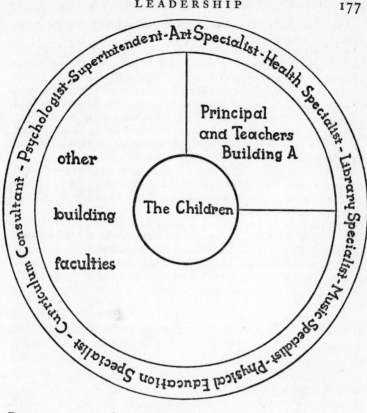

RELATIONSHIP OF SERVICE AGENTS TO CHILDREN IN A DEMO-
CRATIC PLAN

From Koopman, Miel, and Misner, *Democracy in School Administration* (New York, D. Appleton–Century Co., Inc., 1943), p. 61.

teachers have worked out a practical rôle for the central official: [27]

The coordinating role of the central staff is often a corequisite to
the exercise of local choice and initiative on the part of a school
faculty or a school-community group. Efforts to alleviate juvenile
delinquency, to promote health campaigns and physical correction,

[27] Charles E. Prall and C. Leslie Cushman, *Teacher Education in Service*
(Washington, D.C., American Council on Education, 1944), pp. 485–486.

and to plan cooperatively with trade and industry require a coordinating committee or official for the system as a whole. These
matters can rarely be delegated to individual faculties. . . . This is
because the full sweep of these problems intersects the operating
areas of many agencies, community groups, and professional bodies
which have no divisions comparable to a school attendance unit.
A school administration which would tempt its faculties to deal
separately with the agencies and organizations concerned with delinquency, with medical and dental practitioners, or hospitals and
public clinics without providing for the constant formulation of
over-all policies, would be courting disaster.

Important as the coordinating role may be, it can be overworked
and overvalued. This is apt to be the case when the desire to accomplish results takes precedence over the desire to add to the stature
of a given staff. For such a tendency there is no inoculation quite so
effective, in our opinion, as actual participation with a staff which is
beginning to reach its own solutions. There can be no real security
for autonomous schools, for schools which are exercising responsible freedom in meeting current challenges, unless there are people
at the center who are gaining the sense of personal participation in
what is going on. It is, of course, a matter of long-time importance
that the way in which a school faculty responds to current challenges—by acquiescence and uniformity, or deliberation and choice
of attack—may become the customary way of handling all other
matters relating to the conduct of the schools.

It appears that, along with their coördinating activities, members of central staffs will, if they are wise, participate as much
as possible with faculty groups at the grass roots of curriculum
development.

The Obligation of Educational Leaders to Generate More Leadership

Professional educators in all sorts of positions have potential
ability for leadership in curriculum change. Responsibility for
leadership should not be confined exclusively to the administrative group but must rest in every individual who deals with
learners. It is likely that a socially motivated faculty group will
readily see the importance of giving to learners and community
adults appropriate opportunities for participation in curriculum
development. There is slim chance that such opportunities will

be provided in situations where they are denied to classroom teachers.

Therefore it seems highly reasonable to recommend that teachers and principals should carry much responsibility for curriculum development. It is axiomatic that, no matter who plans the curriculum, the plans ultimately are carried out by a teacher and group of learners. For this reason, we covet the utmost initiative and ability in the persons who are closest to learners in school. In other words, the greater the amount of effective leadership developed on the part of all members of the professional staff, the greater the probability that the experiences of learners in their charge will be educative.

Learners and community adults too must have their opportunities to exercise leadership on numerous occasions if there is to be the wide increase in leadership ability that seems essential. A functional organization that is expanding to meet needs and in which division of labor is a principle systematically and thoughtfully applied offers manifold opportunities for leadership development among professional personnel, learners, and community adults alike. Every committee chairmanship created, every assignment of special responsibility means more chances for more persons to exercise leadership and to test their effectiveness in actual group situations. These persons can be encouraged to contribute to professional magazines and yearbooks and to house or community organs, to appear before community organizations or on the radio, and to get experience at taking leadership in different situations, such as presiding at meetings of various types, serving on panels, and taking part in community forums.

It helps tremendously if status leaders are generous with praise and recognition for any and all services rendered by members of the group. The praise, however, should be focused on the service and not on the person. As Howard Lane says,[28] "The motivation of individuals to excellence rather than to

[28] Howard Lane, *Group Planning in Education*, 1945 Yearbook of the Department of Supervision and Curriculum Development (Washington, D.C., National Education Association), p. 9.

being of genuine worth is directly contrary to the achievement of intelligent group enterprise. . . . Discriminating praise of the individual," he continues, "seems to act as a habit-forming drug; group appreciation of contributions and achievements seems to be a prime motivator of human action." Most persons blossom under recognition of their contributions and are encouraged to undertake new ventures as a result.

Discovering Leadership in the Community. Help in discovering and developing leadership among community adults may be secured from a list of suggestions worked out by a study group at a state conference on community councils.[29] The group report lists the following means of locating potential leadership material in the community:

1. Ask high school students for names of persons they know who have unusual talents or abilities.
2. Survey abilities and "willingness to lead" among persons who are potential leadership material.
3. Obtain from community leaders the names of persons who have latent leadership abilities.
4. Determine the most "popular" persons in town by casual questioning around community. "Popular" persons are usually better leaders than persons with "prestige."
5. Deputy leadership. An untried assistant for the over-burdened helpful soul.

Suggestions for developing leadership evolving from this same study group include:

1. Giving responsibilities to new leaders only as they are safely able to absorb them with a feeling of security. This security grows from allowing them to feel that they have a source of help and encouragement in experienced people.
2. Giving them a taste of successful participation.
3. Developing a precedent of not overworking leaders so that non-leaders are not deterred from being interested.
4. Providing community forum experiences.
5. Making leadership no monetary drain.
6. Providing program planning institutes so that leaders are not all dressed up with no place to go.

[29] From a mimeographed report of a conference held in Michigan in 1940.

Educational Leaders as Coördinators

An important function of the educational administrator is to make it possible for individuals to pool their abilities and their efforts in the solution of curriculum problems. Group thinking is possible only if a group is assembled under favorable conditions. Expertness can be brought to bear on a situation when and as needed only if a skilled coördinator is at work. A coördinator who knows his job can in most cases keep community adults and professional personnel from working at cross purposes with one another. He can make available to one working group the experience of another group at a time when it will be most helpful. Joint faculty meetings, joint committee meetings, the addition to working groups of experts from within or from outside the community can be arranged by the alert coördinator.

Part of the coördinating function is concerned with strategy and timing of group efforts. While this function is discharged in coöperation with others, it appears that the administrator, especially in the early stages of coöperative curriculum development, should take special responsibility for strategy.

Begin Where People Are. One fundamental principle of strategy is to begin with people where they are. One of the most common errors made by an administrator coming into a new situation is to act as if nothing, or at least nothing good, had transpired in the school before his arrival. The newcomer, naturally, is in a difficult position. He does not share the common memories of the group. For that reason, it is all the more necessary that he proceed carefully, doing more listening and watching than telling and doing. It is usually best to proceed from the known and on-going for continuity is a basic element in desirable social change. Discover first what the school has done and what public and private projects are under way in the community. Take into account the standing in the community and the relationships established by one's predecessor on the job. Learn the history, purposes, and program of teacher organizations and various other organizations in the community. Determine readiness for change in different individuals. Learn specifically what changes are desired. This does not mean that these will necessarily be the changes that should be or will be made. It does mean that clues have been gained as to points where study should begin.[30]

Respect the Need for Security. A second fundamental principle of strategy is to respect, at all stages of the process of change, people's need for security. Familiar ways of working should not be ruled out unless one is sure there is something ready to take their place.

A good example of violation of teacher security comes from an army radio school. In some central office it had been decided that instruction should be made more practical; henceforth teachers should make use of models in demonstrating radio operation. One morning came the order to the commanding officer of the school: "Remove all blackboards from classrooms at once." The order was carried out with military efficiency. All chalk was collected on the instant; by noon not a blackboard remained in a classroom. But—the teaching models had not yet arrived, nor did they come for some time. Eventually, after the models were installed, it was discovered that blackboards were useful in supplementing instruction by means of models, and they were restored to the classrooms.

It is unnecessary to point the moral of this tale. The example is an extreme one, but the same type of action on a more subtle level is taken time and again where teachers in the schools are concerned. The story is told of a teacher's convention where the speaker had been belaboring the audience for their present methods of teaching reading. Finally one listener made bold to ask, "What then would you have us do?" "Well, I wouldn't use flashcards!" was the reply.

It is obvious that this is no way to change the curriculum. People learn when they face a problem and attempt to solve it, but a completely negative approach causes needless strain. The only way to be sure that all who are concerned with curriculum change are adequately prepared to undergo it, is to

[30] For further discussion of this matter see pp. 44 ff.

provide for their participation in planning the change. We may summarize the responsibility of leaders in this matter as follows: Have a conscious policy of change; make provision for changing any and every policy and bit of procedure as need dictates; help people to make changes without losing their sense of security.

Another feature of good strategy is to respect the growth rates of individuals and to respect individual differences. In other words the process of curriculum change cannot be hastened beyond the ability of the individuals to make the often delicate adjustments required.

Avoid Unsound Short-Cuts. It is a great temptation for administrators and supervisors to use all manner of short-cuts to arrive at goals seen and desired by the officer in question. Administrative *fiat* is sometimes used to institute sweeping curriculum changes. Sometimes principals, supervisors, and "key" teachers are "converted" on the assumption that the mine run of teachers will automatically follow suit. Malpractice in progressive education may be attributed to the fact that in so many cases teachers have been forced to accept changes for which they had little readiness or understanding.

Again, there may be reliance on the written word for producing changes in people. Bulletins, courses of study, directions pour from the central office. Evidence as to the relative ineffectiveness of this procedure was given in connection with the discussion of communication.[31]

The attempt to get uniformity and standardization is another favorite method of telescoping the process of curriculum change. We have already pointed out that this method is not really the short-cut that it seems.

An additional temptation is to encourage a low level of co-operation among the group involved for the reason that less finesse and patience are thereby required. The lowest level, that of compulsion, takes on all the varied forms of power tactics, from that of administrative *fiat* mentioned earlier to use of threats of lowered rating, demotion, or dismissal. Administra-

[31] See p. 123.

tors operating on this level should come to realize that pressure does not improve a delicate situation.

More frequently, perhaps, school officials set the standard of coöperation at the level of compromise. This, as was pointed out earlier, is the inevitable result of trying to arrive at curriculum decisions binding on an entire school system. The results really suit no situation within the system.

We offer Urwick's warning to social reformers regarding the danger of overestimation of the "masses" as an appropriate one for the status leaders in school systems: [32]

. . . many of those who are most busily urging reforms of our old institutions and ways of life *are* superior to the mass of their fellow-citizens—not in their moral worth, perhaps, but in the fact that they have reached a much higher level of thought and conscious purpose than is common in their society. And of this superiority they need to be reminded very frequently, lest they forget altogether the 'difficulties of adaptation,' which, presenting little difficulty to them, form insuperable obstacles in the way of quick reform of the masses who are in a different stage of mental development.

Urwick's warning is sound. It is all too easy to overestimate the readiness for change on the part of others when one has himself had experiences that make change seem imperative.

Apply the Principle of Rapidity. Yet, the need for fundamental curriculum change is so great that no strategy can be considered adequate which does not provide for shortening the process as much as possible. Here lies a great opportunity for social invention. Areas in which invention is needed have already been indicated—among them improving human motivations, discovering more functional forms of organization, and extending techniques of group action.

The method of demonstration used in such government projects as the Tennessee Valley development may well be more widely applied to education. In some matters, where technical decisions are required, it may be well quietly to make some change agreed on by the staff and then to submit the results for public approval or disapproval. New procedures in teaching

[32] Urwick, *op. cit.*, p. 115.

reading might be instituted in that way. In other matters, especially those more highly charged with emotion, such as sex education, it probably is best to forestall explosions by planning with parents how such education may best be provided for the young. In still other cases, it may be that the adults of the community believe certain curriculum changes to be long overdue—such as attention to the large percentage of students in high school who will not attend college. Strategy in such an instance might be to use the concern of the community to help the teachers and high-school principal to recognize the desirability of curriculum change.

In many matters of strategy the educational administrator or curriculum director may have to follow his own hunches. Coming into a new situation, he may be able to bring about certain changes with great rapidity by a tacit assumption that he is following a highly reasonable and not at all unusual course. For example, the new leader may begin at once to consult with teachers, asking them to help make certain decisions, without ever requiring the group to verbalize upon the qustion of whether or not it wishes to operate democratically. New ways of working may thus be instituted without fanfare.

SUMMARY

Much remains to be learned in the field of educational leadership and many problems can be solved only in the light of a given set of circumstances. Among them are several raised in the foregoing discussion: (1) most desirable ways of enlisting the initial interest of teachers, learners, and community adults in a process of curriculum change; (2) the amount of diversity which can be tolerated comfortably in a school or school system; (3) ways to help principals, supervisors, and other specialists in the school system to find creative rôles; (4) the amount of freedom desirable for all concerned with curriculum development at different stages of the process. It is to the solving of all such problems relating to curriculum change that the status leader in education must address himself in the years ahead. The patient and painstaking forging of an adequate process of curriculum change for each American school is a task that will require sound and imaginative leadership of groups that are constantly improving their values and their techniques.

All this is not to indicate any belief that fundamental curriculum change is child's play. It is merely to indicate the very substantial assets on which we can count. It is the purpose of this concluding chapter to single out for special emphasis certain suggestions to educational leaders and to summarize the points at which study and experimentation are required.

SUGGESTIONS TO EDUCATIONAL LEADERS

1. *Change*. Provide for change. Continuous attention to curriculum-planning should prevent crystallization of curriculum practice and obviate the necessity of periodic, violent revolutions that so often result in "school fights." Arrangements should be flexible in order that the school curriculum may be releasing rather than standardizing.

2. *Process*. Discover an adequate process for achieving curriculum change. Remember that a curriculum change has not actually occurred until it has been registered in the minds and hearts and habits of people. The process that produces curriculum change must contain its own guarantees of desirable security, growth in socialization, and satisfying and satisfactory accomplishment for the persons participating.

3. *Gradualism and Rapidity*. In all planning, respect the principles of gradualism and rapidity. Remember that human beings need time to make adjustments to new arrangements and new ideas before being expected to make further adjustments, but be mindful also of the need for the greatest possible speed in effecting essential and basic curriculum changes. Be both patient and impatient at the same time.

4. *Values*. Recognize the importance of values for giving direction to the process of curriculum change, but regard efforts to forge a common philosophy of education as a concomitant, not a prerequisite, of that process. Experiences that strain present values may be depended upon to lead to clarification, appraisal, and revision of values if the group has proper leadership.

5. *Dissatisfaction*. Capitalize upon both the minor complaints

of persons connected with the school and their vaguely felt, larger dissatisfaction with the results the school is obtaining to secure initial and continuing interest in the process of curriculum change. Regularize opportunities for giving suggestions regarding the curriculum and thus make more constructive the criticisms that the school is constantly encountering in any case. Regard constructive criticism as a sign of healthy interest in the schools. Regard petty, destructive criticism as evidence that people do not have, or do not realize that they have, proper opportunities for registering dissatisfaction.

6. *Goals.* Take account of the need for self-set goals of two sorts—those that give broad direction to individual and group efforts without limiting opportunity to be creative and individual, and those that mark out more immediate and definite steps toward the distant goal and at the same time are within the present capabilities of individuals and groups. Be mindful of the fact that goals should be flexibly held so that they can be reëxamined frequently and revised if need be.

7. *Organization.* Set up a simple and functional internal organization for curriculum development, giving adequate opportunities for participation to three groups—teachers and other professional personnel, learners, and community adults. Base the organization upon units where there is a large sense of common membership. Develop ways of working together that are tailor-made for the situation in which they are to be used by providing for periodic group evaluation of organizational forms and group planning of needed expansion and restructuring. The proper organization almost automatically carries much of the burden of coördination for which the educational leader is responsible.

8. *Group Solidarity and Heterogeneity.* Strive for a condition of diversity within unity. Promote feelings of common membership in groups of growing size and remoteness, first the individual school and its community or district, next the larger local school unit and community, then area, state, region, nation, and world. At the same time value, develop, and utilize unique contributions of individuals and minority groups. In-

tegrate all possible productive differences into a richer whole.

9. *Knowledge, Desires, and Beliefs.* Help participants in the process of curriculum change to operate increasingly on the basis of new knowledge, yet recognize the necessity of harmonizing desires and beliefs with that knowledge. For in-service education of professional personnel and for adult education this means that group study must move from an academic and over-verbalized plane to the level of that which is tangible and observable in a local setting.

10. *The Expert.* Bring to bear on each situation all available and needed expertness. Sometimes an expert imported into the community may be most effective. Sometimes local experts in the school system or in the community may be utilized with most success. Always it is wise to develop increasing expertness along a growing number of lines in the persons of those who are participating in the process of curriculum change. Always there is the problem of securing recognition and proper use of expertness where it exists—mutual respect must be developed in professional educators and community adults. There is the additional problem of overcoming the undesirable effects of specialization that is too narrow in its conception and basis.

11. *Communication.* Make constructive use of communication. Develop skill both in facilitating face-to-face communication and in utilizing modern inventions for bridging distance. Have a planned program of interpretation, combating bad propaganda with good. Make sure also that communication is a two-way process, a give and take among professional educators and community adults.

12. *Techniques.* Practice and extend techniques of group action. Develop and help others to develop greater skill in discussion, in effecting economies of time and effort through division of labor, and in use of records for guaranteeing continuity of attention to curriculum development. Invent, test, and share other techniques that promise to make group action ever more efficient.

13. *Power.* Build constructive social power in groups and individuals to counteract destructive power tactics commonly

employed by selfish or short-sighted individuals and interest groups in local communities. Plot the present location of power and discover potential sources of additional social power that may be put at the service of wider community interest. Plan strategy, organization, and communication on the basis of this study of the power equation.

14. *Authority*. Regard authority as something residing in a working group to be delegated to any and every person to whom it becomes desirable to assign responsibility. The educational leader who has so little faith in others that he reserves all authority unto himself is placing an undue amount of confidence in the wisdom of a single member of the group. He is placing ultimate reliance upon one solitary method of curriculum change—his personal authority. This is a clumsy tool, indeed, for bringing about genuine changes in persons.

15. *Status Leadership*. Develop expertness along those lines that appear to be requirements of status leaders—expertness in techniques of group action, in organization, in timing and strategy, in coördination. Increase expertness continually along the lines required in the particular position held whether it be school superintendent or principal, supervisor or curriculum director.

16. *Shared Leadership*. Generate as much leadership in others as possible. The need for leadership in school and community is too great to allow further hoarding of opportunities to exercise it. Leadership of certain amounts and kinds can and must be developed in every participant in the process of curriculum change along with the ability to follow the lead of others.

17. *Human Relations*. Become increasingly familiar with principles of human development, studying especially the persons participating in the process of curriculum change. Provide conditions as ideal as possible under which those persons may work together. See to it that each individual has status in the group. Provide for a free flow of ideas. Cut needless red tape. Take into consideration the physical comfort of all participants. Respect the need of all human beings for a rhythm of intensity of motivation and expenditure of energy.

GUIDE FOR LOCAL EXPERIMENTATION AND STUDY

Each of the foregoing suggestions contains its own challenge in that it indicates an area in which judgment and choice is required and therefore points to the need for experimentation and study in each local school community. A few of the questions with regard to curriculum change that may have to be answered in particular situations are:

1. Is a given constellation of habits in a school making for a desirable economy of effort and providing a useful basis of continuity or does it represent a crystallization that is deterring constructive action?

2. Is curriculum change proceeding rapidly enough to prevent further crystallization and to guarantee sufficient accomplishment yet not too rapidly to threaten the security of teachers, parents, and children?

3. How much difference in educational philosophy and teaching procedures can be tolerated from school to school and teacher to teacher? How can those differences be minimized most safely and effectively?

4. How can common goals and values be arrived at most quickly and genuinely?

5. Shall teachers, parents, and children be encouraged to express their current discontents, whether petty or not, or will this merely heighten an existing tendency to find fault with everything?

6. How will initial interest in curriculum change best be secured in a given school-community situation?

7. What internal organization is most satisfactory for a given situation?

8. Will the method of demonstration of the effectiveness of new ways by the school faculty to the community be most effective under given circumstances or is it better to secure community understanding and coöperation from the start in a particular instance?

9. When should an expert from the outside be brought into

the picture and how should his services be utilized on a given occasion?

10. Under what circumstances should bulletins and written announcements replace group meetings?

11. Under what circumstances may a certain individual be given opportunities to practice techniques, such as those of leading a discussion, at the possible expense of group accomplishment?

12. To what extent should educational leaders bow before the unquestioned power of groups and individuals in the community?

13. How shall the matter of authority be managed in a community where teachers, the board of education, and the school patrons apparently expect the administrators and supervisors to operate on an authoritarian basis?

14. How shall time be found for coöperative curriculum development without lengthening the teacher's working day unduly?

15. How can the status leader exert strong leadership without making others unhealthily dependent?

Since no process of curriculum change can be expected to operate automatically, educational leaders must plan always to give attention to improving the process in the interests of bettering the school program in vital ways. Curriculum change is not only one form of deliberate social change; it can be an important means of effecting wider social change. That is the contribution to social betterment which the curriculum director and other status leaders in education can make. Their efforts will be unsuccessful, however, unless they operate in the manner implied in two choice Chinese proverbs: [1]

> You cannot clap your hands with one palm.
>
> In everything let there be standing room.

[1] Quoted by Pearl Buck, *American Unity and Asia* (New York, The John Day Company, 1942), p. 83.

APPENDIX A

Excerpts from Professional Logs

1. A teaching principal writes:

I will never forget those first meetings of our new steering committee when hardly anyone would express herself or himself. But as our supervisors drew them out, they became more vocal and "let down their hair." They admitted that they realized they were not doing the things they really believed in, some because of pressure from above, some because they were afraid of their own ability.

In a very short time it was evident that there was experimentation going on. New ideas and sometimes really revolutionary statements were forthcoming where silence had reigned before.

I can hear one conscientious teacher saying quite discouragedly, "I know I ought to be doing differently but I can't seem to organize my plans even though I have planned with the children. Will you come in and help me?" This was just what the supervisor wanted, an expression of need for her help. The supervisor did help and this teacher grew quickly in modern thinking. I was interested in her case because she had gotten into a rut. This year she made application and was taken into one of the finest schools in this area. This teacher growth has been one of the outstanding outcomes of our committee work.

It was amazing when the "oldsters" who looked askance at our first meetings came out of their shells, started asking for equipment, tolerating a half-finished boat or a Mexican cart or an airplane lying overnight, or taking time out of arithmetic class to visit the half-finished house down the street so they could do their arithmetic there.

One of our seemingly most hopeless cases became the chairman of the arithmetic committee when it was formed this year. At first she declined but was finally persuaded. We have found out that her ability to take such responsibility is more than we ever dreamed of and I know she was surprised herself.

We tried an anonymous question box. The questions were organized in advance of a meeting and discussion was based upon them. Those teachers who felt their questions to be trite or stupid did not have to own them. This we found was one of the fears of teachers, that of feeling insecure when attempting a new method. Often the simplest question was the one most often asked and handling it as an integral part of the program gave it significance and often allayed fears as to the simplest procedures.

2. Four elementary principals write:

Says Principal A: This afternoon in teachers' meeting we discussed the desirability of having well-modulated voices in the classroom. I mentioned the fact that children's voices are somewhat inclined to be high pitched and shrill particularly in moments of excitement when they become enthusiastic over something. We discussed ways of using voices and that led to the point that I wished to develop, the teacher's voice.

There are two or three teachers in the school who talk very loudly and almost yell at the children in their desire to be enthusiastic. The result is that the children also speak loudly and yell right back at the teacher. One teacher admitted that she talked loudly when trying to develop some topic of importance. We were then free to discuss setting a good example in voices, tones, etc.

One teacher remarked that she found herself speaking loudly when she became irritated. Someone remarked that the parents do the same thing at home. Consequently, we find the children talking in loud tones when engaged in arguments, etc. We all agreed that a good example must be set by the parents and teachers if we expect desirable results from the children.

Teachers resolved to be more careful in order that they might set the correct pattern of speech for their class. It was decided that we would try to have some speech expert speak at one of our parent-teacher meetings in order that we may all become more speech conscious.

Says Principal B: The regular mothers' meetings for this semester started today. Tea was served after the mothers observed the class at work for the last hour of the day. This time everyone stayed in the room rather than go downstairs to the cafeteria. A cozy atmosphere was soon set and everyone became well known to each other in a few minutes.

I had planned to get the group into a discussion of something which would be beneficial to them and their children. It wasn't long before the usual questions about homework expected and general school procedures were asked. Then the interest settled on arithmetic. Many questions were asked and we went to the blackboard and showed just how we taught subtraction. Parents then showed how they learned and an understanding was soon reached on why parents shouldn't try to help very much.

One parent wanted to know if we used progressive education. That brought out another interesting discussion of the methods used in our school in all the subjects. Before the meeting was over the mothers were praising the library, the methods used, and the general feeling in the school.

These meetings usually break up within half an hour. This one lasted until five o'clock and they decided another one in two or three months would be a splendid idea. This was a fifth grade.

Had another mothers' meeting today, two days later. We used the same idea of general discussion if possible. It worked again and soon our two kindergarten teachers and I were in the middle of another good situation.

Reading readiness, experiences necessary for kindergarten children, how much to help in writing, reading, putting on clothes, etc. Maybe this is some part of the democracy we have been talking about. I hope so.

Says Principal C: Today we entertained at our school the seventh grade teachers from the Junior High School. I had invited these teachers to meet with us informally in order that we might discuss topics that would be helpful to all of us and particularly to the children.

We met in the library and had coffee and cake after which we had a wonderful discussion.

We asked the teachers from the Junior High School to tell us any particular subject matter weaknesses that they might have observed in the children whom we are sending to them. We also asked them to tell us if there were any things that they wished us to stress in our teaching that would help them.

We are all quite well acquainted and everyone spoke freely knowing that it was for our mutual advantage. I have never attended a more perfect meeting. The Junior High School teachers mentioned so many things in which they felt that our students were unusually prepared. This was very gratifying to the upper grade teachers who work with these students just before they leave the school.

It was suggested that we stress certain forms in arithmetic which are later required for regents examinations. Together we discussed things that we all expected in English, social studies, etc. When the Junior High School teachers were leaving, they asked if they might come again as they had enjoyed the visit so very much and they felt that so much had been gained. It gave us all a very happy feeling of working together with one purpose in mind.

Says Principal D (a New Principal Whose Teachers Had Just Surprised Her with a Birthday Party): We sat around the table for about an hour just chatting and discussing various events of the day. Everyone seemed to enjoy it greatly. Before leaving, I suggested that we should find out the birthday of everyone in order that we might always arrange to get together and wish each other well on these occasions.

3. A classroom teacher writes:

The entire staff has had a little problem in trying to get along with the program director because of not being "let alone." For example, the program director never gives the teachers a chance to use their own initiative and ideas. At a staff meeting, the director does most of the talking. When a teacher begins to say something, the words are taken out of her mouth. She often breaks into what the children are doing just because her idea of how it should be done is a little different. The teachers decided to let her have all the say at the meeting and not start a suggestion or anything. When asked if anyone has a suggestion or anything, each teacher answers "no" very politely. When she comes in to interfere with what the children are doing (which the children resent very much), the teachers just let her take charge. For one week nothing was attempted or started unless it was suggested by the director. During this little "tryout" the relationship of all seems to be very pleasant but it seems to be working. The director seems to feel what it's all about. For the last couple of days she has not done as much interfering, and even asked the staff to hold a meeting and discuss some things at a time when she was absent. Of course, she did not tell the staff that she was going to be absent. There is beginning to be a much better relationship among the whole group.

APPENDIX B

Basic Assumptions for Curriculum Planning in the Public Schools of Philadelphia

C. LESLIE CUSHMAN
Associate Superintendent

If curriculum planning in Philadelphia is to serve effectively in the improvement of teaching, it is necessary that the basic assumptions underlying this planning be widely understood and pretty generally accepted throughout the instructional personnel of our schools.

We Presuppose a Democratic Way of Working. The assumptions which are here stated and discussed have been formulated through extended conference with teachers, principals, supervisors, directors, and superintendents from among the personnel of the Philadelphia Public Schools. It is believed that they are assumptions which our schools are at this time ready to accept in principle and to adopt in practice. It is also important to note that these are assumptions which seem to be in accord with the democratic way of working together. That way is here viewed as one in which the total personnel works together cooperatively and intelligently in the formulation and realization of common ends. Further, the democratic way is here viewed as "by far the most difficult way of life, imposing the sternest obligations for self-control both on the citizens of a truly democratic state, and on those among them who accept the risks and privileges of leadership."

City-Wide Plans Are Set Up on This Foundation. The assumptions that follow are at the present time used as guides in all activities that have to do with city-wide curriculum planning.

They will continue to be so used until some revision seems appropriate. It follows, obviously, that our city-wide curriculum planning will be effective only to the extent that others—teachers, principals, department heads, supervisors, directors, and superintendents—work with these same assumptions in mind.

The assumptions to which reference has been made are as follows:

ASSUMPTION 1: Every teacher [1] should be looked upon as a person capable of developing considerable ability to behave intelligently with reference to the particular teaching situation of which he is a part.

ASSUMPTION 2: Intelligent behavior in a teaching situation means (1) that a teacher studies the interests and needs of the particular pupils of his class, or classes; (2) that he informs himself of the work of other teachers who have dealt with or will in the future deal with the pupils to whom he is assigned; (3) that he takes account of the neighborhood in which the school is located; (4) that he acquaints himself with the full range of instructional materials and specialized services that are available to him; (5) that he seeks continuously to clarify and enrich his objectives; and finally, (6) that he continuously organizes and carries through a program that takes proper account of these elements in the teaching situation.

(The terms "intelligent" and "intelligently" are used here with the particular meaning noted in this assumption. Perhaps "creative" would be a more accurate term. That has not been used because many persons identify the ability to "create" with the rare individual who is something of a genius.)

ASSUMPTION 3: Intelligent teaching is most readily achieved and maintained in a school that has developed the capacity to act unitedly, or as an organic unit.

ASSUMPTION 4. If individual schools are to develop the capacity to act as organic units, it is necessary that they be granted (and that they use wisely) a considerable degree of freedom.

ASSUMPTION 5: Courses of study, curriculum plans, teaching materials, and all activities designed to improve teaching should be developed in full harmony with the foregoing assumptions: that is, they should be such as to promote intelligent teaching (as conceived in Assumption 2) in schools possessing a considerable degree of freedom.

[1] What is said in this statement about teachers also applies to all other divisions of the instructional personnel.

(It is also true that the procedures of administration and supervision should accord with these assumptions. Specific discussion of such matters is not included here because this statement is directed particularly to the subject of curriculum planning.)

QUESTIONS OF INTERPRETATION

Various questions have been raised regarding each of these assumptions. In certain cases such questions indicated doubt or misgiving as to the validity of the statement. In other cases it was evident that clarification and further development were needed. The nature of the discussion that follows has been determined chiefly by these questions.

> ASSUMPTION 1: Every teacher should be looked upon as a person capable of developing considerable ability to behave intelligently with reference to the particular teaching situation of which he is a part.

How Many Teachers Behave "Intelligently"? The wording of the first assumption may well be considered with care. Some may say that reasonably intelligent behavior of the kind here referred to is not within the realm of possibility for ten or twenty per cent of teachers of usual capacity. Others might place the figure higher. In part, such variation might be due to differences in interpretation of what *is* intelligent behavior. But probably in greater part it would be due to differences in the extent to which we should be inclined to trust human capability. These differences are quite possibly produced by differences in the situations in which the individuals have lived and worked.

All Teachers Are not Equally Gifted. There are three things to be noted with reference to the wording of this assumption: First, it is not stated that *all* teachers are or can be made equally or identically intelligent. Secondly, it is not even stated that *all* teachers are capable of developing the ability to behave intelligently. Thirdly, it is not stated that all teachers do now exhibit intelligent teaching behavior, but rather that they should be viewed as "capable of developing considerable ability" to act thus.

But We Must Assume Much Competency. Before proceeding further into what the statement means for school practice, it will be useful to think for a moment about the implications that would follow from *denial* of the validity of this assumption. If a considerable fraction of teachers do not have this capacity for intelligent behavior, such a condition can only exist for one or both of two causes: (1) a faulty process of selection, which has brought to our schools an unusual number of stupid persons; (2) the impossibility of establishing such a favorable condition even with improved methods of selection. With reference to the first of these alternatives, it may be said that while the processes of selecting personnel in the Philadelphia schools can perhaps be improved, it is clear that over a period of years these processes have been much better than in almost any other large city.

Otherwise Democracy Is Hopeless. As to the latter supposition, we may answer that to deny that schools can with comparative ease be staffed with teachers capable of intelligently discharging their professional tasks would seem to be a denial of the postulate upon which democracy itself rests—that men can be educated to govern themselves through intelligent decisions coöperatively derived. The validity of the assumption cannot, however, be established by asserting that not to believe thus would lead to unpleasant results. Further, there is no way by which the assumption can in any complete sense be proved. Rather, it is a statement that one must accept or reject on faith grounded on previous experience and study.

Teachers Rise to What You Expect of Them. An impelling reason for faith in teachers' capacity to work intelligently is to be found in the differences in the average quality of teaching among the different schools of a city. In certain schools it will be found that many or all of the teachers do a superb job, while in other schools of the same city opposite conditions exist. The procedures of assigning personnel to various schools are rarely such as to account for these differences. Indeed, the only adequate way to account for them is by reference to the differences in working conditions within the two groups of schools. Administrative officials in many cities will tell how teachers fail in certain schools and later succeed splendidly in others. All of this tends to support the belief that over a period of time the average teaching level ascends or descends to about what it is assumed teachers are capable of doing. One who believes this naturally prefers to assume that the potential capacity for intelligent behavior is pretty high.

Of Course There Are Exceptions. It is of course true that in every large organization there are certain individuals who demonstrate in one way or another that they either cannot or will not conduct themselves intelligently and coöperatively. This is true even in the best of school systems. For situations involving such individuals it is obvious that protective measures must often be taken in the interest of the common welfare. Such measures, or the threat of such measures, should not, however, be viewed as a means of motivating the larger group. For the competent, intelligent teacher such measures are inappropriate as a means of positive motivation in a democratic society.

But You Must Take Note of a Majority. In short, the matter we must decide is, which attitude will get us further in the long run with the great majority of our professional associates: to permit those of average and less-than-average ability to make a few extra mistakes because we over-estimate their ability; or to develop by underestimating the ability of *everyone* a sense of frustration among those with originality and enthusiasm—those who are ready and able to move ahead? All that has just been stated grows out of a conviction that in a great school system we shall get much further by capitalizing on success than on failure.

ASSUMPTION 2: Intelligent behavior in a teaching situation means (1) that a teacher studies the interests and needs of the particular pupils of his class, or classes; (2) that he informs himself of the work of other teachers who have dealt with or will in the future deal with the pupils to whom he is assigned; (3) that he takes account of the neighborhood in which the school is located; (4) that he acquaints himself with the full range of instructional materials and specialized services that are available to him; (5) that he seeks continuously to clarify and enrich his objectives; and finally, (6) that he continuously organizes and carries through a program that takes proper account of these elements in the teaching situation.

Good Teachers Make a Study of Their Problem. This assumption is a definition or analysis of the elements that constitute intelligent teaching. Some may wish to add other items or to combine those given in some other way. All will recognize that these elements apply in different ways with different subjects of study, and perhaps in teaching pupils of different ages. In general, however, this analysis has seemed to meet with favor. Because the question of objectives often gives rise to differences in point of view regarding their determination and use, special attention may well be given to the topic of objectives in this assumption. It is stated that intelligent teaching requires that one seek "continuously to clarify and enrich his objectives."

All Must Share in Choosing Objectives. It is obviously implied that objectives are not to be chosen arbitrarily (although they may well be suggested) by some central group, and then handed out to be accepted and acted upon by teachers or school groups. Rather each teacher and each school is to share in the determination of objectives. To a limited degree this means that in practice the objectives of each teacher will always be somewhat different from those of other teachers. It may at first appear that this could lead only to hopeless confusion. Actually, however, that need not result.

Aims Grow Out of Individual Experience. The objectives of each teacher are the products of his experience—his reading, his association with others in the profession, his earlier education, his work with pupils, his contacts with the neighborhood of the school, his teaching ability, and the like. If the experience of the teachers in a school or in a school system have common characteristics, the differences in their objectives are not likely to be so great as to cause concern—indeed, those differences may be very beneficial. Where differences in objectives seem too great for the common good, such differences cannot in any real sense be removed by executive order or authoritative declaration. Good teachers are made of sterner stuff. If such differences are to be lessened, that can be done best by providing new and similar experiences for the persons concerned.

Teachers Need to Keep Up Their Growth. This statement regarding objectives also implies that every teacher's purposes are "continuously" to be clarified and enriched throughout his years of service. Such a concept gives needed dignity and zest to the passage of years in service. Indeed, it is only as a teacher "seeks continuously to clarify and enrich his objectives," that he can hope to maintain the enthusiasm required for intelligent teaching as that term is here used.

> ASSUMPTION 3: Intelligent teaching is most readily achieved and maintained in a school that has developed the capacity to act unitedly, or as an organic unit.

Schools Should Direct Their Own Lives. In the case of the third assumption there is need for common understanding of what is meant by "organic unit." The term is used here to indicate that the school should have the characteristics of a biological organism; that is, (1) It should be capable of sensing the relevant facts of its environment; (2) It should be able to formulate a promising plan (or plans) of action with reference to its existence and development in that environment; (3) It should have the power to act as a unit in trying out that plan; and finally, (4) It should be able to evaluate the effectiveness of that plan and to modify its activity in the light of that evaluation.

A School Should Be a Kind of Family Group. It may of course be argued that there should be this same sense of unity among the total personnel of the schools. In reality, however, the full unity that is here implied cannot be achieved to the same extent throughout an entire school system, particularly a system as large as ours. Within the individual school the goal should be a quality of living and working together comparable to that found in a good home. Working together should become "first nature." Only thus can the school provide for each of its pupils a full, well-rounded educational experience. Further, only thus can the individual school constantly move ahead to the new tasks it should accept and perform. Such a degree of unity within the individual school is no more a threat to coöperative action on the part of the total staff than is rich life within the home a threat to coöperative action on the part of the total community—indeed, in both cases coöperative action in the larger unit is dependent upon the lessons of coöperativeness being well learned in the smaller group.

Change Is Inevitable and Essential. What has been said obviously carries the implication that the program of each school should constantly be changing—changing in ways somewhat peculiar to itself. There are two reasons for this: The first, the reason most commonly given, is that the world about us is constantly changing, and that the school also must change its program or fall behind. A second reason for continual change, a reason that is much more important, is that change is essential to life. Any school in which the program isn't constantly undergoing change is dead. Such a statement as the foregoing invites the objection that change and progress are not the same. This is of course true, but it is also true (and this again is more important) that without change there is no chance of progress. Our responsibility is not to stand and shudder at the hazards of change. It is rather to welcome change, and if possible, direct it to ways that are better than the ways of the past or the present.

ASSUMPTION 4: If individual schools are to develop the capacity to act as organic units, it is necessary that they be granted (and that they use wisely) a considerable degree of freedom.

United Action Is a Matter of Slow Growth. The capacity to act as a unit is not a thing that can be decreed for the individual school, or arrived at by wishful thinking. It must be learned over a period of time through the process of planning together, carrying out unitedly what has been planned, and then together viewing the results. And once secured, it can be maintained only through the continuance of such a process of coöperative action. Planning together, trying out the plans that have been made, and then evaluating accomplishment can be done only in schools that have a considerable degree of freedom. There must be freedom to study the particular children, parents, and environment of the school. There must be freedom to canvass the particular educational resources available to the teachers. There must be freedom to take into account the particular strengths and also weaknesses of the school personnel. There must be freedom to act with considered attention to each of the foregoing.

It will be useful at this point to distinguish between a freedom which takes account of local conditions on the one hand, and what may be called "singularity" that goes off into byways known to itself only, on the other. It is fitting that some of the dangers that may come from the misuse of freedom be enumerated:

1. Singularity can be used to produce among schools that serve children of the same age group such variations in practice as to cause confusion and hostility among parents and pupils.
2. Singularity can create such differences between schools that serve the same pupils at different periods in their development as to make adjustment at each new school level unnecessarily difficult.
3. Singularity may be used as an excuse for inactivity in the face of pressing needs.

If we grant, however, as we must, that there are risks incident to freedom, it still remains true that unity within a school organization and intelligent teaching on the part of individuals can be achieved in no way other than through "a considerable degree of freedom." The question may then arise, how much freedom?

Some may think the matter can be resolved by granting freedom as rapidly as a readiness to use it is demonstrated. Such a policy is likely to prove unsatisfactory for two reasons:

1. It fails to take account of the fact that the individual or the group best learns to use freedom through being allowed a good deal of opportunity to make mistakes.

2. It ignores the fact that before this capacity to use freedom wisely has been demonstrated, the person or persons in authority may have become so accustomed to the exercise of their authority as to be reluctant to accept any other procedure.

We Can't Say Just "How Much Freedom." The summation of the matter is that there is no simple way of resolving the question of "how much freedom." Certainly it can't be settled with mathematical exactness. Instead, the question must always be determined through judgment based on careful study, and often on extended discussion. It is of the essence, however, that those parties concerned, those who should share in judgment, should be clear as to what is at stake in any issue. It is not enough to think only of the matter of immediate concern. Always, that matter must be considered along with the question of what effect the judgment will have upon the individual's or the school's sense of responsibility.

With Real Unity, "Authority" Grows Less Important. Experience seems to show that in any organization where there is a real desire to work together coöperatively, the question of "how much freedom" looms less and less important with the passage of time. The number of situations in which there are sharp differences between those in positions of major authority and others with less authority will be found fewer than are often feared. And most, if not all such differences, are likely to be found resolvable with continued, vigorous study in an atmosphere of good will.

> ASSUMPTION 5: Courses of study, curriculum plans, teaching materials, and all activities designed to improve teaching should be developed in full harmony with the foregoing assumptions; that is, they should be such as to promote intelligent teaching (as conceived in Assumption 2) in schools possessing a considerable degree of freedom.

City-Wide Plans Prevent Inbred Thinking. There may of course be those who feel that the best way to promote initiative on the part of individual schools and intelligent teaching behavior on the part of teachers would be to curtail greatly city-wide planning of the curriculum, and to give pretty complete autonomy to individual schools and teachers. Such a step would doubtless stimulate some teachers and some schools to strike out boldly in ways that would attract much attention. It is likely, however, that a much longer number would be driven back to a cautious program, the aims of which would be above all else to avoid trouble. Not many individual teachers or schools are willing or eager to move ahead boldly without knowing that others, too, are going in the same direction.

We Need to Share Thoughts with Others. Through city-wide curriculum planning we should be able to share our ideas and our experiences with regard both to our purposes and practical means for their attainment. Through this we should be able to achieve a much higher type of responsible freedom than could be had through "going it alone." Indeed, we live in a time when freedom achieved in anything other than a co-operative setting is likely to have little meaning. City-wide curriculum planning should not, however, lessen the amount or importance of curriculum planning at other points in the school system—within the district, the individual school, the subject-matter department, or by the individual teacher. City-wide planning should at all times be carried on so as to increase and to give added meaning to planning all along the line.

"Courses of Study" Should Inspire, and not Prescribe. If one accepts what has been said up to this point, he will pretty surely agree that city-wide curriculum planning should be carried on in such ways as "to promote intelligent teaching in schools possessing a considerable degree of freedom." To accept the assumption as valid is, however, one thing, and to adhere consistently to it is quite another. Schools everywhere have much to learn about what courses of study should look like if they are to encourage rather than to hinder initiative on the part of teachers and schools. Courses of study and other curriculum materials have in most cases been directed to the question of *what* to teach: they have called attention primarily to subject matter. Aside from a few noble sentiments by way of introduction, they have usually provided little help to the teacher's or the school's subsequent analysis of all factors needing to be

considered for intelligent teaching. Whether we can do better remains to be determined. The challenge to invent new procedures and new types of materials that will encourage initiative all along the line is one of the factors that makes our work so inviting.

We Have a Huge Task Ahead of Us. A final word—

What has been said in the preceding pages grows out of a hope and a faith that working thus, we may achieve throughout the public schools of Philadelphia the task that is ours to do. That task fully performed is tremendous. Indeed, there are those who believe that the schools here and elsewhere throughout America are incapable of rising to the challenge of our day. Some say the schools are not ready. In a pessimistic mood, they say, "If we could have had another twenty-five or fifty years in which to get a fuller understanding of the nature of the child and to effect a better working relationship with the community, it might have been done."

Let's Unite to Do Our Best. As in all times, however, the tasks that are ours to do are determined by a course of human events in which our wishes and our readiness to act play a minor part. The only choice we can make is either to despair and rest a little on our oars, or to look fully at what is required of us, and to act with all the insight and vigor at our command. If we choose the latter alternative, it seems not unreasonable to believe that together we can succeed in building and maintaining here a school program worthy of the best traditions of this great city, adequate to the great needs of the youth of this generation, and full of rich adventure for each of us.

APPENDIX C

Curriculum Development in Maine as Based upon the Individual Classrooms

WILLIAM H. BURTON

Graduate School of Education, Harvard University
Curriculum Consultant, Maine State Department of Education

A first glance at the state program of curriculum improvement in Maine, now in its second year, might occasion in the casual observer, some surprise. A curriculum is under construction, but with its scope and sequence as yet undefined! A formal statement of aim and philosophy has not been prepared, a survey of state needs has not been made, but activity directed by goals is under way. The usual machinery of curriculum councils and committees is missing, but operations are proceeding.

The Maine program has begun its operations in the classrooms of individual teachers. The primary attack has been upon improving the work of the classroom teachers in doing whatever they are now doing. Out of the activities involved in improving instruction at the level where it is, will come questions, arguments, further study. This in turn will, and is leading to, the formulation by teachers and their superintendents of their own aims, philosophy, scope and sequence. Questions concerning surveys of local needs and for coördination of local needs and for coördination of local efforts have already arisen. Machinery for coördination will be set up as need arises, designed to fit the situation out of which the need and the machinery develop. Any printed or mimeographed course of study that is produced will emerge, it is hoped, out of the curriculum as it develops in the classroom. Conviction that curriculums and courses of study are dynamic and under constant development is emerging and will, it is hoped, dominate the continuing program.

Activity is confined to the elementary schools at present, but a program for the secondary schools, and for the articulation of the whole program will doubtless follow.

Guidance and assistance for the teacher in the improvement of instruction, that is, in the development of his own curriculum, is given by the state department staff, the University of Maine, the four normal schools, and by one outside consultant. The flow within the program is reciprocal but predominantly from the classroom upward.

Leadership of the program now under way is located as far as possible in the local communities. A very loose general plan had to be developed at the very first in order to get the program into motion, but this too was based directly upon questions, comments, and criticisms from the field. The plan for initiating activity gave way as functional plans began to emerge out of the activity.

SALIENT CHARACTERISTICS OF THE MAINE CURRICULUM PROGRAM

1. The primary attack has been based upon improving the work of classroom teachers in doing whatever they are now doing.

The initial stages of the program are based upon questions raised by teachers and superintendents. Questions vary from very specific, often minute queries about daily program and drill devices to broad questions of basic methods, of maturation levels, integration, and the like. Distinct growth has been indicated in the type of question being asked, particularly after a summer workshop held in 1944.

2. Leadership is vested in teachers and their own local district superintendents. Assistance from the state department, the state university and normal schools, and from the consultant is given on a service basis in answer to direct questions.

3. A common understanding of aim and philosophy, of viewpoint, recognition of the necessity for a survey of needs will emerge out of activities involved in improving instruction.

Formal statements and organized surveys will be made by local groups but not until readiness has developed.

4. The scope and sequence will take shape out of the program of activities necessary to the continuous improvement of instruction.

The aim, philosophy, scope and sequence will not be stated in advance and the curriculum squeezed into pre-determined forms; these items will be developed as needed to fit given situations, and by the personnel using them.

5. The machinery or scheme of councils, committees, and channels will be developed as demanded by ongoing activities.
6. The written course of study will grow out of the curriculum.

THE INITIATION OF THE PROGRAM

An initial conference to test opinion and to set the stage for a democratic program. The Commissioner of Education, Mr. H. V. Gilson, after informal conversations with many interested school people and laymen called an informal conference for May 12–13, 1943. State department members, representatives from the normal schools, the university, and twelve superintendents engaged in eleven hours of wholly frank, spirited discussion. Representative teachers were originally invited but were unable to attend on short notice. However, the teaching body has been in the forefront of the program ever since.

Agreement was reached that three areas should be integrated in the state program: (a) the course of study; (b) pre-service selection and training of teachers; (c) in-service improvement of teachers through state and local leadership. The teacher training institutions are thus an integral part of the program. The local superintendents are recognized as key leaders. We are for the moment chiefly concerned with the course of study for which three procedures were considered: (*a*) supplement the present course with a continuing series of bulletins, first on acute current problems and eventually covering all areas; (*b*) rewrite the course through committees into a series of sizable bulletins, one to a subject or other division; (*c*) embark upon a somewhat extensive program for the construction of a new and modern course. The third alternative with a five-year initial program was adopted.

Two erroneous tacit assumptions were permitted to go unchallenged at this time: (*a*) the state department and the consultant would outline an organization, select the personnel, and in general direct the program; (*b*) course of study writing is equivalent to curriculum improvement. Corrections for these views came quite naturally out of the program as it developed.

Superintendents and teachers were asked for their views. The status of affairs was presented to the annual convention of superintendents and to the annual meeting of the teachers associations. Discussion was arranged out of which three suggestions arose: (*a*) that local study groups be formed; (b) that regional conferences be held to supplement the local groups; (*c*) that a curriculum workshop be held in the summer.

The normal schools offered their contribution. Conferences were held at the four normals to secure the views and suggestions of the staff members. The normals participated in the workshop also.

DEVELOPMENT OF THE PROGRAM TO DATE

Local Study Groups and Regional Conferences. A very few local study groups led by alert superintendents existed prior to the state program. The 1944 summer workshop greatly increased local interest in study and try-out led by returning teachers. Local study groups so far are uncoördinated but requests are arising for state wide study of given problems. Requests for bulletins, bibliographies, for definite sources, and for specific guidance in carrying on group discussion are steadily increasing.

Two excellent regional conferences were held before prohibitory regulations became effective. Nine districts, approximately 450 teachers, and 25 lay participants were served. Meetings were based on specific questions submitted by teachers through their superintendents. Meetings will be reinstituted in the near future.

The 1944 summer workshop. Interest was such that enrollments had to be apportioned to districts. A total of 172 participants appeared, including 27 superintendents, two normal school principals, and other staff members. Accomplishments in a three-week "blitz" session were remarkable. *First,* a series of bulletins was suggested by the students. *Second,* approximately fifteen students on their own initiative produced materials for basing teaching upon a survey of local community needs, industries, resources, etc. *Third,* questions leading toward the more remote aspects of the program, well beyond local improvement, began to appear. *Fourth,* the necessity of public participation was recognized and discussed. *Fifth,* the superintendents asked that an unrehearsed teachers meeting be held to demonstrate the coöperative initial planning of a local program. One unlooked for result from the demonstration was an expression from participating teachers that they had gained an understanding not previously possessed concerning the problems of the superintendent.

The first bulletins appear. Bulletins so far issued include:

1. A Summary of Suggestions for Initiating the New Program Locally. (Prepared by workshop group, 1944.)
2. Selected Illustrative Teaching Units. (Prepared by individual members and selected by a committee from the state department.)
3. The Teaching of Art in the Modern Way. (Prepared by a committee of teachers led by a normal school staff member.)

The 1945 summer workshop. Efforts by last summer's students to try out their improved teaching plans resulted in vigorous demands from all over the state for more background supporting the newer methods. (This had been anticipated by the leaders.)

A six-week workshop was held at one of the normal schools

based upon studying children in action in the campus school. Excellent materials were produced and an inclusive bibliography developed. These materials were carried over into the larger workshop which followed.

The 1945 workshop with enrollment up to 192 met the demand for more background by including organized study of the characteristics of learners at different levels of maturity. The program is thus orienting itself toward organization on the basis of the learner and his society and not upon the basis of logical subject matter.

Demands arising during the year resulted in the formation of teacher committees within the workshop to start work on state bulletins:

The Improvement of the Junior-Primary Program
Aiding Teachers to Make the Transition from Traditional to Modern Methods
Aid for Teachers in One Room Rural Schools.

Excellent beginnings were made. Participation will be widened during the year as these materials are worked over by many teachers in the field before being finally edited and published.

Other bulletins proposed. In addition to the three mentioned, three other problems susceptible to bulletin treatment were mentioned but committees did not arise. These will be worked upon by the state department and selected public school personnel during the year.

1. Public Relations for District Superintendents
2. A Guide to Curriculum Development in Maine Districts
3. Principles and Techniques in Handling Group Conferences and Discussions

Four of the six proposals are definitely planned for publication during 1945–46.

Replanning. Replanning conferences concluded that the superintendents as local leaders, and now freed from some war time pressures, should be given aid quickly. Two conferences subsidized by the state were held with 30 superintendents in each. These with the 37 reached in the summer workshop include over two-thirds of the district leaders. Superintendents in these conferences studied the items previously requested from the field and upon which workshop comment had been focused.

1. The Characteristics of Children at Different Levels of Maturity
2. Making the Transition from Older to Newer Methods
3. A Public Relations Program for Superintendents
4. The Development and Management of Local Study Groups
5. The Techniques for Handling Group Discussions

Developments now emerging. The state university has volunteered, first to initiate, through the extension department, study of local communities, methods of survey, etc. Second, both the university and the normal schools in coöperation have offered to aid local study groups with guidance and credit through extension courses. The development of curriculum materials from local resources will be stressed.

Regional conferences will be reinstituted in answer to requests.

Personnel added because of program. The position of Deputy State Commissioner in charge of Curriculum and Instruction was created and filled by Mr. Harland A. Ladd, former superintendent in Bath, Maine. A director of Elementary Education was added to Mr. Ladd's staff and filled by Miss Zeta I. Brown, a former state supervisor called back from another state. The vacancies on the staff of state supervisors have been filled bringing the number to four. The writer has served as consultant since the beginning.

Some Suggestions for Participating in Coöperative Thinking Through Group Discussion

Prepared for the
Michigan Study of Secondary School Curriculum

by

J. CECIL PARKER [1]

1. Each person should do his own thinking. Don't try "to save time" by telling the group the right answer. The leader is not a group instructor, but a social engineer, trying to arrange conditions so that each will do creative thinking.
2. Group discussion is not a debating society. We do not argue for the fun of it. The issues are of great importance; wise men disagree in their views; our task is to find more truth than we bring to any group meeting. We are in a coöperative quest. Our thinking is creative rather than combative.
3. Ask yourself which ideas, experiences, and differences are basic, fundamental, and most worth discussing.
4. When discussion wanders, restate the question and get a new start. Sometimes, if the side-line is especially important, put it up to the group, "Shall we follow this interesting issue that has come up, or shall we return to the plan of discussion originally adopted?"
5. Make short statements; not speeches.
6. Do not pass any important matter that is not clear to you. Sometimes individuals hear unfamiliar terms and assume that everyone else must understand; hence they fear it would be humiliating to ask for explanations or illustrations. This is

[1] Adapted from Goodwin Watson, William H. Kilpatrick, H. S. Elliott, S. A. Courtis, and others.

untrue. Have you not often been glad when someone else asked for clarification on a point on which you had been none too clear? Others may profit too, but you are in the group to learn, and you must not hesitate to ask.

7. If you find yourself talking more than other members of the group, train yourself to pass over minor points and to speak on only a few carefully chosen issues.

8. Use special care to be fair to positions represented by a minority or not represented at all in the group. If you are aware of a position not being adequately represented, present it as its adherents would like to hear it stated, then explain your disagreement.

9. Challenge contributions you cannot fully accept. Do not keep your disagreements quiet in the mistaken notion that it is better manners to pretend to agree when you do not. Make inquiry concerning the assumptions involved in the contribution.

10. The "either-or" attitude is on the whole not fruitful. Search rather for new means which enable both sets of values to be pursued without clash. Our concern in coöperative thinking is not simply to choose between two ways we now know, but if possible to find a way of integrating the values of both, thereby creating an improved solution. However, avoid smoothing over differences. Differences should be probed with questions to make them clear and sharp.

11. When there is some confusion over a diversity of opinions expressed, a minute of silence can do much to help members rise to a clearer perspective of what has been said. In suggesting this pause the chairman should restate the precise issue under discussion. After the pause the members may be more able to coöperate in detecting the root of the disagreements. This may be in the partial nature of the experience and evidence used, or in a difference in the sense of values. Try to keep in mind some ends everyone wants.

12. Be on the lookout for different uses of the same word. Call

for illustrations whenever this difference becomes confusing. Do not wrangle over a verbal definition.

13. Trust the group. There is no person in it who is not superior to the rest in at least one respect. The experience of all is richer than the experience of any. The group as a whole can see further and more truly than its best member. Remember that every member of the group is an individual just as you are.

14. For every discussion there is available a limited amount of time. Each individual should help make it possible to utilize the time more effectively. To attempt too much in too short a time fosters a habit of slipshod and superficial thinking.

15. Summarize (1) whenever a major point is finished before going on to the next; (2) whenever the discussion has been fairly long drawn out or confused; (3) shortly before the close of the period. Try to use the words of members of the group, rather than your translation.

A Supervisor Takes Special Responsibility in the Induction of New Teachers

HAZEL A. KIER

Intermediate Supervisor Kansas City, Kansas

[*Note:* As a supervisor who is concerned with the development of good mental health and the promotion of better human relationships among the people with whom she works, Miss Kier is particularly concerned that the new teacher be given the right induction into the school system. Her concern about the new teacher was intensified during the war years because so many desirable, well-trained young people left the profession. Along with many other educators, she began to ask, "Wherein have we failed to meet the needs, interests and abilities of these young people? How can we help new teachers each year so that they can make proper adjustments and become satisfied, worthwhile and effective educators?" The following account describes some of the ways in which Miss Kier has attempted to facilitate the induction of new teachers into the Kansas City, Kansas, school system.]

Because of the tremendous shortage of teachers countrywide, our city system, with a population of 130,000, has found it impossible to employ the necessary number of well-trained teachers. Those who have been hired, though willing, lack recent training, experience in city systems of any size, and are often faced with home problems of adjustment as well as those which confront them in making necessary adjustment to a new school system. Of the thirty or forty new teachers hired, the majority are married women who are living in the city only as long as the husband is in the service or until his work is completed at a war industry. Many of them are from other sections of the country. The unmarried teachers are from small city or town systems.

Though the work of the supervisor is with all new teachers, her deepest concern lies with those members of both old and new groups, many of whom have potentialities of good leadership, who are interested in becoming permanent teachers. How can she best help them? How can she help keep them in the profession? She must assume the responsibility of giving guidance or seeing to it that others in the system help these new teachers make satisfactory adjustments to the new situations. The classroom teacher has the most significant responsibility of determining the mental health of children. They will succeed to the extent that they themselves enjoy good mental health, that their needs, interests and abilities are taken into account.

The following gives a brief picture of the areas in which the supervisor has assumed responsibility for guidance.

  1. *We have let the new teacher know that members of the administrative staff are just as interested in a successful adjustment to his new home and social life as they are to his new school life.*

The supervisor attempts to know as much about the new teacher as possible before meeting him. She studies his records to discover interests, club and church affiliations, and educational experiences. The first interview is a time of getting acquainted, letting the teacher tell about his preparation and experiences, answering his questions, but for the most part endeavoring to establish a satisfactory rapport that will enable the supervisor to be of maximum assistance in helping this new member of the faculty. The conversation turns to the problems of finding a residence, of making new friends, of things to do, and the teacher is assured that he will have help in solving these problems.

An administrative conference is held soon after the first interviews to discuss the teacher's placement in the school that seems best suited for him.

Following his placement in as conducive a school environment as possible, the supervisor then has a conference with the new teacher not only to talk about the choice and freedom he may have in the use of materials of instruction and course of study, something about the school environment and faculty of the school to which he has been assigned, but also to help him meet his problems of getting settled in a new community. He or she may need assistance in finding a room or apartment; he or she may desire a roommate. The supervisor or the principal of his new building will go through the files with him. Often they know the temperament of a particular landlady or a fellow teacher or the type of neighborhood that would seem best for a new teacher. The teacher might welcome the suggestion of a desirable cleaner, grocer, and other trades people until he has time to investigate and make his own choices.

Arrangements should be made for him to meet one or more teachers in his building and some parents, if at all possible, before the first faculty meeting. One of these teachers should be responsible for introducing the new teacher to other members of the faculty and to see that he meets teachers from other schools at the general meetings.

Within the month the new teacher should be helped to become acquainted with the civic and cultural opportunities of the city. Many new teachers must be shown that social sensitivity and enrichment of personality are dependent partly on activities outside the school. He should be told about the symphony orchestra, lecture series, plays, clubs, Red Cross and canteen services, university cultural classes and church activities in order that he may have opportunity to choose those activities that would be most worthwhile to him. A small town teacher may be hesitant about striking out alone. An interested supervisor can see that he is given the opportunity to meet teachers and lay people with like interests.

A meeting with just the new teachers to talk over and discuss problems peculiar to a new person adjusting to a new situation has been found to be most appreciated.

Above all, one must have a friendly warm feeling for these new members, have faith in their desire to do a good job, and have patience until they find themselves in the new situation.

2. *We have let the new teacher know the measures that are in force to give him a sense of well being and a feeling of security.*

It is the responsibility of every school system to provide professional services that are conducive to good mental health. The Kansas City, Kansas, system has some very worthwhile features that are factors in promoting the mental health of teachers and it rests with someone in the system to give new teachers an overall picture rather than have them get the information through hit or miss channels.

The supervisor finds opportunity to explain the following features which are so very important in building a feeling of professional security:

1. Teacher tenure after three probationary years—the privileges and responsibilities
2. Hospitalization plan
3. Pension system
4. Accident and health insurance plan
5. Accumulative sick leave
6. Group insurance
7. Credit Union
8. Twelve-month salary plan
9. Recent adjustments in salary schedule (to decrease differences in salary)
10. Membership opportunities in local, state and national organizations
11. Standards for professional growth which include professional credit for private lessons, extended trips, and experiences outside school such as war service activities.

There are teacher-initiated organizations that help promote friendly and coöperative human relationships that the new teacher will want to know about—Grade Teachers Club, Teachers Chorus, and All-City Council.

The new teacher will feel more secure if he knows something

about the in-service teacher training program. When a view of the program is given as a whole and the purpose of each type of activity is explained, the program itself does not seem so over-whelming. The following program is carefully explained.

1. Conferences, group and individual
2. Convocation
3. Lecture Series
4. Supervisory Meetings
   (Scheduled throughout the year to avoid conflicts)
   a. Art
   b. Music
   c. Organized physical education
   d. Curriculum
      (1). Sharing materials, techniques, methods
      (2). Discussing common problems
      (3). Learning to use new materials
      (4). Developing materials of instruction
   e. Library
5. Committee Work
   Voluntary—Planned to meet individual needs of teachers in the subject fields.

3. *We have helped the new teacher know his school and com-munity environment and the many opportunities and re-sources they offer for training in effective citizenship.*

It is important that the new teacher gain an early knowledge of the school and city community. This knowledge will give him a background for better understanding those with whom he works. It will be the source of much of the material needed for meeting the needs, interests and abilities of his pupils, and, finally, this knowledge will be useful in his own personal development and enjoyment.

All visits from the supervisor during the first weeks of school are before or after school or by appointment only and are pri-marily for the purpose of helping the teachers gain this knowl-edge of the school and community.

Record keeping is a difficult problem for some new teachers. A thirty-minute explanation often makes the seemingly compli-cated procedure quite simple.

Helpful methods, techniques and procedures are often developed during a church school period when children are at church and the teacher is free to assimilate new ideas.

If an attitude of coöperative planning is developed at each meeting, the new teacher gains in self respect and in knowledge of how to solve his problems.

4. *We have helped the new teacher gradually develop a democratic living situation in his classroom.*

The problem is not so much a matter of modern training as it is a matter of the teacher's own innate development and resourcefulness. If he is thoroughly interested in the welfare of children and concerned that they not lose out in valuable experiences of learning and living together, he will soon adapt himself to the constructive aspects of the individual school program. We have found that if the new teacher is helped to have a constructive, loyal, proud feeling toward his profession and to have a keen appreciation of his shared responsibility in educating the modern youth, he is eager to work coöperatively with pupils, parents and co-workers to meet their needs. The process is slow and much depends on the leadership given.

In summary, the most important help the supervisor can give new teachers is to show them through practice that she is always available for help, that everyone wants them to succeed and stands ready to help them, that they are respected for being persons who hope to achieve the ultimate goals of education and that the supervisor's task is to help each one to that faith in himself and in his profession that will promote the greatest achievement.

A Project in Developing Accumulative Records for Teachers

MARGARET L. GORDON, PRINCIPAL

J. J. Smallwood School, Norfolk, Virginia

I am a new supervising principal without clerical assistance. I suggested the development of the accumulative records in order to become better acquainted with the teachers and in order to keep an objective record of their professional growth and development.

We have an accumulative record folder for each teacher. Each folder contains the questionnaire reproduced below. The items on this questionnaire were decided upon by the teachers of Smallwood School in their professional meetings in the fall. The criterion for selection was simply: "Will the answer to such a question indicate my professional growth or describe me as a person?" Items A–G are filled out by the teacher alone. The remaining items (except "Remarks and Suggestions") are filled out in conference with the principal. Since my time for actual classroom supervision and conferences with teachers is limited, the teachers are free to get their own folders at any time and to jot down on separate paper things to which they wish to call my attention; or to enclose bits of their work, such as case studies of pupils, plans for units of work, class newspapers or bulletins, special notes from parents, etc. I ofttimes write in matters (personal) to which I wish to refer.

As these data accumulate, or fail to accumulate, in a teacher's folder, they tend to indicate how a teacher might need special help or how she might be of special help to others. I hold a conference with each teacher whenever I can find the time, trying to reach each one at least once a month, although some need more conferences than others. We discuss the merits of the things the teacher has contributed to his record. Often I may suggest things he has failed to include or refer to—especially teaching techniques which I have observed as indicative of professional growth.

The teachers seem to enjoy this type of supervision and record-keeping. I expect that they will have many suggestions for improving it as time goes on.

J. J. SMALLWOOD SCHOOL

TEACHERS COOPERATIVE RECORD SHEET

1944–1945

Name _____ Birth day and month _____

Address _____ Telephone _____

A. *Educational Background*

    1. Graduate of: Year   Degree, if any

    High School _____ ____ _____

    Normal School _____ ____ _____

    College _____ ____ _____

    Graduate School _____ ____ _____

    2. Extension Classes Completed:

    Institution   Name of Course   Year

    3. Summer Schools Attended:

    4. Teaching Experience:

    In Norfolk _____ approx. yrs. In Norfolk schools other than J. J. Smallwood (Name of schools) _____

    Have you taught the following? (yes-no) Summer school _____ Night _____ Homebound pupils _____

    Teaching experience outside of Norfolk. (Name place and approx. yrs.)

5. Extensive Travel (Name places visited)

B. *Positions Held in School System* (Give dates)

C. *Community Affiliations* (Church membership, clubs, volunteer organizations, etc. Name the institution and the offices you have held, if any.)

D. *Educational Affiliations* (Local, state, or national)

E. *Positions Held in J. J. Smallwood School* (Current year)
    Volunteered   Elected   Assigned

F. *Participation in P.T.A. Meetings*

G. *Extra-Curricular Associations with Pupils*

H. *Types of Records Kept*   *Condition of Records Kept*
                                    (For temporary use only,
                                    of cumulative value, easily
                                    interpreted, or complex)

I. *Types of Disciplinary Procedures*
    (Brief description of case)   (Disciplinary measure taken)

J. *Outstanding Visits to Homes of Pupils*
    (Name of pupil)   (Result of visit)

K. *Exceptional Relations with Parents, Teachers, Nurse, Visitors, Janitor, Lunchroom Workers, or Administrators*
    (Incident)   (Adjustment or Reactions)

L. *Outstanding Coöperative Educational Activities of Your Pupils*

M. *Professional Books Borrowed from School Library*

N. *Remarks and Suggestions* (The back of this page may be used if needed)

O. *Teaching Techniques Developed* (Brief description)

P. *Educational Contributions* (Written and oral reports, articles, teaching devices, etc.)

SELECTED BIBLIOGRAPHY

Curriculum Development

CASWELL, H. L., "The Function of the Curriculum Director," *Curriculum Journal*, Vol. IX, Oct., 1938, pp. 245–249.

COOK, Lloyd Allen, *Community Backgrounds of Education* (New York, McGraw-Hill Book Company, Inc., 1938).

Department of Supervisors and Directors of Instruction, *Leadership at Work*, Fifteenth Yearbook (Washington, D.C., National Education Association, 1943).

HARAP, Henry, Ed., *The Changing Curriculum* (New York, D. Appleton–Century Company, Inc., 1937).

John Dewey Society, *Democracy and the Curriculum*, Third Yearbook (New York, D. Appleton–Century Company, Inc., 1939).

KOOPMAN, G. Robert, MIEL, Alice, and MISNER, Paul J., *Democracy in School Administration* (New York, D. Appleton–Century Company, Inc., 1943).

MIEL, Alice, "Barriers to Improved Instruction," *Teachers College Record*, Vol. XLVI, Apr., 1945, pp. 434–440.

MORT, Paul R., and CORNELL, Francis G., *American Schools in Transition* (New York, Bureau of Publications, Teachers College, Columbia University, 1941).

MYERS, Alonzo F., KIFER, Louise M., MERRY, Ruth C., and FOLEY, Frances, *Cooperative Supervision in the Public Schools* (New York, Prentice-Hall, Inc., 1938).

National Society for the Study of Education, *Curriculum-Making: Past and Present*, Twenty-Sixth Yearbook (Bloomington, Ill., Public School Publishing Company, 1926), Part I, Chs. 1–5.

PRALL, Charles E., and CUSHMAN, C. Leslie, *Teacher Education in Service* (Washington, D.C., American Council on Education, 1944).

STRONG, Carl L. and Staff, "A School System Goes Democratic," *The Clearing House*, Vol. XVIII, Sept., 1943, pp. 14–18

Group Processes

Department of Supervision and Curriculum Development, *Group Planning in Education*, 1945 Yearbook (Washington, D.C., National Education Association, 1945).

Department of Supervisors and Directors of Instruction, *Cooperation: Principles and Practices,* Eleventh Yearbook (Washington, D.C., National Education Association, 1938).

DE HUSZAR, G. B., *Practical Applications of Democracy* (New York, Harper & Brothers, 1945).

LEWIN, Kurt, "The Dynamics of Group Action," *Educational Leadership,* Vol. I, Jan., 1944, pp. 195-200.

PIGORS, Paul J. W., *Leadership or Domination* (Boston, Houghton Mifflin Company, 1935).

TABA, Hilda, *Dynamics of Education* (New York, Harcourt, Brace and Company, 1932).

TEAD, Ordway, *The Art of Leadership* (New York, McGraw-Hill Book Company, 1935).

WATSON, Goodwin, Ed., *Civilian Morale* (New York, Reynal & Hitchcock, 1942).

Social Theory

DEWEY, John, *Human Nature and Conduct* (New York, Henry Holt and Company, Inc., 1922).

———, *The Public and Its Problems* (New York, Henry Holt and Company, Inc., 1927).

———, "Theory of Valuation," *International Encyclopedia of Unified Science* (Chicago, University of Chicago Press, 1939), Vol. II, No. 4.

FOLLETT, Mary P., *Creative Experience* (New York, Longmans, Green & Company, 1924).

LIPPMANN, Walter, *Public Opinion* (New York, Harcourt, Brace & Company, 1922).

MACIVER, Robert M., *Society* (New York, Farrar & Rinehart, Inc., 1937).

OGBURN, William F., *Social Change* (New York, The Viking Press, 1928).

TODD, Arthur J., *Theories of Social Progress* (New York, The Macmillan Company, 1922).

URWICK, E. J., *A Philosophy of Social Progress* (London, Methuen and Company, Ltd., 1920).

The American and World Scene

ADAMS, James Truslow, *The Epic of America* (Boston, Little, Brown & Company, 1931).

———, *Frontiers of American Culture, A Study of Adult Education in a Democracy* (New York, Charles Scribner's Sons, 1944).

BEARD, Charles A., *The Republic* (New York, The Viking Press, 1943).

———, and BEARD, Mary R., *The American Spirit* (New York, The Macmillan Company, 1942).

COUNTS, George S., *Education and the Promise of America* (New York, The Macmillan Company, 1945).

CURTI, Merle, *The Growth of American Thought* (New York, Harper & Brothers, 1943).

DE TOCQUEVILLE, Alexis, *Democracy in America*, Rev. Ed. (New York, The Colonial Press, 1899).

JONES, Alfred W., *Life, Liberty and Property* (Philadelphia, J. B. Lippincott Company, 1941).

Journal of Educational Sociology, Issue on Community Coordination, Vol. XI, No. 2 (Oct., 1937).

LASKI, Harold, *Reflections on the Revolution of Our Time* (New York, The Viking Press, 1943).

LYND, Robert, *Knowledge for What?* (Princeton, N.J., Princeton University Press, 1939).

———, and LYND, Helen Merrell, *Middletown* (New York, Harcourt, Brace and Company, 1929).

———, *Middletown in Transition* (New York, Harcourt, Brace and Company, 1937).

MERRIAM, Charles E., *The New Despotism and the New Democracy* (New York: McGraw-Hill Book Company, 1939).

———, *Political Power* (New York, McGraw-Hill Book Company, 1934).

MUMFORD, Lewis, *The Condition of Men* (New York, Harcourt, Brace and Company, 1944).

MYRDAL, Gunnar, *An American Dilemma* (New York, Harper & Brothers, 1944).

PARRINGTON, Vernon L., *Main Currents of American Thought* (New York, Harcourt, Brace and Company, 1927–1930), 3 vols.

WARNER, W. Lloyd, HAVIGHURST, R. J., and LOEB, M. B., *Who Shall Be Educated?* (New York, Harper & Brothers, 1944).

WARNER, W. Lloyd, and LUNT, Paul S., *The Social Life of a Modern Community* (New Haven, Conn., Yale University Press, 1941).

ZIMMERMAN, Carle C., *The Changing Community* (New York, Harper & Brothers, 1938).

INDEX

Accomplishment, 25-26

Accumulative records for teachers, 228-230

Action, group, 134 ff., 145-146

Activity program, 4-5

Adaptations, study of, 106

Administrative officers, selection of, 153

Administrator-teacher relationship, 168

Administrators, authoritarian, 151-152

Adults, community, 66, 70, 74, 79, 86, 87, 91, 92, 108, 109, 132, 154-155, 169, 172, 179

Adventures for teachers, 167

Agar, Herbert, 68

Agreements, 39, 80, 93

Aids, teaching, 117

Aims, 8, 54

Aims-and-objectives approach, 49, 53

Ambivalences, 103-104, 109

Antagonisms, 83, 86

Anthropology, cultural, 105, 109

Apathy, 33, 41, 67, 68, 145

Approach, aims-and-objectives, 49, 53; "broken front," 79; city-wide, 73; non-verbal, 111

Arnold, Dwight L., 32

Arrangements for meetings, 135-136

Assumptions for curriculum planning, 200-211

Attack on modern education, 147

Audience, figures and reactions, 111

Authoritarian administrators, 151-152

Authoritarian practices, 152

Authoritarian teacher leadership, 93

Authority, 92, 151, 157, 192

Autocratic leadership, 84, 198-199

Autonomous school, 69, 79, 200-211

Autonomy, individual school, 8, 86, 200-211

"Badministrators," 152

Bakersfield, Calif., 7

Beard, Charles A., 16, 19, 22

Beliefs, 100 ff., 171, 191; determinants of, 102

Benedict, Ruth, 104

Blackboard, need for, 136, 141

Board of education, 95; bulletin of, 115

"Broken front" approach to curriculum development, 79

Bronxville, New York, 114

Brookings Institute, 53

Books, sales of, 111

Buck, Pearl, 100, 194

Bulletins, 55, 108, 115-116, 118, 123, 183

Bureaucracy, 124

Burgess, E. W., 165-166, 167

Burton, William H., 82, 212-218

Carr, Edward H., 61, 67

Case studies of teachers, 168

Caswell, H. L., 9, 78, 175; and Campbell, 9

Central staff, 74, 80, 82, 92, 176-178

Change, 189; attitudes toward, 18-19; control of, 15 ff.; cultural, 62; in curriculum, 10, 14, 95, 98; deliberate, 18; factors in, 18; in participation, 112; in people, 10; in persons, 14, 188; policy of, 183; public opinion, 112; seeing need for, 106-108; social, 10, 15 ff., 96, 109

Channels, 63, 68

Cherrington, Paul T., 119
Child development, materials on, 117
Childs, John L., 22, 36, 84
Choice, 90, 92, 104 ff.
City-wide approach, 73
City-wide program, 69
Clapp, Elsie R., 13
Classes, social, 97; for adults, 111
Cleavages, 78, 83, 98
Cleveland, O., 118
Collaboration in research, 126
Committees, 65, 66, 70, 77, 79, 94, 137-138, 140-141, 151, 195
Common goals, 92-93
Common membership, 65, 84
Common philosophy, 85, 93
Common purpose, 84
Common values, 36-37, 55, 84, 92-93
Communication, 100, 103, 109 ff., 191; face-to-face, 119 ff.; lines of, 71; technical inventions in, 110 ff.
Community, adults, 66, 70, 74, 79, 86, 87, 91, 92, 108, 109, 132, 154-155, 169, 172, 179; coördinating council, 68, 74, 75-77, 86; discovering leadership in, 180; leadership, 73; organization, 68, 73, 74, 86; relations committee, 70, 77; resources, 118; service, 87; stereotypes of schools, 169; study of, 45; teachers members of, 86
Competence of all educational groups, 153, 154, 168
Compromise, 184
Compulsion, 183
Conditions of effective endeavor, 29, 61 ff., 90, 149
Conferences, 80, 94, 109, 137, 152, 167; parent-teacher, 120, 122; small-group, 137-138
Conflict, 96, 97, 171
Consensus, 140, 160
Consultants, use of, 130-132, 174
Contributors to bulletins, 115
Control, of change, 15 ff.; commercial, 112; local, 188; of opinion-forming agencies, 110, 145; social, 110

Conversations, 111, 112
Coöperation, helping people learn, 160-161; of parents, 66; of school with other agencies, 78; through organization, 146
Coördinating committee, faculty, 94
Coördinating council, community, 68, 74, 75-77, 86
Coördination, 77-82, 127, 128, 162; of community participation, 70
Coördinators, leaders as, 181 ff.
Corey, Stephen, 21, 167
Cornell, Francis G., 106
Cosmopolitanism, 169
Council, community coördinating, 68, 74, 75-77, 81, 86; curriculum, 74, 79-82, 86, 94, 138; parent-teacher, 81; service, 81, 130; of specialists, 81; student, 70, 71, 79
Course of study, 8, 11, 55, 116-117, 151, 183; and curriculum, 7; preparation, 9, 10, 65
Criticism, 120
Crystallization, 1 ff., 14, 47, 59; chief characteristics of, 3; defined, 1; manifestations of, 5; in procedures for curriculum-making, 6-9
Cultural, anthropology, 105, 109; change, 62; maladjustment, 15, 27, 40
Culture, teacher, 163-164
Cumulative records for teachers, 167-168
Curriculum, 18; "broken front" approach to, 79; change, 10, 14, 95, 98; committee, 70, 77, 94; council, 74, 79-82, 94, 138; and course of study, 7; defined, 9-10; development, 94, 212-218; director, 81, 174-175; materials, 55, 59, 80, 108, 116-118; planning, 200-211; programs, 6-9, 10; records, 55, 79, 117; revision, 8, 151
Cushman, C. Leslie, 176-178, 200-211

Day of reasonable length, 95
Debate, and discussion, 138
Decision-making, 72, 138-139, 140

Democracy, "do-," 100; repertory of, 100; "talk-," 100
Democratic leadership, 84, 93, 137 ff., 198
Democratic procedures, 99
Democratic techniques, 99-100
Demonstration, by the expert, 127, 184
Denver, Colo., 81, 133
Department of Supervision and Curriculum Development, 13
Desires, 100 ff., 171, 191; education of, 103-104
Development, child, 117; curriculum, 94, 212-218; human, 43, 46, 109, 161, 165, 169, 171; personality, 165
Dewey, John, 22, 34, 36, 37, 62, 63, 73, 104
Differences, 88, 90, 91, 92, 93, 94, 96, 170; individual, 160
Director of curriculum, 81; function of, 175; specialization of, 174-175
Discovering leadership, 180
Discussion, 111, 112; and debate, 138; function of, 138; groups, 122; suggestions for, 219-221; techniques of, 120-121, 134, 138-140, 142
Dissatisfaction, 33, 40 ff., 189-190; relation to apathy and skepticism, 41
Dissemination, of information, 119; of knowledge, 102
Districts, within a school system, 81
Disunity, practices fostering, 86
Diversity, 89, 90
Division of labor, 56, 66, 134, 140-141, 142-143
"Do-democracy," 100
Documents, social, 110-111
Donnelly, John Franklin, 160
Doubts, creation of, 104
Dowagiac, Mich., 77

Economic power, 145, 146
Education, in-service, 80, 108, 154
Educational journalism, 114

Efficiency, 26, 99
Élite theory of leadership, 149-157
Elliott, H. S., 23
Emotional factors, 102
Ends, 90; relation to means, 21, 33, 34, 48
Energy, 32
Everett, Samuel, 13
Evidence, correlation with belief and desire, 102
"Executive" leader, 127
Exhibits, 111
Experimentation, 81, 94
Expert, 80, 100, 118, 122, 123 ff., 144, 191; in elementary school, 129-130; outside, 130-132; in secondary school, 130
Expertness, of community adults, 132; integration of, 175-178; of teachers, 159, 160-161, 172 ff.

Face-to-face communication, 110, 119 ff.
Face-to-face contacts, 69, 176
Fact-finding survey, 74, 175
Factors, in change, 18, 29, 187; emotional, 102; non-rational, 102
Faith, in human potentialities, 169-171; in power of education, 188
Fascism, 150
Fathers' club, 121
Fiat, administrative, 183
Film strips, 118
Films, 118, 119, 121
Flexibility, 85; in goals, 58-59
Follett, Mary P., 41, 90, 96, 134, 139, 146
Follower, rôle of, 156, 158-159, 162
Forum techniques, 136, 138
Free World Association, 28
Freedom, 90, 92

Gates, Arthur I., 101
Georgia, Citizens' Fact-Finding Movement of, 45
Glencoe, Ill., 75-76, 115, 132
Goals, 33, 47 ff., 90, 97, 190; common, 92-93; flexible, 58-59; immediate and remote, 55-58; that

Goals (*continued*)
   limit, 54; open-ended, 52-53, 55;
   self-set, 48-51, 74
Gordon, Margaret L., 168, 228-230
Graded school, 2-3
Gradualism, 27, 162, 189
Greenwich, Conn., 118
Group, action, 134 ff., 145-146; discussion, 122, 219-221; heterogeneous, 88, 95; homogeneous, 88; inarticulate, 64; minority, 89, 95 ff.;
   planning, 84, 136, 139-140, 161,
   172; power, 83; pressure, 72-73,
   114, 145; room, 71, 94, 121-122;
   solidarity, 51, 70, 79, 82 ff., 190-
   191; thinking, 72, 219-221
Grouping of children, 95
Growth, 23-25, 64, 72, 83, 89, 156,
   159, 170
Guarantee, of accomplishment, 25-
   26; of growth, 23-25; of security,
   21-23
Guide for study, 193-194

Handbook for parents, 116
Hanna, Paul, 13
Hartmann, George, 163, 164
Heterogeneity, 51, 82, 87 ff., 190-
   191
Heterogeneous group, 88, 95
Hierarchy, 82
Hollingshead, Arthur D., 50
Homeroom group, 71
Homogeneity, 95
Homogeneous group, 88
Hopkins, L. T., 12, 117
House organ, 116
Human development, 43, 161, 165,
   169, 171; study of, 46, 109
Human relations, 157, 159-160, 163-
   171, 192
Human relationships, 51, 127
Huszar, George B. de, 64, 100, 135-
   136, 139
Hygiene, mental, 165, 169

Idea, 47
Ideal, 34
Illustrations, graphic, 114

"Importance of People," 167
In-service education, 80, 108, 154
Inarticulation, 119, 120
Individual, rôle of, 89 ff.; differ-
   ences, 160
Individual school, 8, 69, 74, 77, 81,
   82, 86, 130, 137, 200-211
Individuals, study of, 165-167
Individuation, 24, 89, 170
Induction of teachers, 222-227
Information, concern for, 112; dis-
   semination of, 119; exchange of,
   120; sources of, 110-112
Innovation, 82, 90; in community
   organization, 68
Innovators, 13
Institutes, 80; leadership training,
   162
Intelligence, method of, 101, 102,
   104
Interpret, opportunities to, 85, 123,
   152
Interpretation, 121-122
Interviews with teachers, 165
Invention, 87; in communications,
   110 ff.; social, 17, 29, 64, 81, 99 ff.,
   184
Iowa University, 84, 159
Isolation, 87

John Dewey Society, 163
Jones, Alfred Winslow, 113
Journalism, educational, 114

Kansas City, Mo., 81
"Key" people, 154-155
"Key" teachers, 94, 183
Kier, Hazel A., 165, 222-227
Kilpatrick, William H., 158, 162
Knowledge, 100 ff., 191; dissemina-
   tion of, 102
Koopman, G. R., 26, 28, 76

Labor, division of, 56, 66, 134, 140-
   141, 142-143
Laissez-faire leadership, 84, 93, 159
Lane, Howard, 23, 179-180
Leader, beloved, 156; as coördina-
   tor, 181 ff.; "executive," 127;

status, 157, 158, 159 ff.; vision of, 172

Leadership, 29, 84, 93, 145, 149 ff.; authoritarian teacher, 93; autocratic, 84, 198-199; democratic, 157 ff., 198; developing further, 159, 161-162, 178-181; discovering, 180; by an élite, 149-157; emerging, 157; shared, 157, 158-159, 192, status, 192; training institutes, 162

Learners, 66, 74, 85, 86, 87, 91, 92, 154-155, 169, 179

Leaves, for teachers, 108

Lectures, 111

Leisure for teachers, 95

Lerner, Max, 20, 105-106, 150

Lewin, Kurt, 48, 56, 89, 138-139, 159

Li Yu Ying, 28

Library, 112; parent, 108; public, 111; rental, 111

Linton, Ralph, 16, 18, 62, 104, 171

Lippitt, Ronald, 83, 84

Lippmann, Walter, 166

Literature, professional, 108

Localism, 169

Logs, daily, 144

Loneliness, 22, 82

Lund, F. H., 102, 113

Lunt, Paul S., 97

Lynd, Robert, 16, 41, 62, 68, 84, 86, 103, 105, 109, 112, 126

Maine, curriculum development in, 212-218

Maladjustment, cultural, 15, 27, 40, 43

Mannheim, Karl, 48, 100

Materials, on child development, 117; curriculum, 55, 59, 80, 108, 116-118

Mayo, Elton, 63

Mead, Margaret, 52, 82

Means, relation to ends, 21, 33

Media of communication, 110 ff.

Meetings, faculty, 108, 137, 195-198; as an instrument, 134 ff.; mothers', 197; parent-teacher, 70, 85, 121

Membership, common, 65, 84

Mental hygiene, 165, 169

Merriam, Charles, 124, 127, 150

Method of intelligence, 101, 102, 104

Michigan, 65

Microphone, two-way, 119

Middle-class mores, 97

Minority, groups, 89, 95 ff.; power of, 145; view, 140

Minutes of meetings, 141

Misner, Paul, 26, 28, 76

Modern education, attack on, 147

Moholy-Nagy, L., 125

Mort, Paul R., 106

Mossman, Lois Coffey, 5

Motion picture, 110, 111, 112, 118-120

Motivations, 29, 32 ff., 103, 147, 149, 169; and discussion, 138

Murphy, Gardner, 33

Museum, school coöperation with, 78

Myrdal, Gunnar, 16, 30, 31

Needs and interests, study of, 108

Newspapers, 110-111, 112, 114; school, 116

Non-parents, 70, 71

Non-rational factors, 102

Non-verbal, approach, 111; methods, 120

Objectives, 8, 48, 50, 54, 55, 65

Office of Education, United States, 6

Officers, selection of, 153; supervisory, 171

Opinion, public, 112

Opinion-forming agencies, 110, 145

Organization, 51 ff., 84, 86, 90, 91, 97, 120, 128, 129, 162, 190; community, 68, 73, 74; of faculty, 77, 79; form of, 63; functional, 64 ff., 171, 179; parent, 71

Over-specialization, 129

Ovid, Mich., 39

Parent-teacher, conferences, 120, 122; meeting, 70, 85, 121

Parents, coöperation of, 66

Park, R. E., 88
Parker, J. Cecil, 139, 219-221
Participation, 23, 61, 62, 67 ff., 79, 91, 93, 94, 112, 129, 136, 171, 183, 188; inter-school, 80; of parents, 132-133; student, 70; unit of, 71, 74, 81
Patrons, 85, 86, 92, 109
Pennsylvania teachers, 106
People, change in, 10
Performances, 111
Person, study of the, 165-167
Personality, development, 165
Persons, change in, 14, 188
Persuasion, primacy in, 102, 113, 114
Philadelphia, 82, 118-119, 142-143
Philosophy, 93; common, 85; of education, 8, 38-39, 50, 55, 65
Placement of teachers, 167
Planning, 92, 100-101; assumptions for, 200-211; continuity of, 66; group, 84, 136, 139-140, 161, 172
Policies, 158; and procedures, 79, 117
Policy of change, 183
Political power, 145
Posters, 111
Potentialities, faith in, 169-171
Power, 191-192; group, 83; motivating, 74; social, 67, 100, 145 ff., 171
Praise, 85, 179-180
Prall, Charles E., 163, 176-178
Prescott, Daniel A., 102, 127, 168
Press, 110, 114, 121
Pressure, 184; groups, 72-73, 114, 145
Primacy in persuasion, 102, 113, 114
Principal, 129, 133, 155; specialization of, 173
Problem-solving, group, 46
Problems, selection of, 74; social, 109
Procedures, 92; democratic, 99; policies and, 79, 117
Process, 19 ff., 189; attitudes toward, 19-20; a configuration, 30; guarantees contained in, 21 ff.; relation to product, 20-21; security in, 19, 22
Product, relation to process, 20-21

Productive differences, 90, 92
Professional literature, 108
Progressive Education, 13
Promotions, premature, 155
Propaganda, 72, 112-113, 145
Psychological environment for meetings, 136-137
Public opinion, level of, 112
Purpose, 48, 54; common, 84; constructive social, 72 ff.; group's own, 72 ff.

Radio, 110, 111, 118-120, 121
Radio station, school coöperation with, 78
Rapidity, 27-28, 162, 184-185, 189
Rating scales, 152
Recognition, 85, 179-180
Record-keeping, 134, 141-142, 143-144; form for, 141-142
Recordings, 118-119
Records, curriculum, 55, 79, 117, 144; daily logs as, 144; exchange of, 143-144; of group experiences, 144; for teachers, 167-168, 228-230
Recreation for teachers, 95
Relations, human, 157, 159-160, 163-171, 192
Relationship, administrator-teacher, 168; service, 79
Relationships, of central staff, 176-178; functional, 71; human, 51, 127; inter-personal, 67 ff.
Repertory of democracy, 100
Reports, convention, 109; to parents, 122
Resource units, 117
Resources, community, 118
Responsibility, 85, 90, 92, 157; of leaders, 159; release from, 156; of teachers, 94
Rocco, Alfredo, 150, 157
Room group, 71, 94, 121-122
Rugg, Harold, 3, 12

Saylor, J. Galen, 8, 87
School, autonomous, 69, 77, 200-211; individual, 8, 69, 74, 77, 81,

82, 86, 137; 200-211; within a school, 70
Schools, uneven support of, 155
Secretary, need for, 141
Security, 21-23, 62, 64, 72, 83, 89, 97, 156, 159, 182-183; through routine, 85
Selection, of administrative officers, 153; of supervisory officers, 153
Self-interest, 24
Sermons, 111
Service, community, 87; council, 81, 130; relationship of specialists, 79
Servility, rôle of, 156
Short-cuts, unsound, 183-184
Skepticism, 33, 41, 42-43, 112, 145
Slides, 118
Small-group conference plan, 137-138
Snyder, Agnes, 25
Social change, 10, 15 ff., 96, 109
Social classes, 97
Social control, 110
Social documents, 110-111
Social invention, 17, 29, 64, 81, 99 ff.
Social power, 67, 100, 145 ff., 171
Social problems, 109
Social realities, 43
Socialization, 24-25, 54, 83, 90, 170
Solidarity, group, 51, 79, 82 ff., 190-191
Sources of information, 110-112
Specialists, 79, 81, 118, 123 ff.
Specialization, 123 ff., 153-154, 162, 176; of administrators, 128, 133; of classroom teachers, 128, 133; of leaders in curriculum development, 172-175
Spence, Ralph, 112
Spread, in policies and procedures, 79; in practice, 80
Staff, central, 74, 80, 82, 92, 176-178
Stage, school coöperation with, 78
Standardization, 92, 183
Standards, 96-97
Status, of individual, 89; leaders, 157, 158, 159 ff.; leadership, 192
Stereotypes, 166; of schools, 169

Strategy, 162, 181 ff.
Stratemeyer, Florence, 12, 117
Straw votes, 140
Strong, Carl L., and staff, 40
Study, of community, 45; continuous, 77; groups, 108; guide for, 193; of human development, 46, 109; of individuals, 165-167; of the person, 165-167; of power-equation, 147; programs, 129; of pupil needs and interests, 108; of social problems, 109; of social scene, 44, 164
Subjects, school, 3-4
Suggestion box, 44
Suggestions, gathering and evaluating, 139
Sumner, W. G., 16, 17, 40, 134
Superintendent of schools, specialization of, 173
Superiority, false assumptions of, 152-154, 164
Supervisor, responsibility for induction of teachers, 222-227
Supervisors, 45, 108, 123, 129, 171, 174; specialization of, 173-174
Supervisory officers, 171; selection of, 153
Supervisory techniques, 123
Support of schools, uneven, 155
Survey, fact-finding, 74, 175; school, 108; talent, 132

Taba, Hilda, 51, 96
Talent, survey, 132
"Talk-democracy," 100
Teacher affairs committee, 70, 77
Teacher culture, 163-164
Teacher load, 165
Teacher placement, 167
Teachers, adventures for, 167; case studies of, 168; cumulative records for, 167-168, 228-230; induction of, 222-227; as people, 165-168; as professional workers, 163-165
Teachers' unions, 97-98
Teaching aids, 117
Techniques, 191; democratic, 99-

Techniques (*continued*)
100; of decision-making, 138-139; of discussion, 120-121, 134, 138-140, 142; forum, 136; of group action, 100, 134 ff., 161, 172; supervisory, 123

Technology, 11, 17

T.V.A., 17, 127, 184

Terms, definition of, 120

Textbooks, 3-4, 59, 151

Theman, Viola, 95

Thinking, group, 72, 219-221

Thomas, W. I., 88

Thompson, Merritt M., 54

Timing, 162, 181

Todd, Arthur J., 101, 103, 164

Transfers, 94-95

Trillingham, C. C., 6-9, 65

Two-way microphone, 119

Understanding, community adults and learners, 168-169; teachers, 163-168

Uniformity, 68, 82, 103

Unions, teachers', 97-98

Unit, of curriculum development,

69; of participation, 71, 74, 81; resource, 117; of work, 4, 171

United States Office of Education, 6

Unity, 39, 83 ff., 89, 90, 92

Urwick, E. J., 47, 52, 88, 124, 138, 170, 184

Values, 21, 33 ff., 90, 97, 189; common, 36-37, 55, 84, 92-93; of the home, 86

Van Antwerp, Harriet, 123

Virginia, 87

Vision, 47, 90; of status leaders, 172; supplementing, 92

Visitation, 87, 108, 167

Volunteering, 93

Warner, William L., 97

"We" feeling, 85

Weinberger, Major Lawrence, 125-126

Woodring, Maxie N., 12, 117

Workshops, 80, 94, 108, 109, 167

Zimmerman, Carle C., 169

(1)